Investing in Shares

3rd Edition

by David Stevenson and Paul Mladjenovic

A Wiley Brand

Investing in Shares For Dummies®, 3rd Edition

Published by: **John Wiley & Sons, Ltd., The Atrium, Southern Gate, Chichester,** www.wiley.com

© 2022 by John Wiley & Sons, Ltd., Chichester, West Sussex

Media and software compilation copyright © 2022 by John Wiley & Sons, Ltd. All rights reserved.

Registered Office

John Wiley & Sons, Ltd., The Atrium, Southern Gate, Chichester, West Sussex, PO19 8SQ, United Kingdom

For general information on our other products and services, please contact our Customer Care Department within the U.S. at 877-762-2974, outside the U.S. at 317-572-3993, or fax 317-572-4002. For technical support, please visit https://hub.wiley.com/community/support/dummies.

Wiley publishes in a variety of print and electronic formats and by print-on-demand. Some material included with standard print versions of this book may not be included in e-books or in print-on-demand. If this book refers to media such as a CD or DVD that is not included in the version you purchased, you may download this material at http://booksupport.wiley.com. For more information about Wiley products, visit www.wiley.com.

A catalogue record for this book is available from the British Library.

Library of Congress Control Number: 2021950170

ISBN 978-1-119-83221-8

ISBN 978-1-119-83222-5 (ebk); ISBN 978-1-119-83223-2 (ebk)

Printed by CPI Group (UK) Ltd, Croydon, CR0 4YY

Contents at a Glance

Table of Contents

Introduction

Houses, gold, tulips, bitcoin . . . our idea of what constitutes a good investment has changed dramatically over time, but one precious, valuable idea still holds true: that shares over the long term have been a great investment and have without doubt made their intrepid 'holders' returns of between 5 and 7 per cent per annum over many decades. Obviously that optimistic assessment requires a huge caveat, perhaps even a flashing warning sign of epic proportions, loudly proclaiming that investing in shares can be a rollercoaster ride!

Anyone piling their hard-earned fortune into the stock market in 2007 or January 2020 would soon have realised that *shares* (also called *equities* or *stocks*) can be hugely volatile and that you can lose your money almost overnight. Remember the dark days of early winter 2008 (or February 2020) when the financial markets stood on the edge of catastrophe and shares were plunging by 5 per cent one day and 10 per cent the next. Scary stuff, but within 12 months, the markets had staged a remarkable recovery and some stocks had more than trebled in value. The moral of the story is simple: Investing in shares can sometimes be fun, often risky, but also frequently rewarding, especially if you're patient, careful and diligent. This book can definitely help you avoid the mistakes others have made and can point you in the right direction.

Explore the pages of this book and find the topics that most interest you regarding the world of share investing. Understanding what not to do can be just as important as working out what to do. The single difference between success and failure, between gain and loss, boils down to one word: knowledge. Take this book as your first step in a lifelong learning adventure.

About This Book

No one knows anything in the paranoid world of investing. Every day experts traipse onto TV screens to discuss where 'the markets' might go tomorrow . . . or next week . . . or even next year. Trust us when we say that it's all hocus pocus – no one knows anything for sure. In fact, you might have a better handle on what really matters in the global markets than the ludicrously overpaid hedge fund maestro sitting in his office in Mayfair. Stock markets are a volatile brew of common sense, wisdom based on decades of experience of 'what works' and an inkling of the ebb and flow of human emotion. Master these criss-crossing currents and you might just build a sensible investment portfolio. Hopefully this book helps you navigate these stormy, ever-changing waters.

This book is designed to give you a realistic approach to making money by investing in shares. It provides the essence of sound, practical share investing strategies and insights that have been market tested and proven from nearly a hundred years of stock market history.

Investing in Shares For Dummies, 3rd Edition, is also a book that is quite different from the 'get rich with shares' titles that cram the bookshelves. It doesn't take a standard approach to the topic; it doesn't assume that shares are a sure thing and the be-all and end-all of wealth building. At times in this book, we tell you *not* to invest in shares. This book can help you succeed not only in up markets but also in down markets. Bull markets and bear markets come and go, but the informed investor can keep making money no matter what. To give you an extra edge, we have tried to include information about the investing environment for shares.

In this third edition of this book, we focus on how investing has been changed dramatically by the advent of new technologies. In particular, we investigate the following:

>> How Internet-based share dealing has changed everything

>> Why robo advisers might be a cheap, easy-to-access way forward for many investors

>> Why technology is driving much of theme-based, big-trend investing and how you can get involved with these big changes

>> How the rise of passive investing through index tracking funds has helped democratise investing

>> How the changed global macroeconomic environment has impacted investing post pandemic

Foolish Assumptions

We reckon you've picked up this book for one or more of the following reasons:

>> You're a beginner and want a crash course on share investing that's an easy read.

>> You're already a share investor, and you need a book that allows you to read only those chapters that cover specific share investing topics of interest to you.

>> You need to review your own situation with the information in the book to see if you missed anything when you invested in that hot share that your sister-in-law recommended.

>> You need a great gift! When Uncle Fred is upset over his poor share picks, you can give him this book so he can get back on his financial feet. Be sure to get a copy for his broker, too. (Odds are that the broker was the one who made those picks to begin with.)

Icons Used in This Book

We use icons, which are little pictures in the margins, to point out information. Here are the icons we use:

TIP

This icon flags a particular bit of advice that just may give you an edge over other investors.

REMEMBER

When you see this icon, we're reminding you about some information that you should always keep stashed in your memory, whether you're new to investing or an old pro.

WARNING

Pay special attention to this icon because the advice can prevent headaches, heart-aches and financial aches.

TECHNICAL STUFF

The text attached to this icon may not be crucial to your success as an investor, but it may enable you to talk shop with investing gurus and better understand the financial pages of your favourite business publication or website.

Beyond This Book

In addition to the material in the print or e-book you're reading right now, this product also comes with some access-anywhere goodies online. Check out the free Cheat Sheet at www.dummies.com. Just search for *investing in shares UK*.

If you do fancy delving a bit more deeply into these ideas, then you may also want to check out David's personal investing blog at www.adventurousinvestor.com or maybe if passive, index tracking funds spark your interest, investigate www.etfstream.com.

Where to Go from Here

We don't expect you to read it cover to cover, although we'll be delighted if you read every word! Instead, this book is designed as a reference tool. Feel free to read the chapters in whatever order you choose. You can flip to the sections and chapters that interest you or those that include topics that you need to know more about.

Because every chapter is designed to be as self-contained as possible, it won't do you any harm to cherry-pick what you really want to read. But if you're like us, you still may want to check out every chapter because you never know when you might come across a new tip or resource that will make a profitable difference in your share portfolio. We want you to be successful so that we can brag about you in the next edition.

1

The Essentials of Investing in Shares

Get a better understanding of the basics of buying shares before you make your first investment.

Identify what you need to scrutinise your own situations and financial goals as much as you scrutinise shares.

Take stock of your current needs, goals and risk tolerance before you invest.

Discover how to determine what you need to know in order to choose the stocks that best suit you.

Chapter **1**

Exploring the Basics

Remember Sid? Back in the 1980s and 1990s investing in shares briefly became insanely popular in the UK. Most cynical Brits had grown up believing that shares were a slightly brutish thing, traded by spivs and sleek stockbrokers and only the preserve of the inveterate gambler. The privatisation of the major utilities (Sid was invoked by the Thatcher government to encourage people to invest in the likes of British Gas and British Telecom) changed everything. Suddenly everyone seemed to have amassed a small portfolio of privatised companies as well as shares in building societies such as Halifax who'd chosen to 'demutualise' and 'list' their shares on the stock market.

Private investors piled into shares in the 1990s as the stock market reached the mania stage at the tail-end of an 18-year upswing (or *bull market*: see Chapter 15 for more information on bull markets). Some years later adventurous types even took to investing in the companies of 'tomorrow' – think Amazon or Google – pumping up an enormous technology-based stock market bubble that eventually burst in spectacular style in the first years of the new millennium (we call this a *bear market* – see Chapter 15 for more on these). Share prices tumbled worldwide and everyone declared that they were much the wiser.

Now, of course, everyone knows that that was an illusion. Shares picked up in value again in the first decade of the new millennium, especially as investors piled into bank shares tempted by the juicy dividends on offer. And then the GFC – the Global Financial Crisis – came along and the rest is history. Perhaps this time everyone has learned their lesson . . . or perhaps not! Shares have bounced back in value, which rather suggests that the animal spirits of investing are alive and kicking. And 2020 experienced another exciting roller coaster ride as markets plunged and then soared, and those stocks such as Amazon and Google that were once a bit 'spivvy' suddenly turned into 'must have'.

One might rather cynically conclude after these serial booms and busts that many investors really hadn't known exactly what they were investing in. If they'd had a rudimentary understanding of what shares really are, perhaps they could have avoided some expensive mistakes. The purpose of this book is not only to tell you about the basics of investing in shares but also to let you in on some solid strategies that can help you profit from the stock market. Before you invest your first fiver, you need to understand the basics of investing in shares, which we discuss in this chapter.

Understanding the Basics

The basics are so basic that few people are doing them. Perhaps the most basic (and therefore most important) thing to grasp is the risk you face whenever you do anything (like putting your hard-earned money in an investment like shares). When you lose track of the basics, you lose track of why you invested to begin with. Find out more about risk (and the different kinds of risk) in Chapter 4.

In an old stand-up routine, the comic was asked 'How is your wife?' He responded 'Compared to what?' You need to apply the same attitude to stocks. When you're asked 'how are your shares?', you may be able to say that they're doing well – especially when compared to an acceptable 'yardstick' like an index (such as the FTSE 100 or the FTSE All Share). Find out more about indices in Chapter 5.

The bottom line is that the first thing you do when investing in shares is not to send your money straight into a stockbroker's account or go to a website to click 'buy shares'. The first thing you do is find out as much as you can about what shares are and how you can use them to boost your wealth.

Getting Prepared before Starting

Gathering information is critical to your plans for investing in shares. You need to gather information on the shares you're planning to buy twice: before you invest . . . and after. You obviously should become more informed before you invest your first few quid. But you also need to stay informed about what's happening to the company whose shares you're buying, about the industry or sector that company is in and about the economy in general. To find the best information sources, check out Chapter 6.

When you're ready to invest, you need an account with a stockbroker. How do you know which broker to use and whether to go online or use paper certificates? Chapter 7 provides some answers and resources to help you choose a broker.

Knowing How to Pick Winners

Once you get past the basics, you can get to the 'meat' of picking shares. Successful share picking isn't mysterious, but it does take some time, effort and analysis. This may sound like a lot of work but it's worth it, because shares are an important part of most investors' portfolios. Read the following section and be sure to 'leap frog' to the relevant chapters.

Recognising the value of shares

Imagine that you like eggs and you're willing to buy them at the supermarket. In this example, the eggs are like companies, and the prices represent the prices that you would pay for the companies' shares. The supermarket is the stock market. What if two brands of eggs are similar, but one costs £1 while the other costs £1.50? Which would you choose? Odds are that you would look at both brands, judge their quality and, if they were indeed similar, take the cheaper eggs – though if you're so minded, you might scrutinise the label for mention of free range.

The eggs at £1.50 are overpriced. The same principle applies to shares. What if you compare two companies that are similar in every respect but have different share prices? All things being equal, the cheaper price has greater value for the investor. But the egg example has another side.

What if the quality of the two brands of eggs is significantly different but their prices are the same? If one brand of eggs is old, of poor quality and priced at £1 and the other brand is fresher, of superior quality and also priced at £1, which would you buy? Of course, you'd take the good brand because they're better eggs. Perhaps the lesser eggs are an acceptable purchase at 50 pence, but they're definitely overpriced at £1. The same example works with shares. A badly run company isn't a good choice if you can buy a better company in the marketplace at the same – or a better – price.

Comparing the value of eggs may seem overly simplistic, but doing so does cut to the heart of investing in shares. Eggs and egg prices can be as varied as companies and share prices. As an investor, you must make it your job to find the best value for your investment cash. (Otherwise you get egg on your face. We bet you saw that one coming.)

Understanding how market capitalisation affects share values

You can determine the value of a company (and thus the value of its shares) in many ways. The most basic way to measure this value is to look at a company's market value, also known as market capitalisation (or market cap). *Market capitalisation* is simply the value you get when you multiply all the number of outstanding shares of a particular company by the price of a single share.

Calculating the market cap is easy. It's the number of shares outstanding multiplied by the current share price. If the company has 1 million shares outstanding and its share price is £10, the market cap is £10 million.

Small cap, mid cap and large cap aren't references to headgear; they're references to how large the company is as measured by its market value. Here are the four basic categories of market capitalisation:

» **Fledglings:** These shares are sometimes known as *micro-caps* or *tiddlers*. They're small and very risky.

» **Small caps:** These shares may fare better than the fledglings and still have plenty of growth potential. The key word is 'potential'.

» **Mid caps:** For many investors, this category offers a good compromise between small caps and blue chips. They offer much of the safety of the big companies while retaining a part of the growth potential of small caps.

» **Blue chips:** These are the established heavy hitters and are ideal for the cautious investors who want the potential for steady appreciation with greater safety. These companies tend to be represented in something called the FTSE 100 Index of top, 'blue chip' companies. We explain more about indices in Chapter 5.

REMEMBER

From a safety point of view, the company's size and market value do matter. All things being equal, large cap companies are considered safer than small cap companies. However, small caps shares have greater potential for growth. Compare these companies to trees: Which tree is stronger – a sturdy oak tree or a newly planted sapling? In a great storm, the oak has a chance of survival, while the young tree has a rough time. But you also have to ask yourself which tree has more opportunity for growth. The oak may not have much growth left, but the sapling has plenty of growth to look forward to – assuming that climate change hasn't resulted in all those saplings dying.

For investment beginners, comparing market cap to trees isn't so far-fetched. You want your money to grow without becoming dead wood.

Although market capitalisation is important to consider, don't invest (or not invest) based on market capitalisation only. It's just one measure of value. As a serious investor, you need to look at numerous factors that can help you determine whether any given share is a good investment. Keep reading – this book is full of information to help you decide.

Sharpening your investment skills

Investors who analyse the company can better judge the value of the shares and profit from buying and selling them. Your greatest asset in investing is knowledge (and a little common sense). To succeed in the world of share investment, keep in mind the following key success factors:

>> **Analyse yourself.** What do you want to accomplish through your investment in shares? What are your investment goals? Chapter 2 can help you figure this out.

>> **Know where to get information.** The decisions you make about your money and the shares to invest in require quality information. If you want help with information sources, turn to Chapter 3.

>> **Understand why you want to invest in shares.** Are you seeking appreciation (capital gains) or income (dividends)? Look at Chapters 8 and 9 for information on these topics.

>> **Do your research.** Look at the company whose shares you're considering, to see whether it's a profitable company worthy of your investment cash. Chapters 10 and 11 help you scrutinise the company.

>> **Choosing a successful share also means that you choose a winning industry.** You frequently see share prices of mediocre companies in 'hot' industries rise higher and faster than solid companies in floundering industries. Therefore, choosing the industry is important. Find out more about analysing industries in Chapter 12.

>> **Understand how the world affects your shares.** Shares succeed or fail in large part due to the environment in which they operate. Economics and

politics make up that world, so you should know something about them. Chapter 14 covers these topics, but also take a look at Chapter 2.

>> **Understand and identify megatrends.** Doing so makes it easier for you to make money. This edition spends more time and provides more resources helping you see the opportunities in emerging sectors and even avoid the problem areas (see Chapter 13 for details).

>> **Use investing strategies like the experts do.** In other words, how you go about investing can be just as important as what you invest in. Chapter 16 highlights techniques for investing to help you make more money from your shares.

>> **Keep more of the money you earn.** After all your great work in picking the right shares and making big money, you should know about keeping more of the fruits of your investing. We cover the taxation of share investment in Chapter 20.

>> **Sometimes, what people tell you to do with shares isn't as revealing as what people are actually doing.** This is why we like to look at company insiders before we buy or sell that particular share. To find out more about insider buying and selling – not to be confused with 'insider dealing', which is illegal – read Chapter 19.

Actually, every chapter in the book offers you valuable guidance on an essential aspect of the fantastic world of shares. The knowledge you pick up and apply from these pages has been tested over nearly a century of share picking. The investment experience of the past – the good, the bad and some of the ugly – is here for your benefit. Use this information to make a lot of money (and make us proud!). And don't forget to check out the Appendixes.

Boning Up on Strategies and Tactics

Successful investing isn't just what you invest in, it's also the way you invest. We are big on strategies such as trailing stop losses. You can find out more about these in Chapter 17.

Buying shares doesn't always mean that you must visit a stockbroker or that it has to be hundreds of shares. You can buy shares for pennies and use programmes such as dividend reinvestment plans. Chapter 18 tells you more.

Getting Good Tips

In Chapter 21 we place our finger firmly on the pulse of the market and look at some major new innovations sweeping through the financial services sector such as and index tracking funds and exchange traded funds (ETFs). We look at why they can be useful and what you need to look out for! Used sensibly, these 'low-cost' funds – the managers charge a very small amount of money in fees – can make a huge difference to your long-term investment plans.

Protecting yourself from the risk of losing money (known as *downside exposure*) is what separates investors from gamblers, and Chapter 23 gives you ten warning signs of a share's decline. We know when we see some of the signs that (at the very least) we need to put on a stop loss order (Chapter 17) so that we can sleep at night. Sometimes the return *on* your money is not as good as the return *of* your money.

If shares give off 'negative signals', then it follows that they give off 'positive' ones as well. Chapter 24 gives you ten of the best signs that are commonly seen before a share is ready to rise. What better time to jump in?

You should be aware about the risks of fraud. It's tough enough to make money from shares in an honest market. Yet we must always be aware of those that would take our hard-earned money from us without our consent. That's why we include Chapter 25 – because there's always a chance of encountering problems when you're dealing with humanity.

Chapter 26 is one of the best chapters in the book. You really need to understand if the environment for a particular share is good or bad. The best shares in the world sink in a tough market while the worst shares can go up in a jubilant and rising market. Ideally, you avoid those shares that are in the tough market and find good shares in a good market. This chapter points you in the direction of those markets.

Chapter **2**

Sizing Up Your Current Finances and Setting Goals

alk to the pros about the topsy turvy world of investing and they'll tell you that to succeed you need two great skills, neither of which have anything to do with reading a share chart or understanding a company's profit and loss statement. The first great skill can loosely be summed up as self-awareness but really it's all about knowing who you are, what your attitude towards risk is and what gets you excited about investing. The other great skill is self-doubt and a willingness to embrace your mistakes, learn from them and then move on! In sum, 'know thyself' before you even attempt to understand the financial markets.

Understanding your current financial situation and clearly defining your financial goals are the first steps to successful investing.

This chapter is undoubtedly one of the most important ones in this book. At first, you may think it's a chapter more suitable for some general book on personal finance. Wrong! Unsuccessful investors' greatest weakness isn't understanding their financial situation and how shares fit in. Often, people should stay out of the stock market if they aren't prepared for the responsibilities of investing in shares – regularly reviewing companies' financial statements and tracking companies' progress. Very often, investors aren't aware of the pitfalls of investing in shares during *bear markets*, that is, periods in which share prices fall generally. Check out Chapter 15 for more on bear markets.

REMEMBER

Investing in shares requires balance. Investors sometimes tie up too much money in shares, putting themselves at risk of losing a significant portion of their wealth if the market plunges. Then again, other investors place little or no money in shares and miss out on excellent opportunities to grow their wealth. Investors should make shares a part of their portfolios, but the operative word is *part*. You should only let shares take up a *portion* of your money. A disciplined investor also has money in bank accounts, bonds and other assets that offer growth or income opportunities. Diversification is key to minimising risk. (For more on risk, see Chapter 4.)

Establishing a Starting Point

Whether you already own shares or you're looking to get into shares, you need to find out how much money you can afford to invest in them. No matter what you hope to accomplish with your share investment plan, the first step you should take as a budding investor is figuring out how much you own and how much you owe. To do this, prepare and review your personal balance sheet. A *balance sheet* is simply a list of your assets, your liabilities and what each item is currently worth, allowing you to arrive at your net worth. Your *net worth* is the total *assets* minus the total *liabilities*. These terms may sound like accounting mumbo jumbo, but knowing your net worth is important to your future financial success, so let's just get on with it. Check out the section, 'Step 4: Calculating your net worth', later in this chapter for more detail.

Composing your balance sheet is simple. Grab a pencil and a piece of paper. For the computer savvy, a spreadsheet accomplishes the same task. Gather together all your financial documents, such as bank and broker statements and other such paperwork – you need figures from these documents. Then follow the steps that we outline in the following sections. Update your balance sheet at least once a year to monitor your financial progress (is your net worth going up or not?).

A second document to prepare is an income statement. An income statement lists your total income and your total expenses to find out how well you're doing. If your total income is greater than your total expenses, then you have net income (great!). If your total expenses meet or exceed your total income, then you're in trouble. You'd better start increasing your income or cutting your expenses. You want to get to the point where you have enough net income to allow you to use that money to fund your share purchases.

REMEMBER

Your personal balance sheet is really no different from balance sheets that big companies prepare. In fact, the more you know about your own balance sheet, the easier it is to understand the balance sheets of companies in which you're seeking to invest.

Step 1: Making sure you have an emergency fund

First, list your cash on your balance sheet (see the next step for more on listing your assets). Your goal is to have, in reserve, at least three to six months' worth of your gross living expenses in cash. The cash is important because it gives you a cushion. Three to six months is usually enough to get you through the most common forms of financial disruption, such as losing your job. Finding a new job can typically take between three and six months.

REMEMBER

If your monthly expenses (or *outgoings*) are £1,000, you should have at least £3,000, and probably closer to £6,000, in a secure, interest-bearing bank or building society account. This account is your emergency fund and not an investment. Don't use this money to buy shares – or anything else.

WARNING

Too many people put themselves at risk because they don't have a basic emergency fund. You wouldn't take the risk of walking across a busy street while wearing a blindfold.

Resist the urge to start thinking of your investment in shares as a savings account generating over 20 per cent per year. This is dangerous thinking! If your investments flop or you lose your job, you'll struggle financially and that will hit your share portfolio (you might have to sell some shares just to get money to pay the bills). An emergency fund helps you through a temporary cash crunch.

Step 2: Listing your assets in decreasing order of liquidity

Liquid assets don't mean beer or lemonade (unless you're Scottish & Newcastle or Schweppes). Instead, *liquidity* refers to how quickly you can convert a particular *asset* (something you own that has value) into cash. If you know the liquidity of your assets, including investments, you have some options when you need cash to buy some shares (or pay a bill). All too often, people are short of cash and have too much wealth tied up in *illiquid investments* such as property. *Illiquid* is just a fancy way of saying that you don't have the immediate cash to meet a pressing need. (We've all been there.) Review your assets and take measures to ensure that you have enough liquid assets (along with your illiquid assets).

Listing your assets in order of liquidity on your balance sheet gives you an immediate picture of which assets you can quickly convert to cash and which ones you can't. If you need money *now*, you can see that cash in your purse or wallet, your current account and your savings account – which are at the top of the list. The items last in order of liquidity become obvious; they're things like property and other assets that you can't sell quickly.

Selling property, even in a seller's market, can take months. Investors who don't have adequate liquid assets run the danger of selling assets quickly and possibly at a loss when they scramble to accumulate cash for short-term financial obligations. For investors in shares, this scramble may include prematurely selling shares that they originally intended to hold as long-term investments.

Table 2-1 shows a typical list of assets in order of liquidity. Use it as a guide for making your own asset list.

TABLE 2-1 John Smith. Investor: Personal Assets as of December 31, 2021

Asset Item	Market Value	Annual Growth Rate (%)
Current assets		
Cash in wallet and in current account	£150	0
Bank and building society savings accounts and National Savings certificates	£500	1 (if you are lucky)
Shares	£2,000	7
Investment trusts	£2,400	7
Other assets	£240	
(Collectibles and so on)		
Total current assets	**£5,290**	
Long-term assets		
Car	£1,800	–10
Home	£200,000	–2 (!)
Buy to let property	£125,000	2
Personal stuff (such as jewellery)	£4,000	
Total long-term assets	**£320,800**	
Total assets	**£326,090**	

Here is a breakdown of Table 2-1:

>> **The first column describes the asset.** You can quickly convert *current assets* to cash – they're more liquid; *long-term assets* have value, but you can't necessarily convert them to cash quickly – they aren't very liquid.

Note: This table lists shares as short-term assets. The reason is that this balance sheet is meant to list items in order of liquidity. Liquidity is best embodied in the question 'How quickly can I turn this asset into cash?' Because a share can be sold and converted to cash very quickly, it's a good example of a liquid asset. (However, that isn't the main reason for buying shares.)

>> **The second column gives the current market value for that item.** Keep in mind that this value isn't the purchase price or original value; it's the amount you would realistically get if you sold the asset in the current market. The third column shows how well that investment is doing, compared to one year ago. If the percentage rate is 5 per cent, that item's value has increased by 5 per cent from a year ago. You need to know how well all your assets are doing. Why? To adjust your assets for maximum growth or to get rid of assets that are losing money. Assets that are doing well are kept (you may even increase holdings), but assets that are down in value are candidates for removal. Perhaps you can sell them and reinvest the money elsewhere. In addition, the realised loss has tax benefits (see Chapter 20).

>> **The third column focuses on the annual growth rate.** Working out the annual growth rate as a percentage isn't difficult. Say that you buy 100 shares in a company called Gro-A-Lot Ltd (GAL), and its market value on December 31, 2020 is £50 a share for a total market value of £5,000 (100 shares at £50 a share). When you check its value on December 31, 2021, you find the stock is at £60 a share (100 shares times £60 equals a total market value of £6,000). The annual growth rate is 20 per cent. You calculate this by taking the amount of the gain (£60 a share minus £50 a share = a gain of £10 a share), which is £1,000 (100 shares times the £10 gain), and dividing it by the value at the beginning of the time period – in this case a year (£5,000). In this case, you get 20 per cent (£1,000 divided by £5,000).

What if GAL also generates a dividend of £2 per share during that period; now what? In that case, GAL generates a total return of 24 per cent. To calculate the total return, add the appreciation (£10 a share times 100 shares equals £1,000) and the dividend income (£2 per share times 100 shares equals £200) and divide that sum (£1,000 + £200, or £1,200) by the value at the beginning of the year (£50 a share times 100 shares or £5,000). The total is £1,200 (£1,000 of appreciation and £200 total dividends), or 24 per cent (£1,200 ÷ £5,000).

The last line lists the total for all the assets and their current market value. The third column answers the question, 'How well did this particular asset grow from a year ago?'

Step 3: Listing your liabilities

Liabilities are simply the bills that you're obliged to pay. Whether it's a credit card bill or a mortgage payment, a liability is an amount of money you have to pay back eventually (with interest). If you don't keep track of your liabilities, you may end up thinking that you have more money than you really do.

Table 2-2 lists some common liabilities. Use it as a model when you list your own. You should list the liabilities according to how soon you need to pay them. Credit card balances tend to be short-term obligations, whereas mortgages are long term.

TABLE 2-2   **Listing Personal Liabilities**

Liabilities	Amount	Interest Rate Charged as a Percentage (%)
Credit cards	£4,000	15
Personal loans	£13,000	10
Mortgage	£100,000	3
Total liabilities	£117,000	

Here's an overview of Table 2-2:

>> **The first column in Table 2-2 names the type of debt.** Don't forget to include student and car loans, if you have them. Don't avoid listing a liability because you're embarrassed to see how much you really owe. Be honest with yourself – doing so helps you improve your financial health.

>> **The second column shows the current value (or current balance) of your liabilities.** List the most current balance to see where you stand with your creditors.

>> **The third column reflects how much interest you're paying for carrying that debt.** This information is an important reminder about how debt can damage your wealth. Borrowing on credit cards, especially store cards, can incur interest at rates of up to 30 per cent. Using a credit card to make even a small purchase costs you if you maintain a balance. Within a year, a £50 jumper at 18 per cent costs £59 when you add the interest.

TIP

If you compare your liabilities in Table 2-2 and your personal assets in Table 2-1, you may find opportunities to reduce the amount you pay in interest. Say, for example, that you pay 15 per cent on a credit card balance of £4,000 but also have a personal asset of £5,000 in a savings account that's earning 2 per cent in interest. In that case, you could consider taking £4,000 out of the savings account to pay off the credit card balance. Doing so saves you £520; the £4,000 in the bank was earning only £80 (2 per cent of £4,000), while you were paying £600 on the credit card balance (15 per cent of £4,000).

TIP

If you can't pay off high-interest debt, at least look for ways to minimise the cost of the debt. The most obvious ways include the following:

>> Replacing high-interest cards with low-interest or no-interest cards. Many companies offer incentives to consumers, including balance transfer deals when you sign up for a new card. Some cards will charge you no interest on the debt you transfer for six, nine or 12 months.

>> Replacing credit card debt with an *unsecured personal loan*, a loan where you don't have to put up any collateral or other asset to secure the debt. Loan rates tend to be lower than expensive plastic credit but you will be paying for a longer term – up to five years is common. However, you can get personal loans at around 3 to 6 per cent instead of the 18 to 30 per cent you'll pay on the most expensive plastic.

WARNING

More and more consumers are accepting that they're taking on too much debt. Don't be one of them. Make a diligent effort to control and reduce your debt, or the debt can become too burdensome. If you don't, you may have to sell your shares just to stay liquid. And, Murphy's Law states that you *will* sell your shares at the worst possible moment. Don't go there.

Step 4: Calculating your net worth

Your *net worth* is an indication of your total wealth. You can calculate your net worth with this basic equation: total assets (Table 2-1) minus total liabilities (Table 2-2) equals net worth (net assets or net equity).

Table 2-3 shows this equation in action with a net worth of £169,090 – a very respectable figure. For many investors, just being in a position where assets exceed liabilities (a positive net worth) is great news. Use Table 2-3 as a model to analyse your own financial situation. Your mission (if you choose to accept it – and you should) is to ensure that your net worth increases from year to year as you progress toward your financial goal.

TABLE 2-3   ## Working Out Your Personal Net Worth

Totals	Amounts (£)	Increase from Year Before (%)
Total assets (from Table 2-1)	**£326,090**	+5
Total liabilities (from Table 2-2)	(£117,000)	–2
Net worth (total assets minus total liabilities)	£209,090	+3

Step 5: Analysing your balance sheet

Create a balance sheet based on the steps you've been through so far in this chapter to illustrate your current finances. Take a close look at it and try to identify any changes you can make to increase your wealth. Sometimes reaching your financial goals can be as simple as refocusing the items on your balance sheet (use Table 2-3 as a general guideline). Here are some brief points to consider:

>> **Is the money in your emergency (or rainy day) fund sitting in an ultra-safe account and earning the highest interest available?** You're likely to earn the highest interest in an online savings account with a bank or building society. But money saved in UK banks isn't entirely 100 per cent guaranteed. There is a guarantee available through the FSCS – the Financial Services Compensation scheme – but it only covers up to £85,000 per eligible person, per bank, building society or credit union. Money invested in National Savings certificates is backed by the Treasury and 100 per cent safe, but the interest rates aren't as good as the best deals offered by banks.

>> **Can you replace depreciating assets with appreciating assets?** Say that you have two computers. Why not sell one and invest the proceeds? You may say, 'But I bought that one two years ago for £500, and if I sell it now, I'll only get £300'. That's your choice. You need to decide what helps your financial situation more – a £500 item that keeps shrinking in value (a *depreciating asset*) or £300 that can grow in value when invested (an *appreciating asset*).

>> **Can you replace low-yield investments with high-yield investments?** Maybe you have £5,000 in a savings account earning 1 per cent. You can certainly shop around for a better rate at another bank or building society, but you can also seek alternatives that offer a higher yield, such as savings bonds.

>> **Can you pay off any high-interest debt with funds from low-interest assets?** If, for example, you have £5,000 earning 1 per cent in a taxable bank account, and you have $£2,500 on a credit card charging 18 per cent, you may as well pay off the credit card balance and save on the interest.

>> **If you're carrying debt, are you using that money for an investment return that is greater than the interest you're paying?** Carrying a loan with

an interest rate of 5 per cent is acceptable if that borrowed money is yielding more than 5 per cent elsewhere. Borrowing money to invest in the stock market isn't advisable in virtually any circumstance.

>> **Can you sell any personal stuff for cash?** You can replace unproductive assets with cash from car boot sales and auction websites, but be warned: the taxman is beginning to monitor these sites to tax any income.

>> **Can you use your home equity to pay off consumer debt?** Borrowing against your home has more favourable interest rates but you'll be repaying the debt for longer. (Be careful about your debt level. See Chapter 22 for warnings on debt and other concerns.)

WARNING

Paying off consumer debt by using funds borrowed against your home is one way to wipe the slate clean. It might be a relief to get rid of your credit card balances but you'll still be repaying the debt, just at a lower rate and for longer. And you might be tempted to run up the consumer debt again. You can get overburdened and experience financial ruin (not to mention homelessness). Not a pretty picture.

The important point to remember is that you can take control of your finances with discipline (and with the advice we offer in this book).

It's All about the Cash . . . (Flow)!

If you're going to invest money in shares, the first thing you need is . . . money! Where can you get that money? If you're waiting for an inheritance to come through, you may have to wait a long time, considering all the advances being made in healthcare lately. What's that? You were going to invest in healthcare shares? How ironic. Yet, the challenge still comes down to how to fund your share programme.

REMEMBER

Many investors can reallocate their investments and assets to do the trick. *Reallocation* simply means selling some investments or other assets and reinvesting that money in shares. It boils down to deciding what investment or asset you can sell or liquidate. Generally, you want to consider those investments and assets that give you a low return on your money (or no return at all). If you have a complicated mix of investments and assets, you may want to consider reviewing your options with a financial adviser. Reallocation is just part of the answer; your cash flow is the other part.

Ever wonder why there's so much month left at the end of the money? Consider your cash flow. Your *cash flow* refers to what money is coming in (income) and what money is being spent (outgoings). The net result is either a positive cash flow or a negative cash flow, depending on your cash management skills. Maintaining a positive cash flow (more money coming in than going out) helps you increase your net worth. A negative cash flow ultimately depletes your wealth and wipes out your net worth if you don't turn it around immediately. The following sections show you how to analyse your cash flow. The first step is to do a cash flow statement.

Don't confuse a cash flow statement with an income statement (also called a *profit and loss statement* or an *income and expense statement*). A cash flow statement is simple to calculate because you can easily track what goes in and what goes out.

With a cash flow statement (see Table 2-6, later in this chapter), you ask yourself three questions:

>> **What money is coming in?** In your cash flow statement, jot down all sources of income. Calculate it for the month and then for the year. Include everything, including salary, wages, interest, dividends and so on. Add them all up and get a grand total for your income.

>> **What are your outgoings?** Write down all the things that you spend money on. List all your expenses. If possible, categorise them into essential and non-essential items. You can get an idea of all the expenses that you can reduce without affecting your lifestyle. But before you even try to do that, make the list of what you spend money on as complete as possible.

>> **What's left?** If your income is greater than your outgoings, and you have an emergency fund (see the section, 'Step 1: Making sure you have an emergency fund,' earlier in this chapter), then you have money ready and available for investing in shares, no matter how small the amount. We've seen small fortunes built when people started to diligently invest as little as £25 to £50 a week or a month. If your outgoings are greater than your income, then you need to sharpen your pencil. Cut down on non-essential spending and/or increase your income. If your budget is a little tight, put your share investment plans on hold until your cash flow improves.

Step 1: Tallying up your income

Using Table 2-4 as a worksheet, list and calculate the money you have coming in. The first column describes the source of the money, the second column indicates the monthly amount from each respective source and the last column indicates the amount projected for a full year. Include all income, such as wages, business income, dividends, interest income and so on. Then project these amounts for a year (multiply by 12) and enter those amounts in the third column.

TABLE 2-4   **Listing Your Income**

Item	Monthly £ Amount	Yearly £ Amount
Salary and wages		
Interest income and dividends		
Business net (after tax) income		
Other income		
Total income		

REMEMBER

This is the amount of money you have to work with. To ensure your financial health, don't spend more than this amount. Always be aware of and carefully manage your income.

Step 2: Adding up your outgoings

Using Table 2-5 as a worksheet, list and calculate the money that's going out. What are you spending, and on what? The first column describes what the expense is, the second column indicates the monthly amount and the third column shows that amount projected for a full year. Include all the money you spend, including credit card and other debt payments; household expenses, such as food, utility bills and travel expenses; and money spent for non-essential expenses such as cigarettes (they're banned in most places now anyway) and elephant-foot umbrella stands.

Tax is just a category in which to lump all the various taxes that you pay the government. If you're employed and pay your tax by PAYE you may not need to list much in this category. You should include all the tax you pay through the self-assessment process. If you're self-employed, you'll have a higher tax figure to include. Feel free to put each individual tax on its own line if you prefer. The important thing is to create a comprehensive list that's meaningful to you. You may notice that the outgoings don't include items such as payments into pensions or ISAs or other savings vehicles. Yes, these items do impact your cash flow, but they're not expenses; the amounts that you invest (or your employer invests for you) are essentially assets that benefit your financial situation versus an expense that doesn't help you build wealth. If you pay into a company pension fund, that will probably be taken care of in the income table if you have included your *net salary* (what's left after tax and other deductions).

TABLE 2-5   **Listing Your Expenses (Outgoings)**

Item	Monthly £ Amount	Yearly £ Amount
Tax		
Rent or mortgage		
Utilities		
Food		
Clothing		
Insurance (car, household, travel and so on)		
Telephone and mobile		
Council tax		
Car expenses		
Charity donations		
Hobbies		
Credit card payments		
Loan payments		
Other		
Total		

Step 3: Creating a cash flow statement

Okay, you're almost at the end. The last step is creating a cash flow statement so that you can see (all in one place) how your money moves – how much comes in and how much goes out and where it goes.

Plug the amount of your total income (from Table 2-4) and the amount of your total expenses (from Table 2-5) into the Table 2-6 worksheet to see your *cash flow*. Do you have positive cash flow – more coming in than going out – so that you can start investing in shares (or other investments), or are expenses overpowering your income? Doing a cash flow statement isn't just about finding money in your financial situation to fund your shares plan. First and foremost, it's about your financial well-being. Are you managing your finances well, or not?

TABLE 2-6 **Looking at Your Cash Flow**

Item	Monthly £ Amount	Yearly £ Amount
Total income (from Table 2-4)		
Total outgoings (from Table 2-5)		
Net inflow/outflow		

Step 4: Analysing your cash flow

Use your cash flow statement to identify sources of funds for your investment plan. The more you can increase your income and the more you can reduce your outgoings, the better. Scrutinise your data. Where can you improve the results? Here are some questions to ask yourself:

» How can you increase your income? Do you have hobbies, interests or skills that can generate extra cash for you?

» Can you get more paid overtime at work? How about a promotion or a job change?

» Where can you cut expenses?

» Have you categorised your expenses as either 'necessary' or 'non-essential'?

» Can you lower your debt payments by switching your personal loans and credit card balances to low-cost or no-cost credit?

» Have you shopped around for cheaper insurance or utility bills?

» Have you analysed how much tax you pay to ensure you are not overpaying?

Finding investment money in tax savings

Research has shown that the average worker in the UK pays more than half of her earnings to the government in direct and indirect taxation. Sitting down with your accountant or financial adviser to try to find ways to reduce your tax is always a good idea. Running a business from home, for example, is a great way to gain new income and to write some expenses off against tax. Doing so can result in a lower tax burden. Your accountant might have ideas that could work for you.

One tax strategy to consider is doing your investing in shares in a tax-sheltered account such as an Individual Savings Account (ISA). Again, check with your accountant or financial adviser about tax deductions and strategies that are available to you. For more on the tax implications of investing in shares, see Chapter 20.

Setting Your Sights on Your Financial Goals

Consider shares as tools for living, just like any other investment – no more, no less. They're the tools you use (one of many) to accomplish something – to achieve a goal. Yes, successfully investing in shares is the goal that you're probably aiming for if you're reading this book. However, you must complete the following sentence: 'I want to be successful in my share investing programme to accomplish . . .' You must consider investing in shares as a means to an end. When people buy a computer, they don't (or shouldn't) think of buying a computer just to have a computer. People buy a computer because doing so helps them achieve a particular result, such as being more efficient in business, playing fun games or spending hours on the Internet.

Know the difference between long-term, medium-term and short-term goals and then set some of each. *Long-term goals* are a reference to projects or financial goals that need funding five or more years from now. *Medium-term goals* refer to financial goals that need funding two to five years from now. *Short-term goals* need funding soon – less than two years from now.

In general, shares are best suited to long-term goals, such as:

>> Achieving financial independence (think retirement funding)

>> Paying for higher education

>> Paying for any long-term expenditure or project

Some categories of shares (such as conservative or blue chip) may be suitable for medium-term financial goals. If, for example, you plan to retire four years from now, conservative shares may be appropriate. If you're optimistic about the stock market and confident that share prices will rise, then go ahead and invest.

Shares generally aren't suitable for short-term investing goals because share prices can be very volatile in price over a short period of time. Shares fluctuate from day to day, so you don't know what they'll be worth in the near future. You may end up with less money than you expected. For investors seeking to reliably accrue money for short-term needs, short-term savings bonds or certificates or guaranteed stock market bonds are more appropriate.

WARNING

In recent years, investors have sought quick, short-term profits by trading and speculating in shares. Lured by the fantastic returns generated by the stock market in recent decades, some investors saw shares as a get-rich-quick scheme and jumped into the day trading game, where they were betting on the direction of a share (or market) on a day-by-day basis. Big mistake! It's extremely important for you to understand the difference between *investing*, *saving* and *speculating*. Which one do you want to do? Knowing the answer to this question is crucial to your goals and aspirations. Investors who don't know the difference tend to get burned. Here's some information to help you distinguish between these three actions:

>> *Investing* **is the act of putting your current funds into securities or tangible assets for the purpose of gaining future appreciation, income or both.** You need time, knowledge and discipline to invest. The investment can fluctuate in price, but has been chosen for long-term potential.

>> *Saving* **is the safe accumulation of funds for a future use.** Savings don't fluctuate and are generally free of financial risk. The emphasis is on safety and liquidity.

>> *Speculating* **is the financial world's equivalent of gambling.** An investor who speculates is seeking quick profits gained from short-term price movements in that particular asset or investment. Some people make money from speculating (even spread-betting, which is another form of speculation), but most don't!

The key message from this process of self-analysis and scrutiny involves returning to our starting thought in this chapter – know thyself. Short-term speculation can work if you're the right kind of investor but, for most people, it's all about getting the household budget in shape and hunkering down for long-term saving and investing.

Chapter **3**

Defining Common Approaches to Investing in Shares

Read this chapter carefully. Millions of investors are at risk because the market sees as much mis-investing activity in shares as it does investing. We know it sounds weird, but the situation is similar to your mad Aunt Jean reversing into the garden wall when she should be heading out onto the road on her way to the shops – she knows she needs to do something, but she chooses the wrong mechanism. Shares are tools you can use to build your wealth. When used wisely, for the right purpose, and in the right environment, they do a great job. But when improperly applied, they can lead to disaster.

In this chapter, we show you how to choose the right investments, based on your short- and long-term financial goals. We also show you how to decide on your reason for investing (for growth or income) and the style of investing – cautious or aggressive – that you need to take.

Matching Shares and Strategies with Your Goals

There are, on any one day, literally thousands of different shares available to invest in and dozens of different strategies and investment approaches. The key to success in the stock market is matching the right kind of share with the right investment situation and investment strategy. You have to choose the share and the approach that match your goals. (Refer to Chapter 2 for more on defining your financial goals.)

Before investing in a share, ask yourself, 'When do I want to reach my financial goal?' Shares are a means to an end. Your job is to figure out what that end is – or, more importantly, when that end is. Do you want to retire in ten years or next year? Must you pay for your child's university education next year or 18 years from now? The time you have before you need the money you hope to earn from investing determines what shares you should buy. Table 3-1 gives you a few guidelines for choosing the kind of shares best suited to your type of investor considering the goals that you have.

TABLE 3-1   Types of Investors, Financial Goals and Shares

Type of Investor	Time Frame for Financial Goals	Type of Share Most Suitable
Cautious (worries about risk)	Long term (more than 10 years)	Blue-chip and large-cap shares
Aggressive (high tolerance to risk)	Long term (more than 10 years)	Small-cap and mid-cap shares
Cautious (worries about risk)	Medium term (3 to 10 years)	Blue-chip and large-cap shares, preferably with dividends
Aggressive (high tolerance to risk)	Medium term (3 to 10 years)	Small-cap and mid-cap shares
Short term	1 to 2 years	Shares aren't suitable for the short term. Instead, look at tax-efficient savings accounts such as a cash ISA, savings with MS&I and guaranteed investment bonds.

TECHNICAL STUFF

Dividends are payments made to an owner (unlike *interest*, which is payment to a creditor). Dividends are a great form of income, especially if you reinvest those dividend cheques back in the underlying shares. For more information on dividend-paying shares, see the 'Investing for a Reason' section later in this chapter, and also Chapter 9.

Table 3-1 gives you general guidelines, but keep in mind that not everyone can fit into a particular profile. Every investor has a unique situation, set of goals and level of risk tolerance. Remember that the terms *large-cap*, *mid-cap* and *small-cap* refer to the size (or *market capitalisation*, also known as *market cap*) of the company. All factors being equal, large companies are less risky than small companies. For more on market caps, refer to the section, 'Investing in Your Personal Style,' later in this chapter.

Investing for the Future

Are your goals long term or short term? Answering this question is important because individual shares can be either a great or a horrible choice, depending on the time period you want to focus on. Generally, the length of time you plan to invest in shares can be short term, medium term or long term. The following sections outline what kinds of shares are most appropriate for each term length.

REMEMBER

Investing in shares becomes less risky as the time frame lengthens. Share prices tend to fluctuate on a daily basis, but they also have a tendency to follow an upward or downward trend over an extended period of time. Even if you invest in a share that goes down in the short term, you may see it rise and possibly go above your initial investment if you have the patience to wait it out and let the share price appreciate.

Focusing on the short term

Short term generally means one year or less, although some people extend the period to two years or less.

Every person has short-term goals. Some are modest, such as setting aside money for a holiday next month or paying for a new kitchen. Other short-term goals are more ambitious, such as building up a deposit for a new home within six months. Whatever the expense or purchase, you need a predictable accumulation of cash soon. If your goals are essentially short term, stay away from the stock market!

WARNING

Because shares can be so unpredictable in the short term, they're a bad choice for short-term considerations. We get a kick out of market analysts on television saying things such as, 'At £10 a share, XYZ is a solid investment, and we feel that its share price should hit our target of £20 within six to nine months.' You know that an eager investor hears that and says, 'Wow, why bother with 1 per cent at the bank when this share will double? I'd better call my broker.' It may hit that target (or surpass it), or it may not. Most of the time, the share doesn't reach the target price, and the investor is disappointed. The share may just as easily go down. The reason that target prices are frequently (usually) missed is that the analyst is just one person, and it's difficult for them to work out what millions of investors will do in the short term. The short term can be volatile, perhaps even irrational, because so many investors have so many reasons for buying and selling that analysis becomes difficult. If you want to use the money you invest for an important short-term need, you can't afford to lose any of it on the stock market during that time.

REMEMBER

Short-term share investment is highly unpredictable. You can better serve your short-term goals with stable, interest-bearing investments (like bank or building society savings accounts).

Considering medium-term goals

Medium term refers to financial goals that you plan to reach within five years. If, for example, you want to accumulate cash as the deposit for an investment in property four years from now, growth-orientated investments might be suitable.

Although some shares *may* be appropriate for a two- or three-year period, not all shares are good medium-term investments. Different types and categories of shares exist. Some shares are fairly stable and hold their value well, such as shares in much larger or established dividend-paying companies. Other shares have prices that jump all over the place, such as volatile small-cap mining stocks or the shares of small, untested technology companies that haven't been in existence long enough to develop a consistent track record.

TIP

If you plan to invest in the stock market to meet medium-term goals, consider large, established companies or dividend-paying companies in industries that provide life's essentials (such as food and drink or utilities).

Preparing for the long term

Investing in shares is best suited to making money over a long period of time, preferably 10 to 20 years. Even investors who bought shares during the depths of the Great Depression saw profitable growth in their share portfolios over a ten- or twenty-year period.

In fact, if you examine any ten-year period over the past 50 years, you see that shares win over other financial investments (such as bonds or bank investments) in almost every single ten-year period when measured by total return (taking into account reinvesting and compounding of capital gains and dividends). Chapters 8 and 9 cover growth and income, and Chapter 18 gives you the lowdown on reinvestment and compounding. As you can see, long-term planning allows shares to shine. Of course, your work doesn't stop at deciding on a long-term investment. You still have to do your homework and choose shares wisely because, even in good times, you can lose money if you invest in companies that go out of business. Part 3 shows you how to evaluate specific companies and industries, and alerts you to factors in the general economy that can affect share price behaviour. Appendix A provides plenty of resources you can turn to.

REMEMBER

Because you can choose between many different types and categories of shares, virtually any investor with a long-term perspective should consider adding shares to their investment portfolio. Whether you want to save for a young child's university education or for future retirement goals, carefully selected shares have proven to be a superior long-term investment in the past.

Investing for a Reason

When a woman was asked why she bungee-jumped off the bridge that spanned a massive ravine, she answered, 'Because it's fun!' When someone asked a man why he dived into a pool full of alligators and snakes, he responded, 'Because someone pushed me.' Your investment in shares shouldn't happen unless you have a reason that you understand, like investing for growth or investing for income. Even if an adviser pushes you to invest, be sure that they give you an explanation of how their choice of share fits your purpose.

Take the example of a nice, elderly lady who had a portfolio brimming with aggressive-growth shares because she had an overbearing stockbroker. Her purpose should've been cautious, and she should have chosen investments that would preserve her wealth rather than grow it. Obviously, the stockbroker's agenda got in the way. Shares are just a means to an end. Figure out your desired end and then match the means. To find out more about dealing with stockbrokers, go to Chapter 7.

Growth investing

When investors want their money to grow, they look for investments that appreciate in value. *Appreciate* is just another way of saying 'grow'. If you have a share that you bought for £8 a share and now its value is £30 a share, your investment has grown by £22 a share – that's appreciation. We know we would appreciate it.

Appreciation (also known as *capital gain*) is probably the number one reason why people invest in shares. Few investments have the potential to grow your wealth as conveniently as shares. If you want the stock market to make you bumper returns over a relatively short period of time (and we still mean years!), head to Chapter 8, which takes an in-depth look at the risky world of investing for growth.

WARNING

Shares are a great way to grow your wealth, but they're not the only way. Many investors seek alternative ways to make money, but many of these alternative ways are more aggressive and carry significantly more risk. You may have heard about people who made quick fortunes in areas such as commodities (like gold, oil or coffee), options and other more sophisticated investment vehicles. Keep in mind that you should limit risky investments to only a portion of your portfolio, such as 10 per cent of your investible funds. Experienced investors, however, can go as high as 20 per cent. Chapter 8 goes into greater detail about growth investing.

Income investing

Not all investors want to take on the risk that comes with making a killing. Some people just want to invest in the stock market as a means of providing a steady income. They don't need share values to go through the ceiling. Instead, they need shares that perform well consistently.

If your reason for investing in shares is to create income, you need to choose shares that pay dividends. Dividends are usually paid twice a year to shareholders listed on the company register.

Distinguishing between dividends and interest

Don't confuse dividends with interest. Most people are familiar with interest, because that's what's added to your money over the years in the bank. The important difference is that *interest* is paid to creditors, and *dividends* are paid to owners or shareholders (if you own shares, you're a shareholder because your shares represent the parts of a publicly traded company that you own).

REMEMBER

When you buy shares, you buy pieces of that company. When you put money in a bank (or when you buy bonds), you basically lend your money. You become a creditor, and the bank or bond issuer is the debtor, and as such, it must eventually pay your money back to you with interest.

Recognising the importance of an income share's yield

Investing for income means that you have to consider your investment's *yield*, the percentage return on your investment. If you want income from a stock market investment, you must compare the yield from one particular share with alternatives. Looking at the yield is a way to compare the income you expect to receive from one investment with the expected income from others. Table 3-2 shows comparative yields.

TABLE 3-2   ## Comparing the Yields of Various Investments

Investment	Type	Amount Invested	Pay Type	Payout	Yield (%)
Smith Co.	Stock	£50/share	Dividend	£2.50	5.0
Jones Co.	Stock	£100/share	Dividend	£4.00	4.0
Acme Bank	Bank account	£500	Interest	£25.00	1.0
Acme Bank	Bank account	£2,500	Interest	£131.25	1.25
Acme Bank	Bank account	£5,000	Interest	£287.50	1.75
Brown Co.	Bond	£5,000	Interest	£300.00	2.0

To understand how to calculate yield, you need the following formula:

Yield = Payout ÷ Investment Amount

Yield enables you to compare how much income you'd get for a prospective investment compared with the income you'd get from other investments. For the sake of simplicity, this exercise is based on an annual percentage yield basis (compounding would increase the yield).

Jones Co. and Smith Co. are both typical dividend-paying shares, and in the example presented in Table 3-2, presume that both companies are similar in most respects except for their differing dividends. How can you tell whether a £50 share with a £2.50 annual dividend is better (or worse) than a £100 share with a £4.00 dividend? The yield tells you.

Even though Jones Co. pays a higher dividend (£4.00), Smith Co. has a higher yield (5 per cent). Therefore, if you had to choose between those two shares as an income investor, you'd choose Smith Co, all else being equal (of course, all else is rarely equal and choosing dividend shares is more complicated than this).

REMEMBER

Shares that pay strong, regular dividends can also increase in value. They may not always have the same growth potential as growth shares, but, at the least, they have a greater potential for capital gain than a bank's savings accounts or bonds. We cover dividend-paying shares (investing for income) in Chapter 9.

Investing in Your Personal Style

Your investing style has nothing to do with the jeans versus pinstripes debate. It refers to your approach to investing in shares. Do you want to be cautious or aggressive? Would you rather be the tortoise or the hare? Your investment personality greatly depends on your reason for investing and the term over which you're planning to invest (see the previous two sections in this chapter). The following sections outline the two most common investment styles.

Cautious investing

Cautious investing means that you put your money into something proven, tried and true. You invest your money in safe and secure places, such as banks and government-backed securities. But how does that apply to shares? (Table 3-1 gives you suggestions.)

Cautious stock market investors want to place their money in companies that have exhibited the following qualities:

>> **Proven performance, also known as 'quality':** You want companies that have shown increasing sales and earnings year after year. You don't demand anything spectacular, just a strong and steady performance. In sum, you want a quality company with a strong business franchise.

>> **Market size:** Companies should be large-cap (short for large capitalisation). Cautious investors believe that bigger is safer. Mostly they'd focus on shares in the FTSE 100 (see Chapter 5 for more on this).

>> **Market leadership:** Companies should be leaders in their industries.

>> **Perceived staying power:** You want companies with the financial clout and market position to weather uncertain market and economic conditions. It shouldn't matter what happens in the economy or who gets elected.

As a cautious investor, you don't mind if the companies' share prices jump (who would?), but you're more concerned with steady growth over the long term. Shares in blue-chip companies are your ideal.

Aggressive investing

Aggressive investors can plan long term or look only over the medium term, but in both cases, they want shares that resemble young greyhounds – able to race ahead of the pack. Aggressive stock market investors want to invest their money in companies that have exhibited the following qualities:

>> **Great potential:** The company must have superior goods or services or smarter working practices than the competition, which suggest that it should grow quickly in future.

>> **Capital gains possibility:** Dividends aren't your first consideration. You may even dislike dividends. You feel that the money is better reinvested in the company. This reinvestment, in turn, can spur greater growth.

>> **Innovation and exploration:** Companies should have technologies, ideas or certain creative methods that make them stand apart from other companies. Alternatively, they might own large tracts of land under which sit vast reserves of oil/gold/copper/iron ore . . . you get the drift! Increasingly, innovation means exploring new areas for huge reserves of natural resources.

Aggressive investors usually seek out small capitalisation stocks, known as *small-caps*, because they have plenty of potential for growth. Take the tree example, for instance: a sturdy oak may be strong, but it may not grow much more, whereas a brand-new sapling has plenty of growth to look forward to. Why invest in stodgy, big companies when you can invest in smaller enterprises that may become the leaders of tomorrow? Aggressive investors have no problem investing in obscure companies because they hope that such companies may become another Tesco. Find out more about investing for growth in Chapter 8.

Chapter **4**

Assessing the Risks

nvestors face many risks, many of which we cover in this chapter. The simplest definition of risk for investors is 'the possibility that your investment will lose some (or all) of its value'. Yet you don't have to fear risk if you understand and plan for it. You need to get familiar with the concept of risk. You must understand the oldest equation in the world of investing – risk versus return. This equation states the following:

> If you want a greater return on your money, you need to tolerate more risk. If you don't want to tolerate more risk, you must tolerate a lower rate of return.

Everyone needs to remember that risk isn't a four-letter word. Well, it is a four-letter word, but you know what we mean. Risk is present no matter what you do with your money. Even if you simply stick your money under the mattress, risk is involved – several kinds in fact. You have the risk of fire. What if your house burns down? You have the risk of theft. What if burglars find your stash of cash? You also have relative risk. (Your relatives may find your money!)

Be aware of the different kinds of risk, and you can easily plan around them to keep your money growing.

Exploring Different Kinds of Risk

Think about all the ways in which an investment can lose money. You can list all sorts of possibilities. So many that you may think, 'Aaargh! Why invest at all?'

Don't let risk frighten you. After all, life itself is risky. Just make sure that you understand the different kinds of risk before you start navigating the investment world. Be mindful of risk and find out about the effects of risk on your investments and personal financial goals.

Financial risk

The financial risk of investing in shares is that you can lose your money if the company whose shares you buy loses money or goes belly up. This type of risk is the most obvious because companies do go bankrupt.

You can greatly enhance the chances of your financial risk paying off by doing an adequate amount of research and choosing your shares carefully (which this book helps you do – see Part 3 for more details). Financial risk is a real concern even when the economy is doing well. Diligent research, a little planning and a dose of common sense help you reduce your financial risk.

Internet and technology shares littered the graveyard of stock market catastrophes during 2000/2001, 2008/9 and 2020 because investors didn't see (or didn't want to see) the risks involved with companies that didn't offer a solid record of results (profits, sales and so on). Remember that when you invest in companies without a proven track record, you're not investing, you're speculating.

REMEMBER

In terms of financial risk, the bottom line is . . . well . . . the bottom line! A healthy *bottom line* (an accounting term for the net profit a company makes) means that a company is making money. And if a company is making money, then you can make money by investing in its shares. However, if a company isn't making money, you're unlikely to make money if you invest in it (unless you can hang on until it does make money). Profit is the lifeblood of any company.

Interest rate risk

Interest rate risk may sound like an odd type of risk, but in fact, it's a common consideration for investors. Probably because investors have been living in an era of low or even zero interest rates, they've forgotten that it hasn't always been like this. Be aware that interest rates change on a regular basis, causing challenging moments.

Banks set their own interest rates, but they generally follow the base rate set by the Bank of England's monetary policy committee. When the Bank of England raises or lowers interest rates, banks and building societies raise or lower interest rates on mortgages and savings, accordingly. Interest rate changes affect consumers, businesses and, of course, investors. And boy can the effects be major – since 2008 interest rates in the UK, for instance, have barely budged above 0.5 per cent and in fact dozens respectable banks are offering savings rates of precisely . . . 0 per cent!

The scenario outlined in the following paragraphs gives you a generic introduction to the way fluctuating interest rate risk can affect investors in general.

Suppose that you buy a long-term, high-quality corporate bond and get a yield of 5 per cent. Your money is safe, and your return is locked in at 5 per cent. Great! That's a guaranteed 5 per cent. Not bad, eh? But what happens if, after you commit your money, suddenly, out of nowhere, interest rates shoot up from 0.5 per cent to 8 per cent? You lose the opportunity to get that extra 3 per cent interest. The only way to get out of your 5 per cent bond is to sell it at current market values and use the money to reinvest at the higher rate.

The only problem with this scenario is that the 5 per cent bond is likely to drop in value because interest rates rose. Why? Say that the investor is called Bob and the bond yielding 5 per cent is a corporate bond issued by Acme Enterprises (AE). According to the bond agreement, AE must pay 5 per cent (called the *face rate* or *nominal rate*) during the life of the bond and then, upon maturity, pay the principal. If Bob buys £10,000 of AE bonds on the day they're issued, he gets £500 (of interest) every year for as long as he holds the bonds. If he holds on until maturity, he gets back his £10,000 (the principal). So far, so good? The plot thickens, however.

Say that he decides to sell the bond long before maturity and that, at the time of the sale, interest rates in the market have risen to 8 per cent. Now what? The reality is that no one is going to want his 5 per cent bond if the market is offering bonds at 8 per cent. What's Bob to do? He can't change the face rate of 5 per cent, and he can't change the fact that only £500 is paid each year for the life of the bond. What has to change so that current investors get the *equivalent* yield of 8 per cent? Of course, *the bond's value has to go down*. In this example, the bond's market value needs to drop to £6,250 so that investors buying the bond get an equivalent yield of 8 per cent. (For simplicity's sake, we have left out the time it takes for the bond to mature.) Here's how it works out:

New investors still get £500 annually. However, £500 is equal to 8 per cent of £6,250. Therefore, even though investors get the face rate of 5 per cent, they get a yield of 8 per cent because the actual investment amount is £6,250. In this example, no financial risk is present, but you see how interest rate risk presents itself. Bob finds out that you can have a good company with a good bond, yet still lose more than £3,500 because of the change in the interest rate. Of course, if Bob doesn't sell, he doesn't realise that loss. (For more on when to sell, see Chapter 17.)

REMEMBER

You can lose money in an apparently sound investment because of something that sounds as harmless as 'interest rates have changed'.

Understanding the adverse effects of rising interest rates

Rising and falling interest rates offer a special risk to stock market investors. Historically, rising interest rates have had an adverse effect on share prices. We outline several reasons why in the following sections.

Hurting a company's financial condition

Rising interest rates have a negative impact on companies that carry a large current debt load or that need to take on more debt because, when interest rates rise, the cost of borrowing money rises, too. Ultimately, the company's profitability and ability to grow are reduced. When a company's profits (or earnings) drop, its shares become less desirable, and its share price falls.

Affecting a company's customers

A company's success comes when it sells its products or services. But what happens if increased interest rates negatively impact its customers (specifically, other companies that buy from it)? The financial health of its customers directly affects the company's ability to grow sales and earnings.

Impacting investors' decision-making considerations

When interest rates rise, investors start to rethink their investment strategies, resulting in one of two outcomes:

>> Investors may sell any shares that they hold in interest rate–sensitive industries. These include utilities, property and the financial sector. Although increased interest rates can hurt these sectors, the reverse is also generally true: falling interest rates boost the same industries. Keep in mind that interest rate changes affect some industries more than others.

>> Investors who favour increased current income (versus waiting for the investment to grow in value to sell for a gain later on) are definitely attracted to investment vehicles that offer a higher rate of return. Higher interest rates can cause investors to switch from shares to bonds or high-interest savings accounts.

Hurting share prices indirectly

High or rising interest rates can have a negative impact on any investor's total financial picture. What happens when an investor struggles with burdensome debt, such as a second mortgage or credit card debt? They may sell some shares in order to pay off part of the high-interest debt. Selling shares to service debt is a common practice that, when taken collectively, can hurt share prices.

TIP

Because of the effects of interest rates on share portfolios, both direct and indirect, successful investors regularly monitor interest rates in both the general economy and in their personal situations. Although shares have proven to be a superior long-term investment (the longer the term, the better), every investor should maintain a balanced portfolio that includes other investment vehicles, such as gilts, savings bonds and/or bank accounts.

REMEMBER

A diversified investor has money in vehicles that do well when interest rates rise. These vehicles include savings accounts and certificates and other variable-rate investments whose interest rates rise when market rates rise. These types of investments add a measure of safety from interest rate risk to your stock portfolio.

Market risk

People talk about *the market* and how it goes up or down, making it sound like a monolithic entity instead of what it really is – a group of millions of individuals making daily decisions to buy or sell shares. No matter how modern the society and economic system is, you can't escape the law of supply and demand. When masses of people want to buy a particular share, it becomes 'in demand', and its price rises. That price rises higher if the supply is limited. Conversely, if no one's interested in buying a share, its price falls. Supply and demand are the nature of market risk. The price of the share you purchase can rise or fall according to the fickle whim of market demand.

Millions of investors buying and selling each minute of every trading day affect the price of your shares. This fact makes it impossible to judge which way your shares will move tomorrow or next week. This unpredictability is why shares aren't appropriate for short-term financial growth.

REMEMBER

Investing requires diligent work and research before putting your money in quality investments with a long-term perspective. Speculating is attempting to make a relatively quick profit by monitoring the short-term price movements of a particular investment. Investors seek to minimise risk, whereas speculators don't mind risk because it can also magnify profits. Speculating and investing have clear differences, but investors frequently become speculators and ultimately put themselves and their wealth at risk. Don't be one of them.

Consider the married couple nearing retirement who decided to play with their money to see if they could make their pending retirement more comfortable. They borrowed a sizeable sum by tapping into the equity in their home to invest in the stock market. What did they do with these funds? You guessed it; they invested in the high-flying shares of the day. Within eight months, they lost almost all their money.

WARNING

Understanding market risk is especially important for people who are tempted to put their nest eggs or emergency funds into volatile investments such as growth shares (or unit trusts that invest in growth shares or similarly aggressive investment vehicles). Remember, you can lose everything.

Inflation risk

Inflation is the artificial expansion of the quantity of money so that too much money is used in exchange for goods and services. To consumers, inflation shows up in the form of higher prices for goods and services. Inflation risk is also referred to as *purchasing power risk*. This term just means that your money doesn't buy as much as it used to. For example, £1 that bought you a sandwich in 2000 barely buys you a . . . sandwich today. Wait, didn't we get that wrong? No. Inflation rates have been low, but that doesn't mean that prices didn't change. They did, but maybe that sandwich you buy today is smaller or contains fewer premium ingredients. For you, the investor, this risk means that the value of your investment (a bond, for example) may not keep up with inflation.

Say that you have money in a savings account currently earning 1 per cent. This account has flexibility – if the market interest rate goes up, the rate you earn in your account also goes up. Your account is safe from both financial risk and interest rate risk. But what if inflation is running at 5 per cent? At that point, you're losing money.

Tax risk

Tax (such as income tax or capital gains tax) doesn't affect your stock market investment directly. Tax can obviously affect how much of your money you get to keep. Because the entire point of investing in shares is to build wealth, you need to understand that taxes take away a portion of the wealth that you're trying to build. Taxes can be risky because if you make the wrong move with your shares (selling them at the wrong time, for example), you can end up paying higher tax than you need to. Because tax laws change so frequently, tax risk is part of the risk-versus-return equation, as well.

It pays to mug up on how tax can impact your wealth-building programme before you make your investment decisions. Chapter 20 covers in greater detail the impact of tax.

Political and governmental risks

If companies were fish, politics and government policies (such as tax, laws and regulations) would be the pond. In the same way that fish die in a toxic or polluted pond, politics and government policies can kill companies. Of course, if you own shares in a company exposed to political and governmental risks, you need to be aware of these risks. For some companies, a single new regulation or law is enough to send them into bankruptcy. For other companies, a new law may help them increase sales and profits.

What if you invest in companies or industries that become political targets? You may want to consider selling them (you can always buy them back later) or consider putting stop-loss orders on the stock (see Chapter 17). For example, a few years ago tobacco companies were the targets of political firestorms that battered their share prices. Now, the enormous social media companies are in the firing line. Whether you agree or disagree with the political machinations of the day isn't the issue. As an investor, you have to ask yourself, 'How do politics affect the market value and the current and future prospects of my chosen investment?' (See Chapter 14 for more on how politics can affect the stock market.)

Personal risks

Frequently, the risk involved with investing in the stock market may not be directly related to the investment or factors directly related to the investment; sometimes the risk is with the investor's circumstances.

Suppose that investor Ralph puts £15,000 into a portfolio of ordinary shares. Imagine that the market experiences a drop in prices that week and Ralph's shares drop to a market value of £14,000.

Because shares are good for the long term, this type of decrease usually isn't an alarming incident. Odds are that this dip is temporary, especially if Ralph carefully chose high-quality companies. Incidentally, if a portfolio of high-quality shares *does* experience a temporary drop in price, it can be a great opportunity to get more shares at a good price. (Chapter 17 covers orders you can place with your broker to help you do that.)

Over the long term, Ralph would probably see the value of his investment grow substantially. But, what if during a period when his shares are declining, Ralph experiences financial difficulty and needs quick cash? He may have to sell his shares to get money.

This problem occurs frequently for investors who don't have an emergency fund or a rainy-day fund to handle large, sudden expenses. You never know when your company may lay you off or when your roof may leak, leaving you with a huge repair bill. Car accidents, household emergencies and other unforeseen events are part of life's bag of surprises – for anyone. Be sure to set money aside for sudden expenses before you buy shares. Then you aren't forced to prematurely liquidate your stock market investments to pay emergency bills. (Chapter 2 provides more guidance on having liquid assets for emergencies.)

REMEMBER

You probably won't get much comfort from knowing that losses from shares are tax deductible – a loss is a loss (see Chapter 20 regarding tax). However, you can avoid the kind of loss that results from prematurely having to sell your shares if you maintain an emergency cash fund. A good place for your emergency cash fund is in an instant access ISA or other savings account.

Emotional risk

What does emotional risk have to do with shares? Emotions are important risk considerations because the main decision makers are human beings. Logic and discipline are critical factors in investment success, but even the best investor can let emotions take over the reins of money management and cause loss. For stock market investing, you're likely to be side-tracked by three main emotions: greed, fear and love. You need to understand your emotions and what kinds of risks they can expose you to. If you get too attached to a sinking share, then you don't need a book on investing in shares, you need a doctor.

Paying the price for greed

In the period between 2001 and 2007, millions of investors threw caution to the wind and chased bumper dividends paid out by huge, global investment banks. The pound signs popped up in their eyes (just like slot machines) when they saw that easy street was lined with large, supposedly safe institutions paying out dividend yields of 5, 6 or even 8 per cent per annum. The rest is history as the global financial crisis (GFC) swept into town and the banks teetered on the edge and stopped paying their dividends!

Unfortunately, the lure of easy money can easily turn healthy attitudes towards growing wealth into unhealthy greed that blinds investors and discards common sense (such as investing for quick short-term gains in dubious 'hot tips', rather than doing your homework and buying shares of solid companies with strong fundamentals and a long-term focus).

Recognising the role of fear

Greed can be a problem, but fear is the other extreme. People who are fearful of loss frequently avoid suitable investments and end up settling for a low rate of return. If you have to succumb to one of these emotions, at least fear exposes you to less loss.

Looking for love in all the wrong places

Shares are dispassionate, inanimate vehicles, but people can look for love in the strangest places. Emotional risk occurs when investors fall in love with a share and refuse to sell it even when the share is plummeting and shows all the symptoms of getting worse. Emotional risk also occurs when investors are drawn to bad investment choices just because they sound good, are popular or are pushed by family or friends. Love and attachment are great in relationships with people, but can be horrible with investments.

INVESTMENT LESSONS FROM THE GLOBAL FINANCIAL CRISIS OF 2007–2009

The dark days of 2008 in particular seem distant now, but investors all peered collectively over the edge and didn't like what they saw. Rumours of cash machines running out of money spread, stock markets plunged at an alarming rate and banks were folding right, left and centre – remember names such as Lehman Brothers, Northern Rock and Bradford and Bingley. The financial world very nearly caved in and many, many investors lost a great deal of money. But there were – and are – some crucial lessons that can be learnt from these dark days:

- **Diversify your portfolio.** Investors should always spread their risk exposure and invest in different industries and sectors. Don't just pile head-long into bank stocks . . . or technology stocks . . . or even commodity stocks. Keeping your portfolio diversified is a time-tested strategy that is more relevant than ever before.

(continued)

(continued)

- **Review and reallocate.** The global financial crisis hit some sectors especially hard, but some markets (although not many) did well. Monitor your portfolio and ask yourself whether it's overly reliant on or exposed to events in specific sectors. If so, reallocate your investments to decrease your risk exposure.

- **Check for signs of trouble.** Techniques such as trailing stops (explained in Chapter 17) come in handy when your shares plummet because of unexpected events. Even if you don't use these techniques, you can make analysing your shares and checking for signs of trouble, such as debts or P/E ratios that are too high, a regular habit. If you see signs of trouble, consider selling anyway.

Minimising Your Risk

Before you go mad thinking that investing in shares carries so much risk that you may as well not get out of bed, take a breath. Minimising your risk is easier than you think. Although wealth-building through the stock market doesn't take place without some amount of risk, you can act on the following tips to maximise your profits and still keep your money secure. The following sections explain what you need to know.

Gaining knowledge

Some people spend more time analysing a restaurant menu to choose a £10 main course than analysing where to put their next £5,000. Lack of knowledge constitutes the greatest risk for new investors, but diminishing that risk starts with gaining knowledge. The more familiar you are with the stock market – how it works, factors that affect share value and so on – the better you can navigate around its pitfalls and maximise your profits.

The same knowledge that enables you to grow your wealth also enables you to minimise your risk. Before you put your money anywhere, you want to know as much as you can. This book is a great place to start – check out Chapter 6 for a rundown of the kinds of information you want to know before you buy shares, as well as the resources that can give you the information you need to invest successfully.

Staying out . . . for now

If you don't understand shares, don't invest. We know this book is about investing in shares, and we think that most people would do well to own some shares. But that doesn't mean you should be 100 per cent invested 100 per cent of the time. If you don't understand a particular share (or don't understand shares, full stop), stay away until you do understand. Instead, give yourself an imaginary sum of money, such as £100,000, give yourself reasons to invest, and just pretend. Pick a few shares that you think may increase in value and then track them for a while and see how they perform. Begin to understand how the price of a share goes up and down, and watch what happens to the shares you chose when various events take place. As you find out more about investing in shares, you get better at picking individual shares, and you haven't risked – or lost – any money during your apprenticeship period. A number of websites are available for doing your 'imaginary' investing, including www.ft.com or www.citywire.co.uk/. You can design your own shares portfolio and see how well you do.

Getting your financial house in order

We could write a whole book on what to do before you invest. The bottom line is that you want to make sure that you are, first and foremost, financially secure before you take the plunge into the stock market. If you're not sure about your financial security, look over your situation with a financial adviser. (You can find more on financial advisers in Appendix A.)

REMEMBER

Before you buy your first share, here are a few things you can do to get your finances in order:

>> **Have a cushion of money.** Set aside three to six months' worth of your gross living expenses somewhere safe, such as in an instant access savings account, in case you suddenly need cash for an emergency.

>> **Reduce your debt.** Overindulging in debt is a major problem for many people in the UK, with both bankruptcy and home repossession rising. Be sure that you can cope with any debts you have.

>> **Make sure that your job is as secure as you can make it.** Are you keeping your skills up to date? Is the company you work for strong and growing? Is the industry that you work in strong and growing?

>> **Make sure that you have adequate insurance.** You need enough insurance to cover you and your family's needs in case of illness, death, disability and so on.

Diversifying your investments

Diversification is a strategy for reducing risk by spreading your money across different investments. It's a fancy way of saying, 'Don't put all your eggs in one basket'. But how do you go about divvying up your money and distributing it among different investments? The easiest way to understand proper diversification may be to look at what you should *not* do:

>> **Don't put all your money in just one share.** Sure, if you choose wisely and select a hot stock, you may make a bundle, but the odds are hugely against you. Unless you're a real expert on a particular company, it's a good idea to have small portions of your money in several different shares. As a general rule, any money you tie up in a single share should be money you can do without.

>> **Don't put all your money in one industry.** We know people who own several shares, but the shares are all in the same industry. Again, if you're an expert in that particular industry, it may work out. But just understand that you're not properly diversified. If a problem hits an entire industry, you may get hurt.

>> **Don't put all your money in just one type of investment.** Shares may be a great investment, but you need to have money elsewhere. Bonds, bank accounts, gilts, property and precious metals are perennial alternatives to complement your shares portfolio. Some of these alternatives can be found in unit trusts or exchange traded funds (ETFs – more on these newish funds in Chapter 21).

Okay, now that you know what you *shouldn't* do, what *should* you do? Until you become more knowledgeable, follow this advice:

>> **Only keep 20 per cent (or less) of your investment money in a single share.** Why 20 per cent? First off, if you look at professional fund managers and their regulations, you'll quickly find that they tend to keep to a limit of 20 per cent or even 10 per cent in any one stock in their portfolios. It's regarded as good practice. The logic is simple – don't overexpose your portfolio to just one big bet.

>> **Invest in four or five different shares that are in different industries.** Which industries? Choose industries that offer products and services that have shown strong, growing demand. To make this decision, use your common sense (which isn't as common as it used to be). Think about the industries that people need no matter what happens in the general economy, such as food, energy and other consumer necessities. See Chapter 12 for more information about analysing industries.

>> **Use a diversified fund (a unit trust, investment trust or ETF) that invests in a number of different companies in a sector or different sectors.** Doing so is a great way to reduce your potential risk – but be aware of the charges made by the fund manager for this fund management service.

Weighing Risk against Return

How much risk is appropriate for you, and how do you handle it? Before you try to figure out what risks accompany your investment choices, analyse yourself. Here are some points to keep in mind when weighing risk versus return in your situation:

>> **Your financial goal:** In five minutes with a financial calculator, you can easily see how much money you're going to need to become financially independent (presuming that financial independence is your goal). Say that you need £500,000 in ten years for a worry-free retirement and that your financial assets (such as shares, bonds and so on) are currently worth £400,000. In this scenario, your assets need to grow by only 2.25 per cent a year to hit your target. Getting investments that grow by 2.25 per cent safely is relatively easy to do because that is a relatively low rate of return.

The important point is that in this case you don't have to knock yourself out trying to double your money with risky, high-flying investments; some run-of-the-mill savings accounts will do just fine. All too often, investors take on more risk than is necessary. Figure out what your financial goal is so that you know what kind of return you realistically need.

>> **Your investor profile:** Are you nearing retirement, or have you just left university? Your life situation matters when it comes to looking at risk versus return. If you're just beginning your working years, you can certainly tolerate greater risk than someone facing retirement. Even if you lose big time, you still have a long time to recoup your money and get back on track. However, if you're approaching retirement, risky or aggressive investments can do much more harm than good. If you lose money, you don't have as much time to recoup your investment, and the odds are that you need the investment money (and its income-generating capacity) to cover your living expenses after you're no longer employed.

>> **Asset allocation:** The term asset allocation is a bit jargon laden but actually refers to something hugely important. Asset allocation is a theory that attempts to work out how to mix and match different stock markets and 'asset classes'. Asset classes might consist of the big two, namely bonds and equities, but 'also-rans' such as commercial property, gold or other

commodities could also feature. These 'alternative assets' can be very useful and sometimes rewarding, and the sensible investor mixes and matches these asset classes in order to build a diversified portfolio. On balance, the thinkers who do the hard work in asset allocation suggest that older investors approaching retirement may want to weight their mix of assets towards cautious markets such as bonds, cash or even gold. Younger, thrusting investors might be better off looking at racier investments in the world of equities, such as small-caps or even stocks in emerging markets (think China or India). But remember – always check with your financial adviser to find the right mix for your particular situation.

Chapter **5**

Getting to Know the Stock Markets

'**H**ow's the market doing today?' is the most common question that interested parties ask about the stock market. This is followed by, 'What did the Footsie do?' and 'How about the S&P 500?' Invariably, people asking these questions want to know whether the market has risen or fallen that day. 'Well, the Footsie fell 5.3 points to 6798.6, while the S&P rose 30.05 to 3256.' When we refer to these numbers, we're talking about *indices*, which are general guides to the performance of stock markets. They give you a basic idea of how well (or how badly) the overall market is doing. In this chapter, we focus our attention on these stock market indices.

Knowing How Indices Are Measured

An *index* is a statistical measure that represents the value of a batch of shares. Investors use this measure as a barometer of the overall progress of the market (or a segment of the market).

The oldest stock market index is the Dow Jones Industrial Average (DJIA or simply 'the Dow'). It was created in 1896 by Charles Henry Dow, one of the founders of Dow Jones, publisher of the *Wall Street Journal*, and originally covered only 12 stocks. The number of stocks covered increased to 30 in 1928, and remains the same today. Dow worked long before the age of computers, so he kept the calculation of his stock market index simple – he worked it out on a piece of paper. Dow added up the stock prices of the 12 companies and then divided the total by 12. Technically, this number is an *average* and not really an index (hence the word 'average' in the name). But for simplicity's sake, we refer to it as an index. Today, the number gets tweaked to account for changes such as stock splits (for more on stock splits see Chapter 19). In the UK, the most important index is the *Footsie* or *FTSE 100* (the Financial Times Stock Exchange 100 Index, to give it its proper name), but we discuss it more in the section 'The FTSE 100 Index', later in this chapter.

However, you need to know that indices get calculated differently. The primary difference between an 'index' and an 'average' is the concept of weighting. *Weighting* is the relative importance of the items when they're computed within the index. Several kinds of indices exist, including:

- >> **Price-weighted index:** This kind of index tracks changes based on the change in the price per share.

  To give you an example, suppose that you own two shares: Share A worth £20 a share and Share B worth £40 a share. A price-weighted index allocates a greater proportion of the index to the share at £40 than to the one at £20. Therefore, if you had only these two shares in an index, the index number would reflect the £40 share as being 67 per cent (two-thirds of the number), whereas the £20 stock would be 33 per cent (one-third of the number).

- >> **Market-value weighted index:** This kind of index tracks the proportion of a share based on its *market capitalisation* (or market value, also called *market cap*). Refer to Chapter 2 for more on market cap.

  Say that in your *portfolio* (the collection of all the different shares you own) you have 10 million £20 shares (in Company A) and one million £40 shares (in Company B). Company A's market cap is £200 million, whereas Company B's market cap is £40 million. Therefore, in a market-value weighted index, Company A shares represent £200 million of a total £240 million in the portfolio – 83 per cent of the index's value – because of its much larger market cap.

- >> **Composite index:** This is an index or average that's a combination of several averages or indices. An example is the FTSE All-Share.

Using the Indices

You may be wondering what to do with all the indices out there and which one or ones you should be checking out. The following sections give you an idea of how to put all the pieces together.

Tracking the indices

Investors get an instant snapshot of how well the market is doing from indices. Indices offer a quick way to compare the performance of one investor's share portfolio or unit trusts with the rest of the market. If the Footsie goes up 10 per cent in a year and your portfolio shows a cumulative gain of 12 per cent, then you know that you're doing well. Appendix A lists resources to help you keep up with various indices.

The problem with indices is that they can be misleading if you take them too literally as an accurate barometer of company success. The Dow, for example, has changed its list of companies many times since 1896. Had it not, the Dow's general upward trajectory in the past few decades would have been very different. Flagging companies have been dropped and replaced with others that have shown more promise. Many of the original companies in the DJIA in 1896 did go out of business, or other companies, that aren't reflected in the index, bought them out.

Investing in indices

Can you invest directly in indices? If the market is doing well but your shares aren't, can you find a way to invest in the index itself? With investment funds based on indices, you can invest in the market in general or in a particular industry.

Say that you want to invest in the Footsie. After all, why try to 'beat the market' if just matching it is sufficient to boost your wealth? Why not have a portfolio that directly mirrors the Footsie? Well, unfortunately investing in all 100 companies that are in the Footsie is too impractical and expensive. Fortunately, you have other ways to accomplish investing in indices.

REMEMBER

Here are the best ways:

>> **Tracker funds:** A *tracker fund* is a unit trust fund that only invests in shares that match as closely as possible the basket of shares that are in a particular index – usually the Footsie or the FTSE All-Share (a broader index that includes the FTSE 100 as well as mid-caps and small-caps). These funds can be

purchased as tax-efficient Individual Savings Accounts (ISAs). Financial advisers or stockbrokers can tell you more about trackers.

» **Exchange-traded funds (ETFs):** ETFs are one of the secrets of stock market investing – they're cheap, simple and hugely effective for the long-term, passive investor. Rather like an index tracking unit trust fund, an ETF can reflect a basket of shares that mirrors a particular index – much like a tracker – but the ETF can be traded like a share itself. You can transact ETFs like shares, in that you can buy them, sell them or speculate that they'll fall in value. You can put stop-loss orders on them to sell them when they fall by a certain amount. ETFs can give you the diversification of trackers coupled with the versatility of shares. You can buy ETFs that track indices including the Footsie, the Dow and Nasdaq – in fact, the choice is nearly endless. You can find out more about ETFs from a stockbroker or financial adviser.

Checking Out Major Markets

Although most people consider the Footsie and the American S&P 500 index to be the stars of the financial press, literally hundreds of different indices exist, many of which track alternative assets and smaller emerging markets.

TIP

You can check out other less-sexy indices that cover specific sectors and industries. If you're investing in mining stock, you should also check the FTSE Basic Materials Index to compare what your stock is doing when measured against the index. You can find indices that cover industries such as transportation, retailers, computer companies and even crypto currencies. FTSE International runs some of these indices, and you can find information about them at www.ftse.com. The S&P Dow Jones and MSCI run other major indices. You can find indices to consult for almost every market in the world, so if you're considering investing in a wide portfolio of shares from different countries these indices are useful. Beginners may find it easier to stick to their home markets initially.

The FTSE 100 Index

The most famous stock market barometer in the UK is the FTSE 100 Index, more commonly known as the Footsie. Its name stands for Financial Times Stock Exchange although the Financial Times doesn't have much to do with the index any more. When someone asks how the market is doing, most investors in the UK quote the 'Footsie'.

The FTSE tracks the top 100 companies in the UK and is updated every three months. Started in January 1984 with an initial value of 1,000, the index covers the 100 largest companies traded on the London Stock Exchange (based on market capitalisation). These stocks represent about 80 per cent of the value of all trading on the exchange. Because the index is weighted by market cap, its largest component stocks have the greatest influence on the FTSE's value. The index is quite unusual in that it re-weights its component stocks daily to represent the actual state of the market. And every three months the index is fully rebalanced when companies are demoted or promoted based on their market caps.

REMEMBER

People refer to companies in the Footsie as *blue chips*. Table 5-1 provides the current top ten companies tracked and their stock exchange codes. You can find the whole index from the same date in Chapter 21.

TABLE 5-1:

The Top Ten Shares of the FTSE 100 Index in April 2021

EPIC or Ticker	Name	Weight (%) in FTSE 100
ULVR	UNILEVER PLC	5.65
AZN	ASTRAZENECA PLC	5.37
HSBA	HSBC HOLDINGS PLC	4.55
DGE	DIAGEO PLC	3.97
GSK	GLAXOSMITHKLINE PLC	3.57
RIO	RIO TINTO PLC	3.48
BATS	BRITISH AMERICAN TOBACCO PLC	3.35
BP	BP PLC	3.15
RDSA	ROYAL DUTCH SHELL PLC	3.01
RDSB	ROYAL DUTCH SHELL PLC CLASS B	2.6

Note: The weighting of the index tells you how much of the overall market cap of the index of 100 stocks comprises of each stock in the list.

The Footsie has grown hugely in popularity as a gauge of stock market activity since it was founded in 1984. Although it's an important indicator of the market's progress, it has one drawback: it tracks only 100 companies. Regardless of their prominent status in the market, the companies represented are only a sample. This means that if the biggest companies in the index – the most valuable – hit a bad patch, they can have a significant impact on the index. You also need to be aware that the stocks in the FTSE 100 are internationally diversified and derive most of their profits from abroad. That means that the FTSE 100 isn't necessarily a great guide to the UK economy. In fact, we'd go so far as to say that it's an increasingly lousy way to track the fortunes of the UK economy, because many of the stocks in the index are international and make most of their money in dollars and euros from international operations.

FTSE International has several indices, including the FTSE4Good, which measures socially responsible company share performance, and the FTSE All-World Index covering companies whose capitalisation represents 90–95 per cent of the world's investible market capitalisation.

The FTSE 250

The FTSE 250 Index is a capitalisation-weighted index of 250 companies on the London Stock Exchange (LSE). While you may expect it to be made up of the top 250 companies, this would be a mistake. The companies are selected quarterly as being the 101st to 350th largest companies with a primary listing on the exchange. Companies that rise and fall in value can be promoted to, or demoted from, the index. Changes, when required, take place quarterly in March, June, September and December. A number of the companies in this index are investment trusts.

The FTSE All-Share

The FTSE All-Share Index is another capitalisation-weighted (or *market value weighted*) index, comprised of companies traded on the London Stock Exchange. It covers around 600 companies and aims to represent at least 98 per cent of the capital value of UK companies.

FTSE All-Share is the aggregation of the FTSE 100 Index, the FTSE 250 Index and the FTSE SmallCap Index, which covers smaller companies.

Even though the index covers many hundreds of companies, more than 80 per cent of the index by value is made up of the largest 100 companies. Medium cap companies make up around 13 per cent of the value, and smaller companies only 4 per cent.

Although the FTSE All-Share is a reliable indicator of the market's overall status, it does have its limitations. Despite the fact that it tracks more than 600 companies, the top 10 companies encompass around 30 per cent of the index's market value. This situation can be a drawback because those 10 companies have a greater influence on the All-Share's price movement than other groups of companies.

Identifying Markets for Smaller Companies

Although most new investors in the UK cut their teeth on shares listed on the London Stock Exchange, there are other markets to consider. These markets allow smaller companies to trade their shares and can offer investors rich opportunities to profit from growing young firms.

The Alternative Investment Market

The Alternative Investment Market (AIM) is a market regulated by the London Stock Exchange but with less demanding rules than the main market. No capitalisation requirements exist, and companies don't need to issue a certain number of shares. When it was launched in 1995, the aim of the AIM was to offer an easy route to market for smaller companies, but it has also attracted larger companies looking for an easier regulatory ride.

AIM has helped raise money for more than 3,916 companies since its launch. Some companies that started out on AIM have since moved on to a full LSE listing but in the last few years, significantly more companies transferred from a full listing to AIM. More than 822 companies are currently quoted, with an aggregate market capitalisation of more than £137 billion.

AIM has also started to become an international exchange, often as the result of its low-regulatory burden, especially in relation to the Sarbanes–Oxley Act – which imposes regulatory costs on companies listed in the United States. One hundred twelve foreign companies have been admitted to AIM, with more than a few in previous years from unusual places such as China.

The FTSE Group has three indices for measuring AIM:

>> The FTSE AIM UK 50 Index

>> The FTSE AIM 100 Index

>> The FTSE AIM All-Share Index

Further afield: International indices

Investors need to remember that the whole world is a vast marketplace that interacts with and exerts tremendous influence on individual national economies and markets. Whether you have one share or one unit trust, you should keep tabs on how world markets affect your investment. The best way to get a snapshot of international markets is, of course, with indices. A few of the more widely followed international indices are

- » **The Dow Jones index (US):** This index is called 'the Dow' for short. The Dow is one of the most important indices in the world.

- » **Standard & Poor's 500 (S&P 500) (US):** This is another important index. Created by publishing firm Standard & Poor's, this index tracks the 500 largest publicly traded companies in the US – measured by market cap, although in reality actually 505 stocks are in the index at the moment. The S&P 500 is a better representative of the overall market performance than the Dow, which features only 30 companies. In the US, money managers and financial advisers watch the S&P 500 more closely than the Dow. However, like the FTSE All-Share, it has its limitations. Although it tracks 500 companies, the top ten companies encompass roughly a quarter of the index's market value.

- » **Nasdaq Composite Index (US):** Nasdaq became a formalised market in 1971. The name used to stand for 'National Association of Securities Dealers Automated Quote' system, but now it's simply 'Nasdaq' (as though it's a name, like Ralph or Mary). The Nasdaq index is similar to other indices in style and structure. The only difference is that it covers the 2,485 plus companies traded on the Nasdaq. The companies encompass a variety of industries, but the index's concentration has primarily been on technology, telecom and Internet industries.

  The Nasdaq Composite Index hit an all-time high of 15041 in August 2021. It's also worth noting that there's an increasingly popular alternative version of the index called the Nasdaq 100; this widely followed stock market index includes 100 of the largest domestic and international nonfinancial companies listed on the Nasdaq Stock Market based on market capitalisation.

- » **Nikkei (Japan):** This index is considered Japan's version of the Dow. If you've invested in Japanese shares or in companies that do business in Japan, you want to know what's up with the Nikkei. It's worth remembering that another alternative index tracks the Japanese blue-chip market – the TOPIX – which is run by the Tokyo Stock exchange.

- » **CAC-40 (France):** This index tracks the 40 company shares traded on the Paris Stock Exchange.

- » **DAX (Germany):** This index tracks the 30 largest and most active shares traded on the Frankfurt Exchange.

You can track these international indices (among others) at major financial websites, such as www.ftse.com, www.bloomberg.com and www.marketwatch.com. You may find international indices useful in your analysis as you watch your shares' progress. What if you have shares in a company that has most of its customers in

Japan? Then the Nikkei can help you get a general snapshot of how well the major companies are doing in Japan, which in turn can be a general barometer of its economy's well-being . . . which is probably not well given the lacklustre returns from the land of the rising sun over the last few decades.

Considering international markets

This section focuses on investing internationally. Building some geographic diversification can make sense from a risk perspective and in addition many international markets allow the UK investor to track different industries and ideas. This section guides you through this increasingly easy process of building a diverse mix of stocks from around the world.

Investing has never been easier

Virtually every major online and offline broker allows you to buy and sell shares in US stocks at very low cost. In fact, for some brokers buying US shares is actually easier than UK shares. The US markets and the brokers serving those markets have become so deep and efficient – translation: very competitive – that prices for US dealing have collapsed. A few decades ago, you might have to pay as much as £50 or more to trade in US stocks, whereas now you can find an ever longer list of UK brokers who make no charge at all, or just charge roughly the same as UK trades.

In some respects, the US markets are even *ahead* of the Brits, especially in the use of what is called fractional shares. We discuss fractional shares in more detail in Chapter 7, but here's a basic overview. Say a share costs $1,000 each. If you're a small, private investor who is a princely sum to invest in a single share, especially if you're investing say a few hundred pounds a month in your account. Fractional shares give you part ownership of that $1,000 share, with the broker – using their back office administrative partners – organising the sharing out of the portions. So you could put an order in to buy say $50 equivalent of that $1,000 share and you then get . . . you guessed it, 0.05 share of the share.

Unfortunately, although fractional shares have become extremely popular in the US, they aren't offered in the UK – more's the pity in our view but that's another story.

WARNING

Dealing in US fractional shares is a doddle, but there is one big exception: ETFs. Chapter 21 discusses ETFs in more detail, but for now know it's almost impossible for UK–based investors to buy (or sell) US–listed index tracking ETFs. The technology is there and the fund managers (and brokers) are willing, but the regulators have put up all sorts of barriers around documentation for UK investors. The net effect is that you can forget about investing in US–listed ETFs.

Dealing in international shares requires currency conversion. For instance, when you buy a US share, your broker will need to transfer your £ sterling into dollars. That's easy-peasy, but there's what's called an *FX spread*, a difference in between the buy and sell rates. As the dealing costs for brokers have come down, cynical observers have noticed that new fees and charges have started to emerge to make up for the lower headline rates, which has had an impact on the supposedly smooth FX transfer process. Many brokers now have spreads of more than 1 per cent in the FX rates whereas some more competitive brokers charge less than 0.50 per cent. In reality institutional level dealing spreads are closer to the 0.10 per cent to 0.30 per cent level, so you can probably make up your own mind about what happens to the difference between what are called the wholesale spreads and the spreads you're charged.

Investing in most European exchanges, especially those in France, Germany and northern Europe (the Netherlands and the Nordics) is easy. After Europe and the US, dealing in internationals stocks becomes much more difficult. Very few mass-market brokers offer dealing in Australian or Asian stocks. Canadian stocks are by contrast fairly accessible. As for Chinese stocks, forget it.

Investing in managed funds

You can also invest in managed funds either actively through investment trusts or passively through ETFs that invest in a major single country. Sometimes you can do this through a major national index such as the Nikkei (refer to the section, 'Further afield: International indices', earlier in this chapter), or through a country-specific fund that invests in a range of local stocks. You can even scale up and invest in whole regions or international subclasses of stocks such as large companies in the emerging markets.

2

Before You Start Buying

Know the different types of shares that exist for different objectives when you're ready to begin investing in shares.

Understand how to switch between strategies based around generating an income and those built on buying into long-term growth.

Gather information that can help you make informed decisions.

Discover what brokers can do for you and where you can find them.

Find out how technology has enabled some online services to help you build a low-cost, diversified portfolio.

IN THIS CHAPTER

» Using stock exchanges to get investment information

» Applying accounting and economic know-how to your investments

» Exploring financial issues

» Deciphering the financial pages

» Interpreting dividend news

» Recognising good (and bad) advice when you hear it

Chapter **6**

Gathering Information

Knowledge and information are two critical success factors in share investment. (Isn't that true about most things in life?) People who plunge headlong into shares without sufficient knowledge of the stock market in general, and current information in particular, quickly absorb the lesson of the eager diver who didn't find out ahead of time that the pool was only an inch deep (ouch!). In their haste to avoid missing so-called golden investment opportunities, investors too often end up losing money.

REMEMBER

Opportunities to *make* money in the stock market will always exist, no matter how well or how poorly the economy and the market are performing in general. Don't believe that there's such a thing as a single (and fleeting) magical moment, and don't feel that if you let an opportunity pass you by, you'll always regret that you missed your one big chance.

For the best approach to investing in shares, you want to build your knowledge and find quality information first. Then buy shares and make your fortunes more assuredly. Basically, before you buy shares, you need to know that the company you're investing in is

>> Financially sound and growing

>> Offering products and services that are in demand by consumers

>> In a strong and growing industry (and general economy)

Where do you start and what kind of information do you want to acquire? Keep reading.

Looking to Stock Exchanges for Answers

Before you invest in shares, you need to be completely familiar with the basics of investing in them. At its most fundamental, investing in shares is about using your money to buy a piece of a company that gives you value in the form of appreciation or income. Fortunately, many resources are available to help you find out about investing in shares. Some of our favourite places are the stock exchanges themselves.

TECHNICAL STUFF

Stock exchanges are organised marketplaces for the buying and selling of shares, or stocks as they're known in the US (and other securities). The London Stock Exchange (LSE), the leading European exchange, provides a framework for share buyers and sellers to make their transactions. The LSE makes money not only from a piece of every transaction but also from fees (such as listing fees) charged to companies and brokers that are members of its exchanges.

The LSE is the main exchange for most investors in the UK, closely followed by the Alternative Investment Market (AIM), which is owned by the LSE. Investors are also finding it increasingly easier to invest in shares listed on overseas exchanges such as the New York Stock Exchange and the Nasdaq. Chapter 5 gives more details about all of these exchanges. Because exchanges and markets benefit from the increased popularity of, and continued demand for, investing in shares, they offer a wealth of free (or low-cost) information and resources for investors. Go to the websites of these exchanges and you find useful resources such as:

>> Tutorials on how to invest in shares, common investment strategies and so on

>> Glossaries and free information to help you understand the language, practice and purpose of investing in shares

>> A wealth of news, press releases, financial data and other information about companies listed at the exchange or market, accessed usually through an on-site search engine

>> Industry analysis and news

>> Share price quotes and other market information related to the daily market movements of shares, including data such as volume, new highs, new lows and so on

>> Free tracking of your share selections (you can input a sample portfolio, or the shares you're following, to see how well you're doing)

What each exchange/market offers keeps changing or is updated, so go and explore them at their websites:

>> London Stock Exchange: www.londonstockexchange.com

>> Alternative Investment Market: www.londonstockexchange.com/raise-finance/equity/aim

Understanding Shares and the Companies They Represent

Shares represent ownership in companies. Before you buy individual shares, you want to understand the companies whose shares you're considering and find out about their operations. Doing so may sound like a daunting task, but you can digest the point more easily when you realise that companies work similarly to how you work. They make decisions on a day-to-day basis just as you do.

Think about how you grow and prosper as an individual or as a family, and you see the same issues with companies and how they grow and prosper. Low earnings and high debt are examples of financial difficulties that can affect both people and companies. You can understand companies' finances when you take the time to pick up information in two basic disciplines: accounting and economics. These two disciplines play a significant role in understanding the performance of a company's shares.

Accounting for taste and a whole lot more

Accounting. Yuck! But face it: Accounting is the language of business, and believe it or not, you're already familiar with the most important accounting concepts. Just look at the following three essential principles:

>> **Assets minus liabilities equal net worth.** In other words, take what you own (your assets), subtract what you owe (your liabilities) and the rest is yours (your net worth). Your own personal finances work the same way as Tesco's

(except yours have fewer zeros at the end). See Chapter 2 to figure out how to calculate your own net worth.

A company's balance sheet shows you its net worth at a specific time (such as 31 December). The net worth of a company is the bottom line of a company's asset and liability picture, telling you whether the company is *solvent* (has the ability to pay its debts without going out of business). The net worth of a successful company is regularly growing. To see whether your company is successful, compare its net worth with the net worth from the same point a year earlier. A company that has a £4 million net worth on 31 December 2019 and a £5 million net worth on 31 December 2020 is doing well; its net worth has gone up 25 per cent (£1 million) in one year.

>> **Income less expenses equal net income.** In other words, take what you make (your income), subtract what you spend (your expenses) and the remainder is your *net income* (or net profit or net earnings – your gain).

A company's profitability is the whole point of investing in its shares. As it profits, the company becomes more valuable, and in turn, its shares become more valuable. To discover a company's net income, look at its income, or *profit and loss* (P&L), statement. Try to determine whether the company uses its gains wisely, reinvesting them for continued growth or paying down debt.

>> **Do a comparative financial analysis.** That's a mouthful, but just a fancy way of saying how a company is doing now, compared with something else (such as a prior period or a similar company).

If you know that a company you're looking at had a net income of £50,000 for the year, you may ask, 'Is that good or bad?' Obviously, making a net profit is good, but you also need to know whether the profit is good compared to something else. If the company had a net profit of £40,000 the year before, you know that the company's profitability is improving. But if a similar company had a net profit of £100,000 the year before and in the current year is making £50,000, then you may want to avoid that company or see what went wrong (if anything).

Accounting can be as simple as this list. If you understand these three basic points, you're ahead of the curve (in investing in shares as well as in your personal finances). For more information on how to use a company's financial statements to pick good shares, see Chapter 11.

Understanding how economics affects shares

Economics. Double yuck! No, you aren't required to understand 'the inelasticity of demand aggregates' (thank heavens!) or 'marginal utility' (what?). But a working knowledge of basic economics is crucial (and we mean crucial) to your success and proficiency as an investor in shares. The stock market and the economy are joined at the hip. The good (or bad) things that happen to one have a direct effect on the other.

Getting the hang of the basic concepts

Alas, many investors get lost on basic economic concepts (as do some so-called experts that you see on television). Be aware of these important economic concepts:

>> **Supply and demand:** How can anyone possibly think about economics without thinking of the ageless concept of supply and demand? *Supply and demand* can be simply stated as the relationship between what's available (the supply) and what people want and are willing to pay for (the demand). This equation is the main engine of economic activity and is extremely important for your share investment analysis and decision-making process.

>> **Cause and effect:** If you pick up a prominent news report and read, 'Companies in the table industry are expecting plummeting sales', do you rush out and invest in companies that sell chairs or manufacture tablecloths? Considering cause and effect is an exercise in logical thinking, and believe us, logic is a major component of sound economic thought.

When you read business news, play it out in your mind. What good (or bad) can logically be expected given a certain event or situation? If you're looking for an effect ('I want a share price that keeps increasing'), you also want to understand the cause. Here are some typical events that can cause a share's price to rise:

- **Positive news reports about a company:** The news may report that a company is enjoying success with increased sales or a new product.

- **Positive news reports about a company's industry:** The media may be highlighting that the industry is poised to do well.

- **Positive news reports about a company's customers:** Maybe your company is in industry A, but its customers are in industry B. If you see good news about industry B, that may be good news for your company.

- **Negative news reports about a company's competitors:** If they're in trouble, their customers may seek alternatives to buy from, including your company.

>> **Economic effects from government actions:** Political and governmental actions have economic consequences. As a matter of fact, nothing has a greater effect on investing and economics than government. Government

actions usually manifest themselves as taxes, laws or regulations. They also can take on a more ominous appearance, such as war or the threat of war. Government can wilfully (or even accidentally) cause a company to go bankrupt, disrupt an entire industry or even cause a depression. Its decisions can affect money supply, credit and all public securities markets.

What happens to the papier mâché umbrella stand industry if the government passes a 50 per cent sales tax for that industry? Such a sales tax certainly makes a product uneconomical and encourages consumers to seek alternatives to papier mâché umbrella stands. It may even boost sales for the wicker basket industry.

The opposite can be true as well. What if the government passes a tax credit that encourages the use of solar power in homes and businesses? That obviously has a positive impact on industries that manufacture or sell solar power devices. Just don't ask us what happens to solar-powered papier mâché umbrella stands.

Gaining insight from past mistakes

Because most investors ignored basic observations about economics in the first decade of the new millennium, they subsequently lost millions in their share portfolios in 2007 and 2008 and then again in 2020. Over the first few decades the world has experienced the greatest expansion of debt in history, coupled with a record expansion of the money supply. The growing debt has resulted in more consumer (and corporate) borrowing, spending and investing. This activity hyper-stimulated the stock market and caused the share prices of everything from banks through to mines to rise.

Of course, you should always be happy to make a decent gain every year on your investments, but such returns can't always be sustained and encourage speculation. This monetary pump priming by the central banks resulted in the following:

>> More and more people depleted their savings. After all, why settle for 1 per cent in the bank when you can get 25 per cent in the stock market?

>> More and more people bought on credit. If the economy is booming, why not buy now and pay later? Consumer credit hit record highs.

>> More and more people borrowed against their homes. (Why not borrow and get rich now? I can pay off my debt later.)

>> More and more companies sold more goods as consumers took more holidays and bought bigger cars, more electronic goods and so on. Companies then borrowed to finance expansion, open new shops and so on.

It was only a matter of time before this particular money-induced bubble burst and back in 2008 it did so in spectacular style, taking the global economy to the edge of a great depression in the great GFC, the global financial crisis. This sudden downturn caused a sudden slow-down in spending. However, companies had acquired too much in the way of overhead costs, capacity and debt because they had expanded too eagerly. At this point, companies were caught in a financial bind. Too much debt and too many expenses in a plummeting economy means only one thing: profits shrink or even vanish! Companies, to stay in business, had to do the logical thing – cut expenses. What is usually the biggest expense for companies? People! To stay in business, many companies started laying-off employees. As a result, consumer spending dropped further because more people were laid off or had second thoughts about their own job security.

As people had little in the way of savings and too much in the way of debt, they had to sell their shares to pay their mortgages. The lessons learnt from 2007 and 2008 are still important ones for investors today:

>> Shares aren't a replacement for savings accounts. Always have some money in the bank.

>> Shares should never occupy 100 per cent of your investment funds.

>> When anyone (including an expert) tells you that the economy will keep growing indefinitely, be sceptical and read diverse sources of information.

>> If shares do well in your portfolio, consider protecting your shares (both your original investment and any gains) with stop-loss orders. (See Chapter 17 for more on these strategies.)

>> Keep debt and expenses to a minimum.

>> Remember that, if the economy is booming, a decline is sure to follow as the ebb and flow of the economy's business cycle continues.

Staying on Top of Financial News

Reading the financial news can help you decide where or where not to invest. Many websites, magazines and newspapers offer great coverage of the financial world. Obviously, the more informed you are, the better, but you don't have to read everything that's written. The information explosion in recent years has gone beyond overload, and you can easily spend so much time reading that you have little time left for investing.

The most obvious publications of interest to those investing in shares are the *Financial Times* and *MoneyWeek.* These excellent publications report the news and stock market data on a daily and weekly basis. Some of the more obvious websites are (`www.ft.com`), (`www.citywire.co.uk/`), and Bloomberg (`www.bloomberg.com`). These websites can actually give you news and share data within 15 to 20 minutes of an event occurring. (And don't forget the exchanges' websites.)

Appendix A provides more information on these resources, along with a treasure trove of some of the best publications, resources and websites to assist you.

Figuring out what a company's up to

Before you invest, you need to know what's going on with a company. When you read about a company, from the company's literature (its annual report, for example) or from media sources, be sure to get answers to some pertinent questions:

>> **Is the company making more net income – income after tax – than it did last year?** You want to invest in a company that's growing.

>> **Are the company's sales greater than they were the year before?** Remember, you won't make money if the company isn't making money.

>> **Is the company issuing press releases on new products, services, inventions or business deals?** All these achievements indicate a strong, vital company.

Knowing how the company is doing, no matter what's happening with the general economy, is obviously important. To better understand how companies tick, see Chapter 11.

Discovering what's new with an industry

As you consider investing in a company, make a point of knowing what's going on in that company's industry. If the industry is doing well, your company is likely to do well, too. But then again, the reverse is also true.

Yes, we have seen investors pick successful shares in a failing industry, but those cases are exceptional. By and large, investors find it easier to succeed with a share when the entire industry is doing well. As you're watching the news, reading the financial pages or viewing financial websites, check to see whether the industry is strong and dynamic. See Chapter 12 for information on analysing industries.

Knowing what's happening with the economy

No matter how well or how poorly the overall economy is performing, you want to stay informed about its general progress. The value of shares is more likely to keep going up when the economy is stable or growing. The reverse is also true; if the economy is contracting or declining, the share has a tougher time keeping its value. Some basic items to keep tabs on include the following:

>> **Gross domestic product (GDP):** This is roughly the total value of output for a particular nation, measured in the sterling amount of goods and services. GDP is reported quarterly, and all else being equal a rising GDP bodes well for your shares. When the GDP is rising at 3 per cent or more on an annual basis, that's solid growth. If it rises at more than zero but less than 3 per cent, that's generally considered less than stellar (or mediocre). GDP below zero (or negative GDP) means that the economy is shrinking (heading into recession).

>> **Economic indicators:** The Office of National Statistics produces a flood of economic statistics each month that provide a snapshot of economic activity from the preceding month. Each statistic helps you understand the economy in much the same way that barometers (and windows!) help you understand what's happening with the weather. Economists don't just look at an individual statistic; they look at a set of statistics to get a more complete picture of what's happening with the economy. Chapter 14 goes into greater detail on ways that the economy affects share prices.

Seeing what the politicians and government bureaucrats are doing

Being informed about what public officials are doing is vital to your success as an investor in shares. Because governments pass many laws every year, monitoring the political landscape is critical to your success. The news media report what the Prime Minister and Parliament are doing, so always ask yourself, 'How does a new law, tax or regulation affect my shares?' Pay particular attention to what the Chancellor of the Exchequer announces in their Budget (usually in March or April).

TIP

Because government actions have a significant effect on your investments, make sure that you know what's going on. The best way to keep up with proposed changes to laws is through the news media. Proposals are usually laid out in an initial parliamentary consultation document called a Green Paper, which is followed some months later, after consultation and amendment, by a White Paper. The White Paper contains the final suggestions to be debated and voted on by

Parliament. Specialist reporters and consumer groups tend to make a noise if they find issues of interest in Green or White Papers.

Checking for trends in society, culture and entertainment

As odd as it sounds, trends in society, popular culture and entertainment affect your investments, directly or indirectly. For example, headlines such as 'The grey pound – how companies cater for the growing pensioner population' may give you some important information that can make or break your share portfolio. With that particular headline, you know that as more and more people age, companies that are well positioned to cater to this growing market's wants and needs will do well – meaning a successful share for you.

TIP

Keep your eyes open to emerging trends in society at large. What trends are evident now? Can you anticipate the wants and needs of tomorrow's society? Being alert, staying a step ahead of the public and choosing shares appropriately gives you a profitable edge over other investors. If you own shares in a solid company with growing sales and earnings, other investors eventually notice your company. As more investors buy up your company's shares, you're rewarded as the share price increases.

Reading (and Understanding) the Financial Pages

The stock market data in major business publications, such as the *Financial Times*, are loaded with information that can help you become a savvy investor – *if* you know how to interpret them. You need the information in the tables for more than selecting promising investment opportunities. You also need to consult the tables after you invest to monitor how your shares are doing. If you bought HokySmoky ordinary shares last year at £12 per share and you want to know what they're worth today, check out the stock tables printed daily in the financial pages of national newspapers or using websites for real-times prices. You can, of course, also find this information online at some of the websites already mentioned.

If you look at these tables without knowing what you're looking at or why, you're doing the equivalent of reading *War and Peace* backwards through a kaleidoscope. Nothing makes sense. But we can help you make sense of it all (well, at least the tables!). Table 6-1 shows a sample table for you to refer to as you read the sections that follow.

TABLE 6-1 Deciphering Tables

52-Wk High	52-Wk Low	Name (Code)	Div	Vol	Yld	P/E	Price	Chg
21.50	8.00	SkyHighPLC (SH)		3,143		76	21.25	+.25
47.00	31.75	LowDownPLC (LD)	2.35	2,735	5.9	18	41.00	−.50
25.00	21.00	ValueNowPLC (VN)	1.00	1,894	4.5	12	22.00	+.10
83.00	33.00	DoinBadlyPLC (DB)		7,601			33.50	−.75

REMEMBER

Every newspaper's financial tables are a little different, but they give you basically the same information. Updated daily, this section isn't the place to start your search for a good share; this section is usually where your search ends. The tables are the place to look when you already know what you want to buy and you're just checking to see the most recent price, or to look when you already own it and you want to check how your investment is doing.

Each item gives you some clues about the current state of affairs for that particular company. The sections that follow describe each column to help you understand what you're looking at.

52-week high

The column labelled '52-Wk High' (refer to Table 6-1) gives you the highest price that particular share has reached in the most recent 52-week period. Knowing this price lets you gauge where the share is now versus where it has been recently. SkyHigh's (SH) shares have been as high as £21.50, while their last (most recent) price is £21.25, the number listed in the 'Price' column. (Flip to the 'Price' section later in this chapter for more on understanding this information.) SkyHigh's shares are trading high at the moment because the company is hovering right near its overall 52-week high figure.

Now, take a look at DoinBadly's (DB) share price. It seems to have tumbled big time. Its share price has had a high in the past 52 weeks of £83, but the company is currently trading at £33.50. Something just doesn't seem right here. During the past 52 weeks, DB's share price fell dramatically. If you're thinking about investing in DB, find out why the share price fell. If the company is a strong company, it may be a good opportunity to buy shares at a lower price. If the company is having tough times, avoid it. In any case, research the company and find out why its shares have declined in value.

52-week low

The column labelled '52-Wk Low' gives you the lowest price that particular share reached in the most recent 52-week period. Again, this information is crucial to your ability to analyse shares over a period of time. Look at DB in Table 6-1, and you can see that its current trading price of £33.50 is close to its 52-week low.

REMEMBER

Keep in mind that the high and the low prices just give you a range of how far that particular share's price has moved within the past 52 weeks. They can alert you that a company has problems, or they can tell you that a share's price has fallen enough to make it a bargain. Simply reading the 52-Wk High and 52-Wk Low columns isn't enough to determine which of those two scenarios is happening. They basically tell you to get more information before you commit your money.

Name and code

The 'Name (Code)' column is the simplest in Table 6-1. It tells you the company name (usually abbreviated) and the code assigned to the company, also known in the trade as the *ticker*. When you have your eye on a share as a potential purchase, get familiar with its code. Knowing the code makes it easier for you to find your company in the financial tables, which list shares in alphabetical order by the company's name. Share codes are the language of stock market investing, and you need to use them in all communications about your shares, from getting a quote from your broker to buying shares online.

Dividend

Dividends (shown under the 'Div' column in Table 6-1) are basically payments to owners (shareholders). If a company pays a dividend, this dividend is shown in the dividend column. Newspapers usually carry this column in their weekend tables. The amount you see is the annual dividend paid out on one share. If you look at LowDown PLC (LD) in Table 6-1, you can see that you get £2.35 as an annual dividend for each share that you own. Companies usually pay the dividend half-yearly as an interim dividend and a final dividend.

If you own 100 shares of LD, the company pays you £235 in total per year, in two instalments – the instalments don't have to be equal. Some UK companies, especially those with business interests in the US, pay dividends four times a year. A healthy company strives to maintain or upgrade the dividend for shareholders from year to year. The dividend is very important to investors seeking income from their share investment. For more about investing for income, see Chapter 9. Investors buy shares in companies that don't pay dividends primarily for growth. For more information on growth shares, see Chapter 8.

Volume

Normally, when you hear the word *volume* on the news, it refers to how many shares were bought and sold for the entire market. Volume is certainly important to watch because the shares that you're investing in are somewhere in that activity. For the 'Vol' column in Table 6-1, though, the volume refers to the individual share.

Volume tells you how many shares of that particular company were traded that day. If only 100 shares are traded in a day, then the trading volume is 100. SH had 3,143 shares change hands on the trading day represented in Table 6-1. Is that good or bad? Neither, really. Usually the business news media only mentions volume for a particular company when that volume is unusually large. If a share normally has volume in the 5,000 to 10,000 range and all of a sudden has a trading volume of 87,000, then you should sit up and take notice.

Keep in mind that a low trading volume for one share may be high trading volume for another. You can't necessarily compare one share's volume against that of any other company. The large-cap stocks like Tesco typically have trading volumes in the millions of shares almost every day, while less active, smaller shares may have average trading volumes in far, far smaller numbers.

The main point to remember is that trading volume that is far in excess of that share's normal range is a sign that something is going on with that company. It may be negative or positive, but something newsworthy is happening. If the news is positive, the increased volume is a result of more people buying the share. If the news is negative, the increased volume is probably a result of more people selling the share. What are the typical events that cause increased trading volume? Some positive reasons include the following:

>> **Good earnings reports:** A company announces good (or better-than-expected) earnings.

>> **A new business deal:** A company announces a favourable business deal, such as a joint venture, or lands a big client.

>> **A new product or service:** A company's research and development department creates a potentially profitable new product.

>> **Indirect benefits:** A company may benefit from a new development in the economy or from a new law passed by Parliament.

Some negative reasons for an unusually large fluctuation in trading volume for a particular share include the following:

>> **Bad earnings reports:** Profit is the lifeblood of a company. When a company's profit falls or disappears, you see more volume.

>> **Governmental problems:** The company is being targeted by government action (such as a lawsuit or Competition Commission probe).

>> **Liability issues:** The media reports that a company has a defective product or similar problem.

>> **Financial problems:** Independent analysts report that a company's financial health is deteriorating.

TIP

Check out what's happening when you hear about heavier than usual volume (especially if you already own shares in the company).

Yield

In general, yield is a return on the money you invest. However, in the tables in the financial pages and online, *yield* ('Yld' in Table 6-1) is a reference to the dividend yield. It shows the percentage return that the dividend pays on the share price. Yield is most important to income investors. Yield is calculated by dividing the annual dividend by the current share price. In Table 6-1, you can see that the daily yield of ValueNow (VN) is 4.5 per cent (a dividend of £1 divided by the company's share price of £22). Notice that many companies have no yield reported; because they have no dividends, yield is zero.

Keep in mind that the yield reported in the financial pages changes daily as the share price changes. Yield is always reported as if you're buying the shares that day. If you buy VN on the day represented in Table 6-1, your yield is 4.5 per cent. But what if VN's share price rises to £30 the following day? Investors who buy shares at £30 per share obtain a yield of just 3.3 per cent. (The dividend of £1 is then divided by the new share price, £30.) Of course, because you bought the shares at £22, you essentially locked in the prior yield of 4.5 per cent. Lucky you. Pat yourself on the back.

P/E

The P/E ratio is the ratio between the share price and the company's earnings. Many investors follow P/E ratios closely, and they're important barometers of value in the world of share investment. The P/E ratio (also called the *earnings multiple* or just *multiple*) is frequently used to determine whether shares are expensive (good value). Value investors find P/E ratios essential for analysing shares as potential investments. As a general rule, the P/E should be 5 to 20 for large-cap or income shares. For growth shares, a P/E no greater than 15 to 35 is preferable.

In the P/E ratios reported in the financial pages, *price* refers to the cost of a single share. *Earnings* refers to the company's reported earnings (profits) per share in the most recent 12 months. The P/E ratio is the price divided by the earnings. In Table 6-1, VN has a reported P/E of 12, which is considered a low P/E. Notice how SH has a relatively high P/E (76). This share is considered too pricey because you're paying a price equivalent to 76 times earnings. Also notice that DB has no available P/E ratio. Usually this lack of a P/E ratio indicates that the company reported a loss in the latest 12-month trading period.

Price

The 'Price' column tells you how trading ended for a particular share on the day represented by the table – usually the day before the newspaper's publication. In Table 6-1, LD ended the previous day's trading at £41. Some newspapers report the high and low for the day as well as the share's closing price for the day.

Change

The information in the 'Chg' column answers the question, 'How did the share price end on the day compared with its trading price at the end of the previous trading day?' Table 6-1 shows that SH shares ended the trading day up 25 pence (at £21.25). This column tells you that SH ended the previous day at £21. On a day when VN ends the day at £22 (up 10 pence), you can tell that the previous day it ended the trading day at £21.90.

Using News about Dividends

Reading and understanding the news about dividends is essential if you're an *income investor* (someone who invests in shares as a means of generating regular income). See Chapter 9 on investing for income.

Looking at important dates

In order to understand how buying shares that pay dividends can benefit you as an investor, you need to know how companies report and pay dividends. Some important dates in the life of a dividend are as follows:

>> **Announcement date:** Also called the *declaration date,* this is when a company reports a half-yearly dividend and the subsequent payment dates.

On January 15, for example, a company may report that it 'is pleased to announce an interim dividend of 50 pence per share to shareholders of record as of February 10'. If you buy the share before, on or after the announcement date, it won't matter with regard to receiving the company's interim dividend. The date that matters is the record date (see that bullet later in this list).

>> **Date of execution:** Not as bad as it sounds. This is the day you actually initiate the share transaction (buying or selling). If you call up a broker (or contact them online) today to buy a particular share, then today is the date of execution, or the date on which you execute the trade. In most cases nowadays, your broker makes the purchase on the same day. For an example, skip to the 'Understanding why these dates matter' section later in this chapter.

>> **Settlement date (closing date):** The closing or settlement date is the date on which the trade is finalised, which usually happens three business days after the date of execution if you're trading online. The settlement date for paper shares (certificates) is usually ten days after the date of execution. This is the date you pay (or are paid) for and become the proud new owner (or happy seller) of the stock.

>> **Date of record:** The date of record is used to identify which shareholders qualify to receive the declared dividend. Because shares are bought and sold every day, how does the company know which investors to pay? The company establishes a cut-off date by declaring a *date of record*. All investors who are official shareholders on the date of record receive the dividend on the payment date even if they plan to sell the shares any time between the date of record and the payment date.

>> **Ex-dividend date:** *Ex-dividend* means *without dividend*. Because it can take three days to process a share purchase before you become an official owner of the shares, you need to pay close attention to ex-dividend dates if you're intending to gain an income from the shares. You aren't entitled to the most-recently announced dividend if you buy your shares in the *ex-dividend period.* This period can be a matter of only two or three days, but buying on these days means you are not on the register of shareholders on the date of record. Go to the 'Understanding why these dates matter' section to see the effect that the ex-dividend date can have.

>> **Payment date:** The date on which a company sends its dividend cheques or authorises electronic payments to shareholders. Finally!

For typical dividends, the events in Table 6-2 happen twice a year.

TABLE 6-2   **The Life of the Half-yearly Dividend**

Event	Sample Date	Comments
Date of declaration	January 15	The date that the company declares the half-yearly (interim or final) dividend
Ex-dividend date	February 7	Starts the period during which, if you buy the shares, you don't qualify for the dividend
Date of record	February 10	The date by which you must be on the shareholders' register to qualify for the dividend
Payment date	February 27	The date that payment is made (an electronic payment or dividend cheque is sent to shareholders who were on the register on February 10)

Understanding why these dates matter

Remember that typically around three business days pass between the date of execution and the closing date. Similarly about three business days usually pass between the ex-dividend date and the date of record. You need to know this if you want to qualify to receive an upcoming dividend. Timing is important, and if you understand these dates, you know when to purchase shares and whether you qualify for a dividend.

As an example, say that you want to buy shares in ValueNow PLC (VN) in time to qualify for the interim dividend of 25 pence per share. Assume that the date of record (the date by which you have to be an official owner of the shares) is February 10. You may have to execute the trade (buy the shares) no later than February 7 to be assured of the dividend. If you execute the trade on February 7 itself, the closing date should occur three days later, on February 10 – just in time for the date of record. But you should always check with your stockbroker.

What if you execute the trade on February 8, a day later? Well, the trade's closing date is February 11, which occurs *after* the date of record. Unless you have an arrangement with your stockbroker, you won't be on the register as an official shareholder on the date of record, so you won't get that interim dividend. In this example, the February 7–10 period is called the ex-dividend period.

Fortunately, for those people who buy shares during their brief ex-dividend period, shares actually trade at a slightly lower price to reflect the amount of the dividend. If you can't get the dividend, you may as well save on the share purchase. How's that for a silver lining?

Evaluating (Avoiding?) Investment Tips

Psssst. Have we got a share tip for you! Come closer. You know what our tip is? Research! What we're trying to tell you is to never automatically invest just because you get a hot tip from someone. Good investment selection means looking at several sources before you decide on a share. No shortcut exists. That said, getting opinions from others never hurts – just be sure to carefully analyse the information you get. In the following list, we present some important points to bear in mind as you evaluate tips and advice from others:

>> **Consider the source.** Frequently, people buy shares based on the views of some market strategist or market analyst. People may see an analyst being interviewed on a television financial show and take that person's opinions and advice as valid and good. The danger here is that the analyst may be biased because of some relationship that isn't disclosed on the show.

WARNING

This scenario happens on TV all too often. A show's host interviews analyst U.R. Kiddingme from the investment firm Foollum & Sellum. The analyst says, 'Implosion Group is a good buy with solid, long-term, upside potential.' You later find out that the analyst's employer gets investment banking fees from Implosion Group. Analysts declare their interests in research papers, but these important details can be edited out of TV and newspaper interviews. And an analyst is pretty unlikely to knock a company that is helping to pay the bills.

>> **Get multiple views.** Don't base your investment decisions on just one source unless you have the best reasons in the world for thinking that a particular, single source is outstanding and reliable. A better approach is to scour current issues of independent financial publications, such as *MoneyWeek,* and other publications (and websites) listed in Appendix A.

TIP

>> **Gather data from the London Stock Exchange (LSE).** When you want to get more objective information about a company, why not take a look at the reports that companies must file with the London Stock Exchange? These reports are the same reports that the pundits and financial reporters read. They include annual results announcements and trading statements, as well as information on directors' share dealings. Many of the announcements filed with the stock exchange are also available on the best company websites.

Notices of directors' share dealings are normally filed on Reuters News Service (RNS) – a specialist news wire where all official company announcements are made public. UK companies that have dual listings in the US also have to file all their documents with the Securities and Exchange Commission (SEC).

IN THIS CHAPTER

» Understanding what brokers do

» Telling the difference between advisory and execution-only brokers

» Selecting a broker

» Exploring the types of brokerage accounts

» Figuring out what brokers' recommendations mean

Chapter **7**

Finding a Broker

When you're ready to dive in and start investing in shares, you first have to choose a stockbroker. This process is a bit like buying a car: you can do all the research in the world and know exactly what kind of car you want to buy; but you still need a venue in which to do the actual transaction. Similarly, when you want to buy shares, your task is to do all the research you can to select the company you want to invest in. Still, you need a stockbroker to actually buy the shares, whether you buy in person, over the phone or online.

For information on various types of orders you can place with a broker, such as targets and stop-loss orders, and so on, flip to Chapter 17.

Defining the Broker's Role

The broker's primary role is to serve as the vehicle through which you buy or sell shares. When we talk about brokers (also known as *stockbrokers*), we're referring to organisations such as Hargreaves Lansdown, AJ Bell's YouInvest, Barclays Stockbrokers, Interactive Investor, Freetrade and many other organisations that can buy shares on your behalf. Brokers can also be individuals who work for such firms. Although you can buy some shares directly from the company that issues them (we discuss direct purchase plans in Chapter 18), to purchase most shares, you still need a broker. And increasingly the vast majority of this trading happens online using the Internet.

Although the primary task of brokers is the buying and selling of securities such as shares (keep in mind that the word *securities* refers to the world of financial or paper investments, and that shares are only a small part of that world), they can perform other tasks for you, including the following:

>> **Providing advisory services:** Investors pay brokers a fee for investment advice. Customers also get access to the firm's research.

>> **Offering limited banking services:** Brokers can offer features such as interest-bearing accounts, cheque writing, direct deposit and pension advice.

>> **Brokering other securities:** Brokers can also buy bonds, investment and unit trusts, options, exchange traded funds (ETFs) and other investments on your behalf.

Personal brokers make their money from individual investors like you through various fees, including the following:

>> **Brokerage commissions:** This fee is for buying and/or selling shares and other securities.

>> **Service charges:** These charges are for performing administrative tasks and other functions. Brokers charge fees to investors for setting up Individual Savings Accounts or other investment vehicles.

>> **Advisory fees:** Many of the online and offline brokers also charge extra fees for providing personalized advice.

REMEMBER

Any broker advising you on investments must be registered with the Financial Conduct Authority (FCA). In addition, the money you deposit with your broker will normally be held in a linked bank account, so it has the same protection as it would have if it were held in the bank. Should your broker default, you should be entitled to most of your money back through the Financial Services Compensation Scheme. However, limits exist on the scheme, including a maximum of £85,000 per individual. To find out whether the broker is registered and reputable, contact the FCA. (See Appendix A for information on the FCA.)

TECHNICAL STUFF

The distinction between personal stockbrokers and institutional stockbrokers is important. Institutional brokers – many owned by large investment banks – make money from institutions and companies through investment banking and securities placement fees (such as initial public offerings, called flotations, and secondary offerings), advisory services and other broker services. Personal stockbrokers generally offer the same services – on a smaller scale – to individuals and small businesses.

Identifying the Options: Online, Offline, Advisory and Leverage

The old-fashioned stockbroking model – as it used to be called in the UK – has changed radically over the last few hundred years. In the days of old, brokers were famous for wearing suits and working in the City of London, facing off to gentlemen clients! The model changed again with the Big Bang series of regulatory changes in the Thatcher era when many of these old stockbrokers turned into investment banks, before changing again with the introduction of first telephone-based broking and then Internet-based service. In this section we spin through this evolution and how it has resulted in a new range of discrete products and services.

The old model: Advisory and discretionary

In the good old days before the Internet dominated the world, brokers fell into two basic categories:

>> **Advisory:** The advisory brokers advised their clients, the investors who open accounts with them, on how to invest their cash. When they opened an account at a brokerage firm, a representative would be assigned to your account.

>> **Execution-only:** This type of representative is usually called an *account executive*, or a *financial consultant* by the brokerage firm. This person is knowledgeable about shares in particular and investing in general.

Your account executive is responsible for assisting you, answering questions about your account and the shares in your portfolio, and transacting your buy and sell orders. These specialists offered guidance, gave you access to research, thought through how to achieve your investment objectives and even made investment decisions for you.

How the old model has changed

These advisory services have become much less common in recent years, and most of the providers are now reluctant to offer these services to new clients. They prefer instead to either shift to an execution-only model – in the next section – or open a full discretionary account. These discretionary accounts provide full management at the portfolio level for all your investments.

What are these discretionary services you are paying for? In simple terms the discretionary manager will make (frequent) changes to your portfolio based on the objectives you both agreed to when the account was first opened. You then get an annual report detailing the events in the portfolio over the year, including buys and sells plus lots of other information for your own accounts and for tax filings.

REMEMBER

You as the investor are now basically removed from the decision-making process. There is also a fair bit more time involved for the advisor, which means they tend to levy additional charges. In turn that means they tend to only want to provide this service for clients with a minimum of anything between £100,000 to £250,000 depending on the firm.

What to watch out for

Although the advisory brokers with their seemingly limitless assistance can make life easy for you, you need to remember some important points to avoid problems:

>> **Brokers and account reps are still salespeople.** No matter how well they treat you, they're still compensated based on their ability to produce revenue for the brokerage firm. They generate commissions and fees from you on behalf of the company. (In other words, they're paid to sell you things.)

>> **Whenever your rep makes a suggestion or recommendation, be sure to ask why and request a complete answer that includes the reasoning behind the recommendation.** A good advisor is able to clearly explain the reasoning behind every suggestion. If you don't fully understand and agree with the advice, don't take it.

>> **Working with an advisory broker costs more than working with an execution-only broker.** Execution-only brokers are paid simply for performing the act of buying or selling shares for you. Advisory brokers do that and more. Additionally, they provide advice and guidance. Because of that, advisory brokers are more expensive (through higher brokerage commissions and advisory fees). Also, most advisory brokers expect you to be prepared to invest a substantial lump sum just to open an account.

> » **Handing over decision-making authority to your rep can be a possible negative because letting others make financial decisions for you is always dicey – especially when they're using *your* money.** If they make poor investment choices that lose you money, you may not have any recourse because you authorised them to act on your behalf.

WARNING

> » **Some brokers engage in an activity called churning.** *Churning* is basically buying and selling shares for the sole purpose of generating commissions. Churning is great for brokers but bad for customers. If your account shows a lot of activity, ask for justification. Commissions, especially to advisory brokers, can take a big bite out of your wealth, so don't tolerate churning or other suspicious activity.

TIP

Before you deal with any broker, advisory or otherwise, check them out by contacting the FCA by calling 0300 500 0597 or visiting the FCA website at www.fca. gov.uk. You can ask whether any complaints or penalties have been filed against that brokerage firm or the individual rep.

Examples of advisory brokers are Killik & Co, and Brewin Dolphin. Some of the banks and building societies offer stockbroking services, which can be a mix of advice and execution-only. All brokers now have websites to give you further information about their services. Make sure you're as informed as possible before you open your account. An advisory broker is there to help you build wealth, not make you . . . er . . . broker.

The rise of the online brokers

Perhaps you don't need any hand-holding from a broker. You know what you want, and you can make your own investment decisions. All you want is someone to transact your buy/sell orders. In that case, go with an online execution-only broker. They don't offer advice or premium services – just the basics required to perform your share transactions.

Execution-only brokers are *cheaper* to engage than advisory brokers (and discretionary managers) and the vast majority of their business is done online. Because you're advising yourself (or getting advice from third parties such as newsletters or independent advisors), you can save on costs that you incur when you pay for an advisory broker.

REMEMBER

If you choose to work with an execution-only broker, you must know as much as possible about your personal goals and needs. You have a greater responsibility for conducting adequate research to make good share selections, and you must be prepared to accept the outcome, whatever that may be.

Until about 1995, most investing in shares was done with a traditional broker sitting in an office – in a bank or building society or in an independent company. Many investors posted their certificates to the relevant office with a request for them to be sold or for other shares to be bought.

When online investing started, about one trade a day was the norm. But nowadays the majority of investing – especially by execution-only brokers – is done online.

What they can do for you

Execution-only brokers offer some significant advantages over advisory brokers, such as:

>> **Lower cost:** This lower cost is usually the result of lower commissions and is the primary benefit of using execution-only brokers.

>> **Unbiased service:** Execution-only brokers let you simply place your buy and sell orders. Because they don't offer advice, they have no vested interest in trying to sell you any particular shares.

>> **Access to information:** Established execution-only brokers offer extensive educational materials at their offices or on their websites.

What to watch out for

Of course, doing business with execution-only brokers also has its negative aspects, including the following:

>> **No guidance:** Because you've chosen an execution-only broker, you *know* not to expect guidance, but the broker should make this fact clear to you anyway. If you're a knowledgeable investor, the lack of advice is considered a positive thing – no interference.

>> **Hidden fees:** Execution-only brokers may shout about their lower commissions, but commissions aren't their only way of making money. Many brokers charge extra for services that you may think are included, such as issuing a share certificate or preparing your annual tax statement. Ask whether they levy fees for managing ISAs or transferring shares and other securities (such as bonds) in or out of your account. And don't expect much in the way of interest on any cash sitting in your brokerage accounts.

>> **Minimal customer service:** If you deal with an Internet brokerage firm, find out about its customer service capability. If you can't get through to the website, make sure that the firm has an alternative helpline to place your order.

Free Share Dealing: What's the Catch?

A valuable old adage says there's no free lunch – except if you're a journalist. This conveys the essential wisdom that free stuff always has a catch. So, the natural reaction to dealing accounts that offer free share dealing is to scoff and look for the catch. And you'll find catches, but they aren't quite as nasty as you'd expect. In fact, free share dealing accounts are proliferating and if handled properly can be a great alternative to traditional phone-based, full-service accounts. The following sections delve deeper into what you need to know about free share dealing.

Recognising the basics to free share dealing

Free share dealing refers to accounts offered by online brokers such as Freetrade, Trading 212, eToro and to a lesser degree IG Markets (their US share dealing service is free, but they make a charge for UK trades). These all offer dealing in thousands of shares for free. Not complicated you might think, and you'd be right. However, you need to watch out for these important things, which the following sections discuss.

Only available through apps

Nearly all these services only operate via a smart phone-based app. That means you need to master the inner workings of an Apple or Android device. You can't use a normal web-based browser.

TIP

When signing up for free broker services, check out the full list of stocks available to buy and sell offered by the free version. If this is unduly limited, you may be better off paying for more choice.

Short on free offerings

Many of these services only offer a short list of stocks (and ETFs) for free. In some cases, this shortlist covers just a few hundred stocks. If you want to buy outside this list, you'll probably need to upgrade your service. In fact, the cheaper broker services, especially those offering free stock dealing, tend to not offer access to less liquid stocks or more obscure (European) stock markets. If you want to be able to buy a much wider range of stock offerings, you'll need to pay up for access to the more expensive, more established brokers.

WARNING

Many investors love to get access to new issues through what are called *initial public offerings (IPOs)*. These are frequently exciting new businesses listing afresh on the stock market. With nearly every free or low-cost dealing service, you won't be able to access these IPOs. It's just not economic for them to offer the service, so they don't.

The Freemium model is common. The basic service is free, but expect to pay an extra charge for a wider choice of shares or dealing options. The standard model for charging is to levy a monthly all-in fee.

Often less than stellar customer service

Don't expect amazing customer service for the free services. Some are better than others, but you don't need to be a genius to understand one way these online, app-only brokers might cut costs – making you interact through the app using text-based services rather than via a telephone number where you speak with a broker. Dealing in shares over the phone with these services is non-existent.

Fees, such as embedded charges

You should also keep an eye on what are called *embedded charges*, which are the less obvious fees levied for say foreign exchange (also known as FX transfers) or, more importantly, the difference between the buying and selling price of shares, known as the *bid-offer spread.* This can creep up alarmingly with some services.

REMEMBER

You get what you pay for. Internet-based dealing is a godsend for most investors, but the machines that implement these trades only do what they're instructed to do. They send over buys and sells and get the best price they can. If you're investing in less mainstream, less liquid stocks and funds where the bid offer spread can be quite hight, you may want to pay for more expensive services that use actual life humans and telephone dealing. In these circumstances, the real live human broker can actually talk to someone and narrow that bid offer, buying/selling spread down.

Other paid for products and services

You'll be encouraged in some services to experiment with premium services based around spread betting – where you can use leverage to increase your potential returns by betting a smaller amount of money to produce larger gains.

TIP

Most investors want to manage their dealing through a tax-efficient account such as an ISA or SIPP (see Chapter 20). Doing so makes absolute sense, but not all the free services offer a tax-efficient wrapper product.

Understanding costs

In reality whether you go for a free share dealing service or a paid-for service, you need to watch out for a number of charges and costs. These include some or all the following:

>> **Trading, buying and selling shares costs:** These costs can vary between free through to roughly £5 to £15 per trade, with some international shares costing a little more with some services. Most free share dealing services offer a core of free trades.

>> **Platform charge:** A *platform charge* is for running your account online and all the boring admin stuff, and it can vary based on two scales:

- **Percentage:** The first is a percentage of your total funds invested – usually between 0.20 and 0.50 per cent per annum plus VAT.

- **Monthly flat fee:** By contrast some platforms – free or otherwise – make a monthly flat fee for their services, which are usually in the £5 to £20 a month range.

REMEMBER

A flat fee for dealing sounds attractive and simple to understand, but if you don't have much money invested, those costs start to eat into your wealth. For example, say you're charged £10 a month or £120 a year. If you only have a few thousand pounds or even £10,000, then those costs are substantial. By contrast, if you have a few hundred thousand pounds in investments, then those flat fees can be quite attractive.

>> **Tax-efficient wrapper fees:** Tax-efficient wrappers such as ISAs and SIPPs – personal pension plans – also come with a separate cost. This amount varies between a per cent of funds invested or a flat fee for the wrapper.

>> **International fees:** You'll pay charges for international dealing. Refer to the next section for more discussion on international costs.

>> **Service fees:** These fees cover services that cover extra add-ons such as telephone dealing, which will probably cost you more in terms of fees. Whereas most share deals tend not to cost more £10 per trade (minimum), telephone trades can cost as much as £50 as a minimum.

TIP

As a broad-brush statement, if you're being charged more than £500 a year for platform charges and tax wrappers, then you should consider checking out the competition for lower priced alternatives.

Being aware of international costs

Over the last few decades access to trading in international shares – mainly those from the US – has opened up significantly. With some of the leading free share dealing app-based services, you may think most deal in US shares. The big tech stocks such as Tesla and Apple are firm favourites on many of these services, and the rise of fractional shares – see the nearby sidebar – has fuelled their popularity. Unfortunately, after you go beyond the US and the UK. to Europe, and beyond, most free share dealing services give up. Freetrade, one of the most popular providers, doesn't offer – at the moment at least – European shares – although that may change in the future.

WARNING

If you do trade in international stock, keep a beady eye on the FX spread on foreign share dealing transactions. Most experts think any spread above 1 per cent is frankly a bit of a rip-off. Most of the market tends to operate around the 0.5 to 1 per cent range, and best in class trades are under 0.50 per cent.

Choosing a Broker

Before you choose a broker, you need to analyse your personal investing style. After you know yourself and the way you invest, then you can proceed to finding the kind of broker that fits your needs. Think of it as almost like choosing shoes;

if you don't know your size, you can't get a proper fit. (And you can be in for a really uncomfortable future.)

When you come to choose a broker, keep the following points in mind:

>> Match your investment style with a brokerage firm that charges the least amount of money for the services you're likely to use most frequently.

>> Compare all the costs of buying, selling and holding shares and other securities through a broker. Don't compare only commissions. Compare other costs, too, such as the interest paid on cash in your account and 'hidden' service charges.

TIP

Finding brokers is easy. They're listed online via your favourite search engine (use a term like *online share dealing*) as well as in many investment publications and on many financial websites. Start your search by using the sources in Appendix A, which includes a list of the major brokerage firms.

Discovering Various Types of Brokerage Accounts

When you decide to start investing in the stock market, you have to somehow actually *pay* for the shares you buy. Most brokerage firms offer investors different types of accounts, each serving a different purpose. The following sections explain the most common types. The basic difference boils down to how you prefer to do business when it comes to buying and selling securities. If you like to see the tangible evidence of your transactions, you may want to buy and sell paper share certificates – though fewer and fewer people do. But if you worry about mislaying those fading paper assets you'll do better with a nominee account. Check out the 'Nominee accounts' section later in this chapter for more info.

REMEMBER

Whichever account you want, you need to go through the same process to open one. This process includes supplying evidence of who you are and where you live so that the broker can be sure that their services aren't being used for *money laundering*, the process by which money obtained through crime is returned to the legitimate economy. You may fill out an application form online but you have to send documentation – such as a passport or utility bill – and your National Insurance number. You also have to send a cheque for the minimum account balance. Setting up your account can take a couple of weeks.

Cash accounts

A *cash account* means just what you think it means. You must deposit a sum of money along with the new account application to begin trading. The amount of your initial deposit varies from broker to broker. Most brokers have a minimum of £1,000, but you may find others that let you open an account with less than this amount. Once in a while you may see a broker offering cash accounts with a very low minimum deposit, usually as part of a promotion. Use the resources in Appendix A to help you shop around. In any case, you still need to prove your identity to open one of these accounts.

With a cash account, your money has to be deposited in the account before the closing (or settlement) date for any trade you make. The settlement occurs three business days after the date you make the trade (the date of execution) unless you're trading paper share certificates, when it may be extended to ten days. In other words, if you call your broker on Monday, 10 October, and order 50 shares of CashLess plc at £20 per share, then on Thursday, 13 October, you'd better have £1,000 in cash sitting in your account (plus commission). Otherwise, the purchase doesn't go through. And you get stung by a fee for missing the settlement date. You may be required to have the money in the account even before the date of execution. See Chapter 6 for details on these and other important dates.

TIP

If you have cash in a brokerage account, check how much interest the broker pays you on the money. Most offer a pretty low rate, so arranging a linked online savings account from which to transfer cash to your broker when you need it is best.

Nominee accounts

A *nominee account* gives you the peace of mind that your shares are in safe hands, because they're stored electronically in your brokers' computer database. You may be sent contract notes for your trades and regular statements but you no longer have to guard your fragile paper certificates against fire, theft, flood or general clumsiness. This kind of account also gives you the flexibility to buy and sell at short notice as you can arrange to sell enough shares in one company to meet the cost of buying your latest favourite share.

Most brokers don't charge you for holding shares in your account, but they may charge for collecting dividends or making transfers to other accounts. You can have one nominee account with a broker linked to other accounts, such as a cash account or an ISA account where some of your shares can be held tax-free.

As well as the security of knowing exactly where your shares are, and never missing dividend payments, most nominee account holders can now get access to all the company documents that paper shareholders are entitled to. Within a few years, paper share trading will probably disappear from the UK market altogether.

Judging Brokers' Recommendations

In recent years, many investors have become enamoured with a new sport: the rating of shares by brokers in financial reports in the newspapers, on TV/ radio and online. Frequently these reports feature a dapper market strategist talking up a particular share. Some shares have been known to jump significantly right after an influential analyst issues a buy recommendation. Analysts' speculations and opinions make for great fun, and many people take their views very seriously. However, most investors should be very wary when analysts make a recommendation. These sections help you clarify what these recommendations may look like and important questions you can ask to clarify.

Clarifying the recommendations

Brokers issue their recommendations (advice) as a general idea of how much regard they have for a particular share. The following list presents the basic recommendations (or ratings) and what they mean to you:

» **Strong buy and buy:** Get in there! These shares are the ones to buy. The analyst loves this pick but the thing to keep in mind, however, is that *buy* recommendations are probably the most common because (let's face it) brokers sell shares.

» **Accumulate and market perform:** An analyst who issues these types of recommendations is positive, yet unexcited, about the pick. This rating is akin to asking friends whether they like your new suit and getting the response 'it's nice' in a monotone voice. They give a polite reply, but you wish the opinion had been more enthusiastic.

» **Hold or neutral:** Analysts use this language when their backs are against the wall but they still don't want to say, 'Sell that loser!' This recommendation is like your mother saying 'If you can't say anything nice, don't say anything at all.' This rating is the analyst's way of saying nothing at all.

» **Sell:** Many analysts should have issued this recommendation during 2008 and 2009, but few actually uttered it. What a shame. So many investors lost money because some analysts were too nice or just afraid to be honest, sound the alarm and urge people to sell.

» **Avoid like the plague:** We're just kidding about this recommendation, but we wish that this advice was available. We've seen plenty of shares that we thought were dreadful investments – shares in companies that made no money and were in a terrible financial condition that should never have been considered at all. Yet investors gobble up millions of pounds' worth of shares that eventually become worthless.

Don't get us wrong. An analyst's recommendation is certainly a better tip than what you'd get from your dentist or your sister-in-law's neighbour – unless she lives next door to a billionaire – but you want to view recommendations from analysts with a healthy dose of reality. Analysts have biases because their employment depends on the very companies that are being presented. What investors need to listen to when a broker talks up a share is the reasoning behind the recommendation. In other words, why is the broker making this recommendation?

Asking questions

Keep in mind that analysts' recommendations can play a useful role in your personal share investing research. If you find a great share and *then* you hear analysts give glowing reports on the same share, you're on the right track! Here are some questions and points to keep in mind:

» **How does the analyst arrive at a rating?** The analyst's approach to evaluating a share can help you round out your research as you consult other sources such as newsletters and independent advisory services.

» **What analytical approach is the analyst using?** Some analysts use *fundamental analysis* (looking at the company's financial condition and factors related to its success, such as its standing within the industry and the overall market). Other analysts use *technical analysis* (looking at the company's share price history and judging past share price movements to derive some insight regarding the share's future price movement). Many analysts use a combination of the two. Is this analyst's approach similar to your approach or to those of sources that you respect or admire?

» **What is the analyst's track record?** Has the analyst had a consistently good record through both bull and bear markets?

» **How does the analyst treat important aspects of the company's performance, such as sales and earnings?** How about the company's balance sheet? The essence of a healthy company is growing sales and earnings coupled with strong assets and low debt.

- >> **Is the industry that the company is in doing well?** Do the analysts give you insight on this important information? A strong company in a weak industry can't stay strong for long.

- >> **What research sources does the analyst cite?** Does the analyst quote the Treasury or industry trade groups to support her thesis? These sources are important because they help provide a more complete picture regarding the company's prospects for success.

- >> **Is the analyst rational when citing a target price for a share?** When she says, 'We think the share will hit £100 per share within 12 months,' is this opinion presenting a rational model, such as basing the share price on projected profits (or earnings) growth? The analyst must be able to provide a logical scenario about why the share has a good chance of achieving the cited target price within the time frame mentioned. You may not necessarily agree with the analyst's conclusion, but the explanation can help you decide whether the share choice was well thought out.

- >> **Does the company that's being recommended have any ties to the analyst or the analyst's firm?** Many analysts' notes come from firms that have an advisory role with the company they're writing about. There's nothing wicked about that, but it does mean that you've got to take everything they say with a big pinch of salt. This conflict of interest is probably the biggest reason that analysts were so wrong in their recommendations during that period. Ask your broker to disclose any conflict of interest.

TIP

The bottom line with brokerage recommendations is that you shouldn't use them to buy or sell a share. Instead, use them to confirm your own research. We know that if we buy shares based on our own research and later discover the same shares being talked up on the financial news, that's just the icing on the cake. The experts may be great to listen to, and their recommendations can augment your own opinions; however, they're no substitute for your own careful research.

Robo Advisers: Letting the Machine Carry the Load

Both developments – the rise of online brokers and the rise of app-based free share trading services – have disrupted the traditional investment market, and both are powered by the Internet. Chapter 21 looks at the remorseless rise of another disruption, one powered less by technology, rather technology: the exchange traded index tracking fund (ETF). These stock market–listed funds allow you to track a major index almost completely automatically at low cost.

Combine the Internet with the rise of ETFs and you end up with another disruptive new idea – a *robo adviser.* These online investment accounts are aimed at taking some of the noise and confusion out of the investing and making it simple to understand and cheap to operate.

Here's how it works: You want to invest £100 a month for the long term. You have some options:

>> **You can find an independent financial adviser willing to take you on as a client.** They'd make all the decisions for you and send you an occasional statement. Truth be told though most of these advisers don't really find it economic to take you on as a client without say investing £100,000 or more.

>> **You can open a share dealing account – free or paid for – and then make all your own decisions about which funds or shares to invest in.** This option works for many investors, but it can also be confusing for many. You have a lot of decisions to make, including which shares to buy, how many, when, in which markets and which indices to track via a fund. That may be too much for you to handle.

>> **You can open a share dealing account and then just buy a small handful of ETFs covering key markets every month.** This option is sometimes called *lazy investing* and isn't that difficult. Your £100 a month can go in say four ETFs: one tracking say the US market (the S&P 500 for instance), one tracking the UK market (the FTSE 100), another in emerging markets and maybe the last choice in a sector you like. With each you invest £25 a month, which is simple, intelligent, lazy investing, but it still involves you making decisions.

>> **You can open an online account with one of the major online investment services and let their specialists do all the work for you.** Examples of these services include Nutmeg, MoneyFarm, Wealthify or Moneybox. In this model your £100 a month is invested in one account, and the service allocates your £100 between their curated mix of ETFs.

Every few months a new robo adviser seems to emerge, and the market is now full of different options and services. As those choices multiply, the questions you need to ask of each provider also grows. In this section we provide a list of important factors to consider.

Identifying what makes them so attractive

Robo advisers are in effect a cheap, online personal wealth adviser. They start you with an online questionnaire, work out your goals and targets and then suggest a mix of different ETFs to achieve those goals. They do all the buying and selling of funds and shares as well as rebalancing every few years, plus they handle all the tax-wrapper stuff (you can invest through an ISA).

REMEMBER

In almost all cases these digital online wealth advisers, use only ETFs and tend to have three broad categories or styles of investing:

» **Adventurous or growth-oriented portfolios:** They're for the more risk-friendly, probably younger investor with a long-time horizon to invest.

» **Middle-of-the-road or balanced portfolios:** Pretty much this does what it says on the tin.

» **Cautious portfolios for the risk averse:** Perhaps this is an older investor who doesn't want too much volatility up or down.

The term *robo adviser* conjures up banks of clever computers, calculating fiendishly portfolios, and changing them every day depending on the markets. Science fiction fans look away now, but this isn't what happens at most robo advisers. Sure, they have computers, especially for word processing and virtual video calls, but in reality, humans perform most of the investment management work. True, the computer does some of the dealing, but that's about it. A real-life human being sits around and works out which ETFs to put in each portfolio. Some of the services do offer a more personalised service where your portfolio is designed individually for you – and that probably does involve a computer or two.

Choosing between robos

The rise of robo advisers has been facilitated by the Internet and computing power. That means the barriers to entry in this fast-evolving market aren't terribly high, and, as a result, a lot of services are available, all offering fairly similar products. 'Put away some money every month and we'll do all the investing bit for you in a globally diversified portfolio of ETFs' might be their collective catchline, assuming they had one, which they don't.

When you're selecting which robo to use, keep the following factors in mind:

» **Cost:** Cheaper isn't always better, but the cost of providing these services varies. The range is usually between 0.25 per cent (extremely cheap and really only for large sums of money) through to a shade less than 1 per cent.

» **Portfolio personalisation:** Does the service offer a personalised, bespoke portfolio specific to you or does it stick your money into broad pools based around our three-part risk model (adventurous, balanced and cautious)?

>> **Returns:** What do their returns look like? This factor is notoriously difficult to identify. Investigate to see how their portfolios have performed over the last few years. Finding this information can be tricky because most of these services are fairly new so they don't tend to have a track record. And if they offer personalised, bespoke portfolios, comparing results is essentially impossible.

>> **Socially responsible and ethical investing:** Many of the leading robo advisers also offer a specific portfolio service where they focus on only investing in sustainable businesses or those that score highly using ESG (environmental, social and governance) measures.

TIP

The robo adviser market has become much more competitive in recent years, and more than a few of the platforms have struggled to compete. Our hunch is that if you flash-forward to ten years in the future, many if not most of the existing advisers will either have been bought up or gone out of business. That suggests you take some care looking at how robust your robo adviser is if you use one. How much money do you have under management? Who are the robo adviser's backers? Ideally, you want to invest in a product that will still be around in ten years' time, which means you might have more than a passing interest in how likely that provider is to survive!

Chapter **8**

Investing for Growth

What's the number one reason people invest in shares? To grow their long-term wealth (also referred to as *capital appreciation*). Yes, some people invest for income (in the form of dividends), but that's a different matter, which we handle in Chapter 9. Investors seeking growth would rather see the money that can be distributed as dividends reinvested in the company so that (hopefully) a greater gain is achieved by seeing the share's price rise – or *appreciate*. People interested in growing their wealth see shares as one of the convenient ways to do it. Growth shares tend to be riskier than other categories of shares, but they can offer excellent long-term prospects for making the big bucks. If you're the type of investor who has enough money so that a loss won't devastate you financially, then growth shares may well be worth a go! As they say: no guts, no glory. The challenge is to work out which shares are going to make you richer quicker.

REMEMBER

Short of starting your own business, investing in shares is the best way to profit from a business venture. We want to emphasise that, to make money from shares consistently over the long haul, you must remember that you're investing in a company; buying shares is just a means for you to participate in the company's success (or failure).

TIP

Why do you need to think of investing in shares as buying a *company* rather than buying a *share*? Invest in a share only if you're just as excited about it as you would be if you were the chief executive in charge of running the company. If you're the sole owner of the company, do you act differently than one of a legion of obscure shareholders? Of course, you do. As the owner of the company, you have a greater interest in the company. You have a strong desire to know how the enterprise is doing. As you invest in shares, make believe that you're the owner, and take an active interest in the company's products, services, sales, earnings and so on. This attitude and discipline can enhance your goals as an investor in shares. This approach is especially important if your investment goal is growth.

Becoming a Value-Orientated Growth Investor

A share is considered a growth share when it grows faster and at a higher level than the overall stock market. Basically, a growth share outperforms its peers in categories such as sales and earnings. *Value shares* are shares that are priced lower than the value of the company and its assets – you can identify a value share by analysing the company's fundamentals and looking at key financial ratios, such as the price-to-earnings ratio. (For more on the topic of ratios, see Appendix B.) Growth shares tend to have better prospects for growth in the immediate future (from one to four years), but value shares tend to have less risk and more steady growth over a longer term.

Over the years, a debate has quietly raged in the financial community about growth versus value investing. Some people believe that growth and value are mutually exclusive. They maintain that large numbers of people buying shares with growth as the expectation tend to drive up the share price relative to the company's current value. Growth investors, for example, aren't put off by high price to earnings (P/E) ratios. Value investors, meanwhile, are too nervous to buy shares at high P/E ratio levels. (See Appendix B for more on P/E ratios.)

However, you *can* have both. A value-orientated approach to growth investing serves you best. Investors looking for long-term growth spend time analysing the company's fundamentals to make sure that the company's growth prospects lie on a solid foundation. But what if you have to choose between a growth share and a value share? Which do you choose? Seek value when you are buying the share and analyse the company's prospects for growth. Growth includes but is not limited to the health and growth of the company's specific industry and the economy at large (see Chapters 12, 13 and 14 for more on analysing the wider environment). In sum, this approach could be described as *growth but at a reasonable price* – or GARP for short.

REMEMBER

The bottom line is that growth is much easier to achieve when you seek solid, value-orientated companies in growing industries. To better understand industries and how they affect share values, see Chapter 12.

Being a value-orientated growth investor probably has the longest history of success versus most other share investment philosophies. The track record for those people who use value-orientated growth, or GARP, investing is impressive.

Getting Tips for Choosing Growth Shares

Although the information in the previous section can help you shrink your share choices from thousands to maybe a few dozen or a few hundred (depending on how well the general stock market is doing), the purpose of this section is to help you cull the so-so growth shares to unearth the go-go ones. Now you can dig deeper for the biggest potential winners. Keep in mind that you probably won't find a share to satisfy all the criteria presented here. Just make sure that your selection meets as many criteria as realistically possible. But hey, if you do find a share that meets all the criteria cited, *buy it quick*!

When choosing growth shares, you should consider investing in a company only *if* it makes a profit and *if* you understand *how* it makes that profit and from *where* it generates sales. Part of your research means looking at the industry (see Chapter 12) and economic trends in general.

Making the right comparison

You have to measure the growth of a company against something to figure out whether you have a growth share. Usually, you compare the growth of a company with growth from other companies in the same industry or with the stock market in general. In practical terms, when you measure the growth of a share against the stock market, you're actually comparing it against a generally accepted benchmark, such as the FTSE 100 Index, known as the Footsie, or the S&P 500. For more on the Footsie or the S&P 500, see Chapter 5.

If a company has earnings growth of 15 per cent per year over three years or more and the industry's average growth rate over the same time frame is 10 per cent, then this share qualifies as a growth share.

A growth share is so-called not only because the company is growing but also because the company is performing consistently well. Having a single year where your earnings do well versus the Footsie's average doesn't cut it. Growth must be consistently accomplished.

Checking out a company's fundamentals

When you hear the word *fundamentals* in the world of share investment, it refers to the company's financial condition and related data. When investors (especially value investors) carry out *fundamental analysis*, they look at the company's fundamentals – its balance sheet, income statement, cash flow and other operational data, along with external factors such as the company's market position, industry and economic prospects. Essentially, the fundamentals provide an indication of the company's financial condition. Chapter 10 goes into greater detail about analysing a company's financial condition but the main numbers you want to look at include the following:

- **» Sales:** Are the company's sales this year surpassing last year's? As a decent benchmark, you want to see sales at least 5 or 10 per cent higher than last year. Although it may differ depending on the industry, 5 per cent is a reasonable, general 'yardstick'.

- **» Earnings:** Are earnings at least 5 per cent higher than last year? Earnings should grow at the same rate as sales (or, hopefully, better).

- **» Debt:** Is the company's total debt equal to or lower than the previous year? The death knell of many a company has been excessive debt.

A company's financial condition has more factors than we mention here, but these numbers are the most important. We also realise that using a 5 or even 10 per cent figure may seem like an oversimplification, but you don't need to complicate matters unnecessarily.

Looking for leaders and megatrends

A strong company in a growing industry is a common recipe for success. If you look at the history of stock market investing, this point comes up constantly. Investors need to be on the alert for megatrends because they help to ensure your success.

REMEMBER

A *megatrend* is a major development that has huge implications for much (if not all) of society for a long time to come. Good examples are the need to reduce the consumption of hydro carbons – oil and gas to you and us – and replace those energy sources with green climate–friendly alternatives. That can mean everything from investing in electric cars through to hundreds of offshore wind farms. This rush to what's called *net zero* is a huge global megatrend and involves spending hundreds of billions of dollars on everything from batteries to power grids. You need to think about not only the megatrend itself but also the companies that supply into that megatrend.

Considering a company with a strong niche

Companies that have established a strong niche are consistently profitable. Look for a company with one or more of the following characteristics:

>> **A strong brand:** Companies such as Tesco come to mind. Yes, other companies out there sell food, but a business needs a lot more than a similar product to topple companies that have established an almost irrevocable identity with the public.

>> **High barriers to entry:** United Parcel Service (UPS) and Federal Express have set up tremendous distribution and delivery networks that competitors can't easily duplicate. High barriers to entry offer an important edge to companies that are already established.

>> **Research and development (R&D):** Companies such as Pfizer and GlaxoSmithKline spend a lot of money researching and developing new pharmaceutical products. This investment becomes a new product with millions of consumers who become loyal purchasers, so these companies are going to grow.

Noticing who's buying and/or recommending the share

You can invest in a great company and still see its shares go nowhere. Why? Because what makes the share go up is demand – having more buyers than sellers of the share. If you pick a share for all the right reasons, and the market notices the share as well, that attention causes the share price to climb. The things to watch for include the following:

>> **Institutional buying:** Are fund managers and pension plans buying up the share you're looking at? If so, this type of buying power can exert tremendous upward pressure on the share's price. Some resources and publications track institutional buying and how that affects any particular share. (You can find these resources in Appendix A.) Frequently, when a fund manager buys a share, others soon follow. Despite all the talk about independent research, a herd mentality still exists.

>> **Analysts' attention:** Are analysts talking about the share on the financial programmes? As much as you should be sceptical about an analyst's recommendation, it offers positive reinforcement for your share. Don't ever buy a share solely on the basis of an analyst's recommendation. Just know that if you buy a share based on your own research, and analysts subsequently rave about it, your share price is likely to go up. A single recommendation by an influential analyst can be enough to send a share skyward.

>> **Newsletter recommendations:** Independent researchers usually publish newsletter, both in hard copy and increasingly online (usually as PDFs). If influential newsletters are touting your choice, that praise is also good for your share. Although great newsletters are out there (find them in Appendix A), and they offer information that's as good or better than the research departments of certain brokerage firms, don't use a single tip to base your investment decision on. But it should make you feel good if the newsletters tout a share that you've already chosen.

>> **Consumer publications:** No, you won't find investment advice here. They may seem unexpected indicators to suggest, but consumer magazines are a source that you should notice. Publications such as *Which?* regularly look at products and services and rate them for consumer satisfaction. If a company's offerings are well-received by consumers, that's a strong positive for the company. This kind of attention ultimately has a positive effect on that company's shares.

Looking to history for investing lessons

A growth share isn't a creature like the Loch Ness monster – always talked about but rarely seen. Growth shares have been part of the financial scene for nearly a century. Examples abound that offer rich information that you can apply to today's stock market environment. Look at past market winners, especially those of the 1970s and 1980s, and ask yourself, 'What made them profitable shares?' We mention these two decades because they offer a stark contrast to one another. The 1970s were a tough, bearish decade for shares, whereas the 1980s were booming bull times. (See Chapter 15 for details on bear and bull markets.)

REMEMBER

Being aware and acting logically are as vital to successful stock market investing as they are to any other pursuit. Over and over again, history gives you the formula for successful share investment:

>> Pick a company that has strong fundamentals, including signs such as rising sales and earnings and low debt (see Chapter 10).

>> Make sure that the company is in a growing industry (refer to Chapter 12).

>> Be fully invested in shares during a bull market, when prices are rising both in the stock market and in the general economy (check out Chapter 15).

>> During a bear market, switch more of your money out of growth shares (such as technology) and into defensive shares (stable and lower-risk shares, in companies such as utilities whose services we'll always need).

>> Monitor your shares. Hold on to shares that continue to grow and sell those shares that are declining.

Evaluating the management of a company

The management of a company is crucial to its success. Before you buy shares in a company, you want to know that the company's management is doing a great job. But how do you do that? If you call up a company and ask, it may not even return your phone call. How do you know whether management is running the company properly? The best way is to check the numbers. The following sections tell you the numbers you need to check. If the company's management is running the business well, the ultimate result is a rising share price.

Return on equity

Although you can measure how well management is doing in several ways, you can take a quick snapshot of a management team's competence by checking the company's *return on equity* (ROE). You calculate the ROE simply by dividing earnings (more commonly called *operating profit*) by equity (often called *shareholders' funds*). The resulting percentage gives you a good idea of whether the company is using its equity (or net assets) efficiently and profitably. Basically, the higher the percentage, the better, but you can consider the ROE solid if the percentage is 10 per cent or higher. Keep in mind that not all industries have identical ROEs.

To find out a company's earnings, check out the company's *profit and loss account* (or P&L). The P&L is a simple financial statement that expresses the equation:

Sales – Expenses = Net Earnings (or Net Income or Net Profit)

You can see an example of a P&L in Table 8-1. (We give more details on P&L accounts in Chapter 10.)

TABLE 8-1

Grobaby PLC P&L Account

	2020	2021
Turnover	£82,000	£90,000
Operating expenses	(£75,000)	(£78,000)
Operating profit	£7,000	£12,000

To find out a company's equity, check out that company's balance sheet. (Chapter 10 also provides more details on balance sheets.) The *balance sheet* is actually a simple financial statement illustrating the fact that total assets minus total liabilities equal net equity. For publicly listed companies, the net assets are called *shareholders' equity* or *shareholders' funds*. Table 8-2 shows a balance sheet for Grobaby PLC.

TABLE 8-2

Grobaby PLC Balance Sheet

	December 31 2020	December 31 2021
Assets	£55,000	£65,000
Liabilities	(£20,000)	(£25,000)
Shareholders' funds	£35,000	£40,000

Table 8-1 shows that Grobaby's operating profit (or earnings before any deductions such as tax or write-offs) went from £7,000 to £12,000. In Table 8-2, you can see that Grobaby increased the shareholders' funds from £35,000 to £40,000 in one year. The ROE for the year 2020 is 20 per cent (£7,000 operating profit divided by £35,000 shareholders' funds), which is a solid number. The following year, the ROE is 30 per cent (£12,000 operating profit divided by £40,000 shareholders' funds), another solid number.

Equity and earnings growth

Two additional barometers of success are a company's profit growth year on year and growth of shareholders' funds. Look at the growth in Table 8-1. Operating profit grew from £7,000 (in 2020) to £12,000 (in 2021), or a percentage increase of 71 per cent (£12,000 minus £7,000 equals £5,000, and £5,000 divided by £7,000 is 71 per cent), which is excellent. In Table 8-2, Grobaby's shareholders' funds grew by £5,000 (from £35,000 to £40,000), or 14 per cent, which is very good – the management is doing good things here.

Insider buying

Watching management as it manages the business is important, but another indicator of how well the company is doing is whether management is buying shares in the company as well. If a company is poised for growth, who knows better than management? And if management is buying up the company's shares en masse, then that's a great indicator of the share's potential. Remember, though, that managers can't base their investment decisions on information that isn't already available to the public; if they did, that would be *insider trading* and could put them in prison. See Chapter 19 for more details on (legal) insider trading.

A company's financial situation does change, and you, as a diligent investor, need to continue to look at the numbers for as long as the share is in your portfolio.

PROTECTING YOUR DOWNSIDE

We become as monotonous as a one-stringed guitar on one topic: trailing stop losses. (See Chapter 17 for a full explanation of trailing stop losses.) *Trailing stop losses* are stop losses (orders to sell a share once the price of the share falls below a particular price) that you arrange to change daily based on the current value of your share. We always advocate using them, especially if you're new to the game of buying growth shares. Trailing stop losses can help you, no matter how good or bad the economy is (or how good or bad the share you're investing in is).

Suppose that you had invested in Enron, a classic example of a phenomenal growth share that went horribly wrong a while back. In 1999 and 2000, when its shares soared, investors were as happy as chocaholics at Cadbury World. Along with many investors who forgot that sound investing takes discipline and research, Enron investors thought, 'Downside risk? What downside risk?'

Here's an example of how a stop-loss order would have worked if you'd invested in Enron. Suppose that you bought Enron in 2000 at $50 per share and set up a stop-loss order with your stockbroker at $45. (Make it a *GTC* (or good-till-cancelled) order. If you do, the stop-loss order stays on indefinitely.) As a general rule, we like to place the stop-loss order at 10 per cent below the market value. As the shares went up, you kept the stop-loss trailing upward like a tail. (Now you know why people call it a 'trailing' stop loss; it trails the share's price.) When Enron hit $70, your stop-loss was changed to, say, $63, and so on. At $84, your new stop-loss was at $76. Then what?

When Enron started its perilous descent, you got out at $76. The new price of $76 triggered the stop loss, and the share was automatically sold – you stopped the loss! Actually, in this case, you can call it a 'stop and cash in the gain' order. Because you bought the shares at $50 and sold at $76, you pocketed a nice capital gain of $26 (52 per cent appreciation – a do-Enron-ron a do-Enron!). Then you safely stepped aside and watched the share continue its plunge.

But what if the market is doing well? Are trailing stop losses a good idea? Because these stop losses are placed below the share price, you're not stopping the share from rising upward indefinitely. All you're doing is protecting your investment from losses. That's discipline!

Exploring Small-Caps and Speculative Shares

Everyone wants to get in early on a hot new share. Why not? You buy Fillyerboots PLC at £1 per share and hope it zooms to £98 before lunchtime. Who doesn't want to buy a share that may become the next IBM or Microsoft? This possibility is why investors are attracted to small–caps.

DON'T RUSH TO BUY NEW ISSUE SHARES

When a company goes public, it means that it undergoes a *flotation* or *new issue*. This process is also called an initial public offering or IPO (the American term that is now also used in the UK). The *new issue* is the process by which a private firm seeks the assistance of an investment banking firm to gain financing by issuing shares that the public purchases. Flotations generate a lot of excitement, and many investors consider them to be that proverbial ground-floor opportunity. After all, some people find it appealing to get a share before its price skyrockets after investors subsequently flock to it. Why wouldn't people find new issues appealing?

New issues aren't guaranteed to soar in their first year and studies periodically carried out by the stockbroking industry have revealed that new issues (more times than not) decline in price by 60 per cent during the first 12 months. However, your interest in new issues should be guided by your attitude to risk. If you're prepared to take the risk that a new issue will do well for you, that's your choice – if not, keep your investment cash for companies that are already established. You can always wait to see how a new issue share and the company perform. Don't worry about missing that great opportunity; if it proves to be a genuine opportunity, you can still do well with an investment after the flotation.

And sticking with the acronym hunt, more recently you'll also run into something called a SPAC, which stands for a Special Purpose Acquisition company (also called a *blank cheque company*). They're in effect blank slate companies that raise some new money with which they then buy into a young, fast-growing business. They're similar to an IPO but quicker in process terms.

Small-cap (or small-capitalisation) is a reference to the company's market size. *Small-caps* are often newer companies that have room to grow. Investors may face more risk with small-caps, but they also have the chance for greater gains.

Out of all the types of shares, small-cap shares continue to exhibit the greatest amount of growth. In the same way that a tree planted last year has more opportunity for growth than a mature 100-year-old oak tree, small-caps have greater growth potential than established large-cap shares. Of course, a small-cap doesn't exhibit spectacular growth just because of its size. It grows when it does the right things, such as increasing sales and earnings by producing goods and services that customers want.

REMEMBER

For every small company that becomes a FTSE 100 firm, hundreds of companies don't grow at all or go out of business. When you try to guess the next great share before any evidence of growth, you're not investing – you're speculating. Have you heard that one before? (If not, flip to Chapter 2 for details.) Of course, you have, and you'll hear it again. Don't get us wrong – speculating isn't a crime. But you must recognise that you're speculating when you're doing it. If you're going to speculate in small shares hoping for the next Cisco Systems, then use the guidelines we present in the following sections to increase your chances of success.

Avoiding new issues, unless . . .

New issues are the birthplace of public shares, or the proverbial ground floor. The *new issue* or *initial public offering* (IPO) is the first offering to the public of a company's shares. This scenario is also referred to as *going public*. Because a company's going public is frequently an unproven enterprise, investing in a new issue can be risky. But some investors in the UK have done very well out of them.

Here are the two types of new issues:

>> **Start-up new issue:** This is a company that didn't exist before the flotation. In other words, the entrepreneurs get together and create a business plan. To get the financing they need for the company, they approach an investment banker to help them go public immediately.

>> **A private company that decides to go public:** In many cases, the new issue is for a company that already exists and is seeking expansion capital. The company may have been around for a long time as a small private concern, but it decides to seek funding through a new issue to enable it to grow. Many successful private companies are owned by private equity fund managers who like to sell out via an IPO.

Of these two types of new issue, which do you think is less risky? That's right! The established company going public. Why? Because the established company is already a proven business, which is a safer bet than a brand-new start-up. That said, we have one caution – quite a few of the private-to-public transitions backed by private equity fund managers haven't had a happy start to life and many investors have tended to view the IPOs as overpriced.

Asking yourself if your small-cap's making money

We emphasise two points when investing in shares:

>> Make sure that a company is established (being in business for at least three years is a good minimum).

>> Make sure that a company is profitable.

These points are especially important for investors in small shares. Plenty of start-up ventures lose money but hope to make a fortune down the road. A good example is a company in the biotechnology industry. Biotech is an exciting area, but many of these young businesses struggle to make a profit while also investing heavily in research and development. In fact, very few biotech companies ever make a profit until many years into their development. You may say, 'But should-n't I jump in now in anticipation of future profits?' You may get lucky, but under-stand that when you invest in unproven, small-cap shares, you're speculating.

Recognising that investing in small-cap shares requires analysis

The only difference between a small-cap share and a large-cap share is a few zeros in their numbers and the fact that you need to do more research with small-caps. By sheer dint of size, small-caps are riskier than large-caps, so you offset the risk by accruing more information on the share in question. Plenty of infor-mation is available on large-cap shares because they're widely followed. Small-cap shares don't get as much media attention and fewer analysts issue reports on them. Here are a few points to keep in mind:

>> **Understand your investment style.** Small-cap shares may have more potential rewards, but they also carry more risk. No investor should devote a large portion of their capital to small-cap shares. If you're considering retirement money, you're better off investing in investment-grade bonds or savings accounts. For example, retirement money should be in investments that are very safe or have proven track records of steady growth over an extended period of time (five years or longer).

>> **Check with online data sources.** Go online and check out services such as the LSEs website or Yahoo! Finance (and Google Finance) for detailed company information. You can also pay for specialist online services, such as Sharepad.co.uk that offer more detailed analysis.

>> **Check other sources.** See whether stockbrokers and independent research services, such as newspaper market columns, are following the company. If two or more different sources like the shares, then investigate further. Check the resources in Appendix A for further sources of information before you invest.

Chapter 9

Investing for Income

nvesting for income means investing in shares that provide you with regular pay-ments (dividends). Income shares may not offer stellar growth, but they're good for a steady inflow of money. What type of person is best suited to income shares? Income shares can be appropriate for many investors, but they're espe-cially well-suited to the following individuals:

» **Conservative investors:** Conservative investors like to see a slow-but-steady approach to growing their money while getting regular dividend cheques.

» **Retirees:** Growth investing is best suited to long-term needs, while income investing is best suited to current needs. Retirees may want some growth in their portfolios, but they're more concerned with regular income that can keep pace with inflation.

» **Dividend reinvestment plan (DRIP) investors:** For those investors who like to compound their money with DRIPs, income shares are perfect. For more information on DRIPs, see Chapter 18.

If you have a low tolerance to risk or if your investment goal is anything less than long term, income shares are your best bet.

Understanding Income Shares

When people talk about gaining income from shares, they're usually talking about dividends. A *dividend* is nothing more than money paid out to the owners of the company – the shareholders. You purchase dividend shares primarily for income – not for spectacular growth potential.

A dividend is quoted as an annual number but is usually paid twice a year. For example, if the company pays a dividend of £1, you're probably paid £50p each half year. If, in this example, you have 200 shares, you're paid £200 every year (if the dividend doesn't change during that period), or £100 every six months. Getting that regular dividend cheque every six months (for as long as you hold the shares) can be a nice perk.

TIP

A good income share is a share that has a higher-than-average dividend (typically 4 per cent or higher).

REMEMBER

Dividend rates aren't guaranteed – they can go up or down, or, in some cases, the dividend can be discontinued. Fortunately, most companies that issue dividends continue them indefinitely and actually increase dividend payments from time to time. Historically, dividend increases have equalled if not exceeded the rate of inflation.

Advantages of income shares

Income shares tend to be among the least volatile of all shares, and many investors view them as defensive shares. *Defensive shares* are shares in companies that sell goods and services that are generally needed no matter what shape the economy is in. (Don't confuse defensive shares with *defence shares*, which specialise in goods and equipment for the military.) Food, beverage and utility companies are great examples of defensive shares. Even when the economy is experiencing tough times, people still need to eat, drink and turn the lights on. Companies that offer relatively high dividends also tend to be large firms in established, stable industries.

Some industries in particular are known for high-dividend shares. Utilities (such as electricity, gas and water) and the energy sector (oil and gas) are places where you definitely find income shares. Yes, you can find high-dividend shares in other industries, but you find a high concentration of them in the previously mentioned industries. For more details, see the sections highlighting these industries later in this chapter.

Disadvantages of income shares

Before you say, 'Income shares are great! I'll get my cheque book and buy a batch right now', take a look at the potential disadvantages (ugh!). Income shares do come with fine print.

What goes up . . .

Income shares can go down as well as up, just as any share can. Obviously, you don't mind your income shares going up in value, but they can go down just as easily. The factors that affect shares in general – politics, economic trends (Chapter 14), industry changes (Chapter 12) and so on – affect income shares, too. Fortunately, income shares don't get hit as hard as other shares when the market is declining because high dividends tend to act as a support to the share price. Therefore, income shares' prices usually fall less dramatically than the prices of other shares in a declining market.

Interest-rate sensitivity

Income shares can be sensitive to rising interest rates. When interest rates go up, other investments (such as corporate bonds, gilts and savings certificates) are more attractive. When your income share is yielding 4 per cent and interest rates shoot back up to say 5 per cent, 6 per cent or even higher, you may think, 'Hmmm. Why settle for a 4 per cent yield when I can get 5 per cent or better elsewhere?' As more and more investors sell their low-yield shares, the prices for those shares fall.

Another point to remember is that rising interest rates may hurt the company's financial strength. If the company has to pay more interest, that may affect the company's earnings, which in turn may affect the dividend.

REMEMBER

Dividend-paying companies that are experiencing consistently falling revenues tend to cut dividends. In this case, 'consistent' means beyond just a year.

Inflation eats into dividends

Although many companies raise their dividends on a regular basis, some don't. Or, if they do raise their dividends, the increases may be small. If income is your primary consideration, you want to be aware of this fact. If you're getting the same dividend year after year and this income is important to you, rising inflation becomes a problem. Say that you have XYZ shares at £10 per share with an annual dividend of 30 pence (the yield is 30 pence divided by £10, or 3 per cent). If you have a yield of 3 per cent two years in a row, how do you feel if at some point in the (probably distant) future inflation rises to 6 per cent one year and 7 per cent the next? Because inflation means that your costs are rising, inflation shrinks the value of the dividend income you receive.

As you can see, even conservative income investors can be confronted with different types of risk. (Chapter 4 covers the topic of risk in greater detail.) Fortunately, the rest of this chapter helps you carefully choose income shares so that you can minimise these potential disadvantages.

The binary problem in recessions

Another 'challenge' you may want to consider is what we call the *binary problem.* This sounds complicated, but it isn't. Investors love it when a big company like say BP pays out juicy dividends, which sometimes helps push up the share price, but if too much cash is being used by the corporate to fund the dividend, a sudden downturn can present problems. Suddenly the board sits around scratching their collective heads and says 'Gee, we're spending all our spare cash on these cheques and not funding new revenue lines or projects'.

The net result is predictable. Kill the cheques and stop the dividends. But all those income–hungry investors who only really bought for the dividend suddenly panic and sell. The binary issue here is for some businesses the cash outflow becomes so huge that paying the dividends is unaffordable, and in an emergency it's better to stop paying entirely. There's no super clever answer we have to this binary challenge except to focus on the affordability of the dividend and whether the yield on offer looks just too generous.

PLAYING IT SAFE

If you're an investor seeking income and you're nervous about potential risks with income shares, here are some non-share-based alternatives:

- **National Savings Certificates:** Although the interest rates aren't always as good as you get from the best bank and building society accounts, these savings vehicles are guaranteed by the Treasury. They're the safest savings in the UK. They come in a variety of guises, including fixed interest offers and bonds aimed at pensioners or young people. New issues are launched regularly and interest rate changes are announced in the national press.

- **Bank and building society accounts:** These are considered pretty safe and are backed by the Financial Services Compensation Scheme. Try to have some cash invested in savings accounts before you start investing in shares.

- **Unit trusts:** Many unit trusts are suitable for income investors. They offer investors diversification and professional management, and investors don't need to have a large lump sum to start investing.

Don't forget the tax inspector

The government usually taxes dividends as ordinary income. Dividends from all UK companies are quoted *net of tax*. Companies paying dividends must first deduct one-ninth of the price and pay this in tax. See Chapter 20 for more information on taxes for investors.

Analysing Income Shares

Look at income shares in the same way you do growth shares when assessing the financial strength of a company. Getting nice dividends comes to a screeching halt if the company can't afford to pay them. If your budget depends on dividend income, then monitoring the company's financial strength is that much more important. Because the bulk of your returns will be earnt from dividends, you really need to understand the financial position of the dividend paying company and its ability to regularly pay out cash – the subject of the next section. You can apply the same techniques in Chapter 8 for assessing the financial strength of growth shares to your assessment of income shares.

Understanding your needs first

You choose income shares primarily because you want or need income now. As a secondary point, income shares have the potential for steady, long-term appreciation. If you're investing for retirement needs that won't occur for another 20 years, maybe income shares aren't suitable for you – better to invest in growth shares because they're more likely to grow your money faster over your stated length of investment term.

TECHNICAL STUFF

MINDING YOUR DIVIDENDS AND INTEREST

Dividends are sometimes confused with interest. However, *dividends* are payouts to owners, while *interest* is a payment to a creditor. A share investor is a part owner of the company he invests in and is entitled to dividends when they're issued. A bank, on the other hand, considers you a creditor when you open an account. The bank borrows your money and pays you interest on it.

If you're certain that you want income shares, do a rough calculation to work out how big a portion of your portfolio you want income shares to occupy. Suppose that you need £25,000 in investment income to satisfy your current financial needs. If you have bonds that give you £20,000 in interest income and you want the rest to come from dividends from income shares, you need to choose companies that pay you £5,000 in annual dividends. If you have £80,000 left to invest, you know that you need a portfolio of income shares that provide £5,000 in dividend income or a yield of 6.25 per cent (£5,000 divided by £80,000 equals a yield of 6.25 per cent).

Use the following table as a general guideline for understanding your need for income.

Item	Your Amounts	Sample Amounts
A. How much annual income do you need?		£10,000
B. The value of your portfolio (or money available for investment)		£150,000
C. Yield necessary to achieve income (divide item A by item B)		6.7%

With this simple table, you know that if you have £150,000 in income shares yielding 6.7 per cent, you receive income of £10,000 – meeting your stated financial need. You may ask, 'Why not just buy £150,000 of bonds (for instance) that yield at least 6.7 per cent?' Well, if you're satisfied with that £10,000, and inflation for the foreseeable future is zero, then you have a point. Unfortunately, inflation is probably around for the foreseeable future. Fortunately, the steady growth that income shares provide is a benefit to you.

TIP

If you have income shares and don't have any immediate need for the dividends, consider reinvesting the dividends in the company's shares. For more details on this kind of reinvesting, see Chapter 18.

REMEMBER

Every investor is different. If you're not sure about your current or future needs, your best choice is to consult with an independent financial adviser.

Checking out yield

Because income shares pay out dividends – income – you need to assess which shares can give you the highest income. How do you decide which shares will pay the most money? The main thing to look for in choosing income shares is *yield* (the percentage rate of return paid on a share in the form of dividends). Looking at a share's dividend yield is the quickest way to find out how much money you can earn from a particular income share versus other dividend-paying shares (or even other investments such as a bank account). Table 9-1 illustrates this point. Dividend yield is calculated in the following way:

Dividend Yield = Dividend Income ÷ Share Investment

TABLE 9-1   **Comparing Yields**

Investment	Type	Investment Amount	Annual Investment Income (Dividend)	Yield (Annual Investment Income ÷ Investment Amount) (%)
Smith PLC	Ordinary shares	£20 per share	£1.00 per share	5
Jones PLC	Ordinary shares	£30 per share	£1.50 per share	5
Wilson Bank	Savings account	£1,000 deposit	£40	4

The next two sections use the information in Table 9-1 to compare the yields from different investments and to see how evaluating yield can help you choose the company to earn you the most money.

REMEMBER

Don't stop scrutinising shares after you acquire them. You may have made a great choice that gives you a great dividend, but that doesn't mean that the shares stay that way indefinitely. Monitor the company's progress for as long as it's in your portfolio. Use resources such as www.ft.com and Yahoo! Finance (see Appendix A for more resources) to track your shares and to monitor how well that particular company continues to perform.

Examining yield

Most people have no problem understanding yield when it comes to savings. If we tell you that a National Savings Certificate has an annual yield of 3.5 per cent, you can easily work out that if you deposit £1,000 in that account, a year later you have £1,035 (slightly more if you include compounding). The National Savings Certificate's market value in this example is the same as the deposit amount – £1,000. That makes it easy to calculate.

How about shares? When you see a share listed in the financial pages, the dividend yield is provided along with the share's price and annual dividend. The dividend yield in the financial pages is always calculated as if you bought the share on the previous day – the day before publication. Just keep in mind that, based on supply and demand, share prices change virtually every day (every minute!) that the market is open. Therefore, because the share price changes every day, the yield changes as well. So, keep the following two things in mind when examining yield:

>> **The yield listed in the financial pages may not represent the yield you're receiving.** What if you bought shares in Smith PLC (see Table 9-1) a month ago at £20 per share? With an annual dividend of £1, you know that your yield is 5 per cent. But what if today Smith PLC is selling for £40 per share? If you look in the financial pages, the yield quoted would be 2.5 per cent. Gasp! Did the dividend get cut in half? No, not really. You're still getting 5 per cent because you bought the stock at £20 rather than the current £40 price; the quoted yield is for investors who purchase Smith PLC today.

Investors who buy Smith PLC shares today pay £40 and get the £1 dividend, and they're locked into the current yield of 2.5 per cent. Although Smith PLC may have been a good income investment for you a month ago, it's not such a hot pick today because the price of the shares doubled, cutting the yield in half. Even though the dividend hasn't changed, the yield has changed dramatically because of the share price change.

>> **Share price affects how good an investment the shares may be.** Another way to look at yield is by considering the amount of investment. Using Smith PLC in Table 9-1 as the example, the investor who bought, say, 100 shares of Smith PLC when they were £20 per share only paid £2,000 (100 shares times £20 – leave out commissions to make the example simple). If the same share is purchased later at £40 per share, the total investment amount is £4,000 (100 shares times £40). In both cases, the investor gets a total dividend income of £100 (100 shares times £1 dividend per share). From a yield perspective, which investment is yielding more – the £2,000 investment or the £4,000 investment? Of course, it's better to get the income (£100 in this case) with the smaller investment (a 5 per cent yield is better than a 2.5 per cent yield).

Comparing yield between different shares

All things being equal, choosing Smith PLC or Jones PLC is a coin toss. Look at your situation and each company's fundamentals and prospects and something may sway you. What if Smith PLC is a motoring company and Jones PLC is a utility serving inner London. Now what? In a difficult economy, the motoring industry struggles, whereas utilities are generally in much better shape. In that scenario,

Smith PLC's dividend would be in jeopardy while Jones PLC's dividend would be more secure. Another issue would be the dividend cover (see the next section). Therefore, having the same yield isn't the same as the same risk. Different companies have different risks associated with them.

Checking the company's dividend cover

You can use the *dividend cover* to work out what percentage of the company's earnings are being paid out in the form of dividends. Keep in mind that companies pay dividends from their net profits or earnings. Therefore, the company's earnings should always be higher than the dividends the company pays out. Here's how to calculate the dividend cover:

Earnings Per Share ÷ Dividend Per Share = Dividend Cover

Say that CashFlow Now PLC (CFN) has annual earnings of £1 million. (Remember that earnings are what you get when you subtract expenses from sales.) Total dividends are to be paid out of £500,000, and the company has 1 million outstanding shares. Using those numbers, you know that CFN has earnings per share (EPS) of £1 (£1 million in earnings divided by 1 million shares) and that it pays an annual dividend of 50 pence per share (£500,000 divided by 1 million shares). The dividend cover is 2 (the £1 earnings per share is twice the dividend of 50 pence). This number is a healthy dividend cover because, even if the company's earnings fall by 10 or 20 per cent, it still has plenty of room to pay dividends. People concerned about the safety of their dividend income should regularly watch the dividend cover. Generally, 2 or higher is considered safe because the company can well afford to pay its dividend. Anything between 1 and 1.5 would be on the risky side and less than 1 would be dangerous as the company is using the previous year's earnings (or worse still, debt) to pay its dividend.

REMEMBER

When a company suffers significant financial difficulties, its ability to pay dividends is compromised. If you need dividend income to help you pay your bills, you need to be aware of the dividend cover. Generally, a dividend cover of 2 or more is safe. Obviously, the higher the number, the safer the dividend.

Diversifying your shares

If most of your dividend income comes from shares in a single company or from a single industry, consider reallocating your investment to avoid having all your eggs in one basket. Concerns for diversification apply to income shares as well as growth shares. If all your income shares are in the electricity industry, then any problems in that industry are potential problems for your portfolio as well. See Chapter 4 for more on diversification.

Examining the company's bond rating

TIP

A company's bond rating is extremely important to income share investors. The bond rating offers insight into the company's financial strength. A *bond* is a type of share by which the authorised issuer owes the holders a debt and is obliged to repay the capital and interest at a later date when the bond is said to *mature*. Bonds get rated for quality for the same reasons that consumer agencies rate products such as cars or toasters.

Standard & Poor's (S&P) is the major independent rating agency that looks into bond issuers. It looks at the issuer of a bond and asks the question, 'Does the bond issuer have the financial strength to pay back the bond and the interest as stipulated in the bond indenture?'

To understand why this rating is important, consider the following:

>> **If the bond rating is good, that means that the company is strong enough to pay its obligations.** These obligations include expenses, payments on debts and dividends that are declared. If a bond rating agency gives the company a high rating (or if it raises the rating), that's a great sign for anyone holding the company's debt or receiving dividends.

>> **If a bond rating agency lowers the rating of a bond, that means that the company's financial strength is deteriorating.** That's a red flag for anyone who owns the company's bonds or shares. A lower bond rating today may mean trouble for the dividend later on.

>> **If the bond rating isn't good, that means that the company is having difficulty paying its obligations.** If the company can't pay all its obligations, then it has to choose which ones to pay. More often than not, a financially troubled company chooses to cut dividends or (in a worst-case scenario) not pay dividends at all.

The highest rating issued by S&P is AAA. The grades AAA, AA and A are considered *investment grade*, or of high quality. Bs and Cs indicate a poor grade, whereas anything lower is considered very risky (the bonds are referred to as *junk bonds*). The lowest ratings tend to be Ds, which usually mean that the company is in default.

Exploring Typical Income Shares

Although virtually every industry has companies that pay dividends, some industries have more dividend-paying companies than others. And some industries are likely to pay higher dividends than others. You won't find too many companies in the computer or biotech industries paying higher than average dividends! The reason is that, when companies need a lot of money to finance expensive research and development (R&D) projects to create new products, they can't afford to pay dividends. Without R&D, the company can't create new products to fuel sales, growth and future earnings. The following sections look closer at Computer, biotech and other innovative industries, which are often better for growth investors.

Utilities

Utilities generate a large cash flow. (If you don't believe us, look at your gas and electricity bills!) Cash flow includes money from income (sales of products and/or services) and other items (such as the selling of assets, for example). This cash flow is needed to cover things such as expenses, loan payments and dividends. Utilities are considered the most common type of income shares, and many investors have at least one in their portfolios. Investing in a utility company isn't a bad idea. Look for the following:

>> **The utility company's financial condition:** Is the company making money, and are its sales and earnings growing from year to year? Make sure that the utility's bonds are rated A or higher. We cover bond ratings in the section 'Examining the company's bond rating', earlier in this chapter.

>> **The company's dividend cover:** Because utilities tend to have a good cash flow, don't be too concerned if the dividend cover reaches 1.5. Again, from a safety point of view, however, the higher the rate, the better. Refer to the section 'Checking the company's dividend cover', earlier in this chapter for more on dividend cover.

>> **The company's geographic location:** If the utility covers an area that's doing well and offers an increasing population base and business expansion, that bodes well for your shares.

Real estate investment trusts (REITs)

Real estate investment trusts (REITs) were introduced to the UK market in January 2007. A *REIT* is an investment that has the elements of both a share and an *investment trust* (a pool of money received from investors that's managed by an investment company). It's like a share in that it's a company whose shares are publicly traded on the stock market, and it has the usual features that you expect from a share – it can be bought and sold easily through a broker; income is given to investors as dividends and so on. A REIT resembles an investment trust in that it doesn't make its money selling goods and services; it makes its money by buying, selling and managing an investment portfolio. In the case of a REIT, the portfolio is full of real estate or property investments. It generates revenue from rents and property leases as any landlord does. In addition, some REITs own mortgages, and they gain income from the interest.

The main advantages to investing in REITs include the following:

>> Unlike other types of property investment, REITs are easy to buy and sell. You can buy a REIT by dealing online, just as you can to purchase any share.

>> REITs in the UK don't yet have the higher-than-average yields seen overseas. But they must distribute at least 90 per cent of their profit from tax-exempt property rental business to their shareholders.

>> REITs involve a lower risk than the direct purchase of commercial property. Because you're investing in a company that buys the property, you don't have to worry about managing the properties – the company's management does that on a full-time basis. Usually, the REIT doesn't just manage one commercial property; it's diversified in a portfolio of different properties.

>> Investing in a REIT is affordable for small investors. REIT shares are affordable and have tax advantages. They can be bought in tax-efficient wrappers such as ISAs, SIPPs and even child trust funds.

REITs do have disadvantages. They have the same inherent risks as investing in commercial property directly. Before 2007 property investment reached record-breaking levels; it then crashed. As a result, many property funds declined in value by over 50 per cent. Whenever you invest in an asset (property and therefore REITs) that has already skyrocketed as the result of artificial stimulants (in the case of property, very low interest rates and too much credit and debt), the potential losses may offset any potential (unrealised) income. You also need to remember that in times of stress those dividends might be for the chop.

When you're looking for a REIT to invest in, analyse it the way you'd analyse a property. Look at the location and type of the property. If shopping centres are booming in Essex and your REIT buys and sells shopping centres in Essex, then you should do well. However, if your REIT invests in office buildings across the country and the office building market is overbuilt and having tough times, so will you.

Chapter **10**

Using Basic Accounting to Choose Winning Shares

uccessful share picking sometimes seems like pulling a rabbit out of a hat. In other words, it seems like you need sleight of hand to choose shares. Perhaps picking shares is more art than science. The other person seems to always pick winners while you're stuck with losers. What does it take? A crystal ball or a system from a get-rich-quick-with-shares book? Well, with the book in your hands now and a little work on your part, we think you can succeed.

This chapter takes the mystery out of the numbers behind the share. The most tried-and-trusted method for picking a good share starts with picking a good company. Picking the company means looking at its products, services, industry and financial strength ('the numbers'). Doing research regarding the company's 'financials' is easier than ever before, thanks to the Internet.

Recognising Value When You See It

If you pick a share based on the value of the company that's issuing it, you're a *value investor* – an investor who looks at a company's value and judges whether you can purchase the share at a good price. Companies have value in the same way many things have value, such as eggs or papier mâché umbrella stands. They also have such a thing as a fair price to buy them at, too. Eggs, for example, have value. You can eat them and have a tasty treat while getting nutrition as well. But would you buy an egg for £1,000 (and, no, you're not a starving millionaire on a desert island)? No, of course not. But what if you can buy an egg for 5 pence? At that point, it has value *and* a good price. This kind of deal is a value investor's dream.

REMEMBER

Value investors analyse a company's fundamentals (earnings, assets and so on) to see if the information justifies purchasing the shares. They see if the share price is low relative to these verifiable, quantifiable factors. Therefore, value investors use fundamental analysis, while other investors may use technical analysis. *Technical analysis* looks at charts and statistical data, such as trading volume and historical share prices. Some investors use a combination of both.

TIP

History has shown that the most successful long-term investors have typically been value investors using fundamental analysis as their primary investing approach.

In the following section we're going to dig a bit deeper into this numbers driven way of investigating a business's true worth — for instance, how much the business and its cashflow is worth and how that value relates to the share price.

Inspecting a company from a value-oriented viewpoint

When you look at a company from a value-orientated perspective, here are a few of the most important items to consider:

>> **The balance sheet to work out the company's net worth:** A value investor doesn't buy a company's shares because they're cheap; they buy the shares because they're *undervalued* (the company is worth more than the price its shares reflect – its market value is as close as possible to its book value).

>> **The profit and loss (P&L) account to figure out the company's profitability:** A company may be undervalued from a simple comparison of the book value and the market value, but that doesn't make it a screaming buy. For example, what if you find out that a company is in trouble and losing money this year? Do you buy its shares then? No, you don't. Why invest in shares in a

losing company? (If you do, you aren't investing – you're gambling or speculating.) The heart of a company's value, besides its net worth, is its ability to generate profit.

>> **Ratios that let you analyse just how well (or not so well) the company is doing:** Value investors basically look for a bargain. That being the case, they generally don't look at companies that everyone is talking about, because by that point, the shares in those companies cease to be a bargain. The value investor searches for shares that will eventually be discovered by the market and then watches as the share price goes up. But before you bother digging into the fundamentals to find those bargain shares, first make sure that the company is making money.

See the section 'Accounting for Value', later in this chapter for more on using balance sheets, P&L accounts and ratios to help you analyse share values.

TECHNICAL
STUFF

Value investors can find thousands of companies that have value, but they can probably buy only a handful at a truly good price. The number of shares that can be bought at a good price is relative to the market. In mature bull markets, a good price is hard to find because most shares have probably seen significant price increases, but in bear markets, good companies at bargain prices are easier to come by.

Understanding different types of value

Value may seem like a murky or subjective term, but value is the essence of good share picking. You can measure value in different ways, so you need to know the difference and understand the impact that value has on your investment decisions.

Market value

When you hear someone quoting a company at £47 per share, that price reflects the company's market value. The total market valuation of a company's shares is also referred to as its *market cap* or *market capitalisation*. How do you determine a company's market cap? With the following simple formula:

Market Capitalisation = Share Price × Number of Shares Outstanding

If Bolshevik PLC's shares are £35 each and it has 10 million shares outstanding (or shares available for purchase), then its market cap is £350 million. Granted, £350 million dollars may sound like a lot of money, but Bolshevik PLC may still be considered a small-cap depending on the relative value of the rest of the market. For more information about small-cap shares, dip into Chapter 8.

Who sets the market value of shares? The market – millions of investors directly and through intermediaries such as fund managers – determines the market value of shares. If the market perceives that the company is desirable, investor demand for the company's shares pushes up the price.

REMEMBER

The problem with market valuation is that it may not always be a good indicator of a good investment. In recent years, plenty of companies have had astronomical market values, yet they proved to be terrible companies and consequently terrible investments. For example, WorldCom was a multi-billion-dollar telecoms company in the US in the 1990s, yet it eventually went bankrupt, and the shares became worthless. Investors (and analysts) misunderstood the difference between the fleeting market value of the company and its true, underlying value.

Book value

Book value (also referred to as *accounting value*) looks at a company from a balance sheet perspective (assets minus liabilities equal net worth or *shareholders' funds*). Book value is a way of judging a company by its net worth to see whether the company's market value is reasonable compared to the company's intrinsic value.

Generally, market value usually tends to be higher than book value. If market value is substantially higher than book value, the value investor becomes more reluctant to buy that particular share because the share is overvalued. The closer the company's market capitalisation is to the book value, the safer the investment.

WARNING

We like to be cautious with a company whose market value is more than twice its book value. If the market value is £1 billion and the book value is £500 million or more, that's a good indicator that the company may be *overvalued*, or valued at a higher price than the company's book value and ability to generate a profit. Just understand that the further the market value is from the company's book value, the more you pay for the company's real potential value.

Earnings and sales value

A company's intrinsic value is directly tied to its ability to make money. In that case, many analysts like to value shares from the perspective of the company's P&L account. Two common barometers of value are expressed in ratios:

>> Price-to-sale ratio

>> Price-to-earnings ratio

In both instances, the price is a reference to the company's market value (as reflected in its share price). Sales and earnings are references to the company's ability to make money. These two ratios are covered more fully in the section 'Playing around with ratios', later in this chapter.

REMEMBER

For investors, the general approach is clear. The closer the market value is to the company's intrinsic value, the better. And, of course, if the market value is lower than the company's intrinsic value, then you have a potential bargain worthy of a closer look. Part of looking closer means examining the company's profit and loss statement, also called the P&L account, or simply, the P&L.

Putting the pieces together

The more ways that you can look at a company and see value, the better. The first thing to look at is the *price-to-earnings ratio* (or P/E ratio). Does the company have one? (If a company is losing money, it may not have one.) Does it look reasonable or is it in triple-digit, nosebleed territory? Is it reasonable or too high? Next, look at the company's debt load. Is it less than the company's equity? Are sales healthy and increasing from the previous year? Does the company compare favourably in these categories versus other companies in the same industry?

Simplicity is best. You may notice that the number '10' comes up frequently in measuring the company's performance, juxtaposing all the numbers that you need to be aware of. If net income is rising by 10 per cent or more, that's fine. If the company is in the top 10 per cent of its industry, that's great. If the industry is growing by 10 per cent or better (sales and so on), that's great. If sales are up 10 per cent or more from the previous year, that's great. A great company doesn't have to have all of these things going for it. But it should have as many of these things happening to ensure greater potential success.

Does every company or industry have to neatly fit these criteria? No, of course not. But it doesn't hurt you to be as picky as possible. You only need to find a handful of shares from thousands of choices. (Hey, this approach has worked for Paul, his clients and his students for more than two decades.)

Accounting for Value

Profit is for a company what oxygen is for people. That's neither good nor bad; it just is. Without profit, a company can't survive, much less thrive. Without profit, it can't provide jobs, pay taxes or invest in new products, equipment or innovation. Without profit, the company eventually goes bankrupt, and the value of its shares evaporates.

In the heady days leading up to the bear market of 2000–2002, many investors lost a lot of money simply because they invested in shares in companies that weren't making a profit. Lots of public companies ended up like flies that just didn't see the windscreen coming their way. Global giants such as Enron and World-Com entered the graveyard of rather-be-forgotten shares, and plenty of less well-known companies joined them. Investors around the world lost billions investing in glitzy companies that sounded good but weren't making money. When their brokers were saying, 'buy, buy, buy', their hard-earned money was saying, 'bye, bye, bye!'

TIP

Investors in shares need to pick up a rudimentary knowledge of accounting to round out their share-picking prowess and to be sure that they're getting good value for their investment cash. Accounting is the language of business. If you don't understand basic accounting, then you're going to find being a successful investor difficult. Investing without accounting knowledge is like travelling without a map. However, if you can run a household budget, using accounting analysis to evaluate shares is easier than you think.

As we discover in the next sections, a household's balance sheet – assets versus liabilities – isn't dissimilar from those of a business, just a lot more complicated. But understanding a balance sheet, which is only ever a snapshot in time, is of immense importance if you're to properly understand the true worth of a business (its underlying value).

Walking on a wire: The balance sheet

A company's balance sheet gives you a financial snapshot of what the company looks like in terms of the following equation:

Assets – Liabilities = Net Worth

The following sections take a closer look at what you need to review on a company's balance sheet and how to figure out a company's financial position.

Examining a company's balance sheet

Analyse the following items that you find on the balance sheet:

>> **Assets:** Have they increased from the previous year? If not, was the lack of increase the result of the sale of an asset or a write-off (uncollectible accounts receivable, for example)?

>> **Stock:** Does the company have more or less stock than last year? If sales are flat but the stock in the warehouse is growing, that may be a potential problem.

>> **Debt:** *Debt* is the biggest weakness on the corporate balance sheet. Make sure that debt isn't a growing item and that any debt is under control. In recent years, debt has become a huge problem for many companies.

>> **Derivatives:** A *derivative* is a speculative and complex financial instrument that doesn't constitute ownership of an asset (such as a share, bond or commodity), but a promise to convey ownership. Some derivatives are quite acceptable because they're used as protective or hedging vehicles (such derivatives aren't our primary concern). However, people frequently use them to generate income and they can then carry risks that can increase liabilities. Options and futures are examples of derivatives. Find out whether the company dabbles in these complicated, dicey, leveraged financial instruments. Find out (from the company's annual report) whether it has derivatives and, if so, the total amount. If a company has derivatives that are valued higher than the company's net equity, it may cause tremendous problems.

>> **Equity:** *Equity* is the company's net worth (what's left in the event that a company uses all the assets to pay off all its debts). Also known as *shareholders' funds,* equity should be increasing steadily by at least 10 per cent per year. If not, find out why.

Figuring out a company's financial position

A balance sheet is an important document that you should look at carefully to make sure that the company is in a strong financial position. By looking at a company's balance sheet, you can address the following questions:

>> **What does the company own (assets)?** The company can own assets, which can be financial, tangible and/or intangible. *Assets* can be anything that has value or that can be converted to or sold for cash. Financial assets can be cash, investments or accounts receivable. Assets can be tangible things such as products and supplies, equipment and/or buildings. They can also be intangible things such as licences, trademarks or copyrights.

>> **What does the company owe (liabilities)?** *Liabilities* are anything of value that the company must ultimately pay to someone else. Liabilities can be invoices (accounts payable) or short-term or long-term debt.

>> **What is the company's net equity (net worth)?** After you subtract the liabilities from the assets, the remainder is called *net worth, net equity* or *net shareholders' funds*. This number is also critical when calculating a company's book value.

As you can see, a balance sheet isn't hard to understand. Finding the relevant financial data on a company isn't difficult in the age of information. Most public companies publish their most recent financial documents, including interim and annual results and annual reports, on their websites.

The assets and liabilities relationship for a company has the same logic as the assets and liabilities in your own household. When you look at a snapshot of your own finances (your personal balance sheet), how can you tell if you're doing well? Odds are that you'd start by comparing numbers. If your net worth is £5,000, you may say, 'That's great!' But a more appropriate remark is something like, 'That's great compared to, say, a year ago.'

TIP

Compare a company's balance sheet at a recent point in time to a past time. You should do this comparative analysis with all the key items on the balance sheet. You do this analysis to see the company's progress. Is it growing its assets and/or shrinking its debt? Most importantly, is the company's net worth growing? Is it growing by at least 5 per cent from a year ago? All too often, investors stop doing their homework after they make an initial investment. You should continue to look at the company's numbers on a regular basis so that you can be ahead of the curve. If the company starts having problems, you can get out before the rest of the market starts getting out (which causes the share price to fall).

Assessing the company's financial strength

To judge the financial strength of a company, ask yourself the following questions:

>> Are the company's assets greater in value than they were three months ago, a year ago or two years ago? Compare current asset size to the most recent two years to make sure that the company is growing in size and financial strength.

>> How do the individual items compare with previous periods? Some particular assets that you want to take note of are cash, stock and accounts receivable.

>> Are liabilities such as accounts payable and debt about the same, lower or higher compared to previous periods? Are they growing at a similar, faster or slower rate than the company's assets? Remember that debt that rises faster and higher than items on the other side of the balance sheet is a warning sign of impending financial problems.

>> Is the company's net worth or equity greater than the previous year? And is that year's equity greater than the year before? In a healthy company, the net worth is constantly rising. As a general rule, in good economic times, net worth should be at least 10 per cent higher than the previous year. In tough economic times (such as a recession), 5 per cent is acceptable. Seeing the net worth growing at 15 per cent or higher is great news.

Looking at the P&L account

Where do you look if you want to find out what a company's profit is? Check out the company's P&L account. It reports, in detail, a simple accounting equation that you probably already know:

Sales – Expenses = Net Profit (or Net Earnings or Net Income)

Look at the following figures on the P&L account:

>> **Sales:** Are sales increasing? If not, why not? By what percentage are they increasing? Preferably, they should be at 5 per cent higher than the year before. Sales are, after all, where the money is coming from to pay for the company's activities and subsequent profit.

>> **Expenses:** Do you see any unusual items? Are total expenses reported higher than the previous year and by how much? If the item is significantly higher – why is that so? A company with large, rising expenses is going to see profits suffer, which isn't good for the share price.

>> **Research and development (R&D):** How much is the company spending on R&D? Companies that rely on new product development (such as pharmaceuticals or biotech firms) should spend an adequate amount because new products mean future earnings and growth.

>> **Profit:** This figure reflects the bottom line. Is total profit (earnings) higher than the previous year? How about operating profit (leaving out expenses such as taxes and interest)? The profit section is the heart and soul of the P&L and of the company itself. Out of all the numbers in the financial statements, profit has the greatest single impact on the company's share price.

Looking at the P&L, an investor can try to answer the following questions:

>> **What sales did the company make?** Companies sell products and services that generate revenue (known as *sales* or *turnover*). Sales are also referred to as the *top line*.

>> **What expenses did the company incur?** In generating sales, companies pay expenses such as payroll, utilities, advertising, administration and so on.

>> **What is the net income?** Also called earnings or net profit, net income is the *bottom line*. After paying for all expenses, what profit did the company make?

The information you glean should give you a strong idea about the company's current financial strength and whether the management are successfully increasing sales, holding down expenses and, ultimately, maintaining profitability. You can find out more about sales, expenses and profits in the sections that follow.

Sales

Sales refers to the money that a company receives as customers buy its goods and/or services. Sales is a simple item on the P&L and a useful number to look at. Analysing a company by looking at its sales is called *top line analysis*.

REMEMBER

As an investor, take into consideration the following points about sales:

» **Sales should be increasing.** A healthy, growing company has growing sales. It should grow at least 10 per cent from the previous year, and you should look at the most recent three years.

» *Core sales* **(sales of those products or services that the company specialises in) should be increasing.** Frequently, the sales figure has a lot of stuff lumped into it. Maybe the company sells widgets (what on earth is a widget, anyway?), but the core sales shouldn't include other things, such as the sale of a building or other unusual items. Take a close look. Isolate the company's primary offerings and ask whether these sales are growing at a reasonable rate (such as 10 per cent).

» **Does the company have odd items or odd ways of calculating sales?** Over the last decade many building companies boosted their sales by aggressively offering affordable financing with easy repayment terms. Say you find out that Suspicious Sales Ltd (SSL) had annual sales of £50 million, reflecting a 25 per cent increase from the year before. Looks great! But what if you find out that £20 million of that sales number comes from sales made on credit that the company extended to buyers? Some companies that use this approach later have to write off losses as uncollectible debt because the customer ultimately can't pay for the goods.

If you want to get an idea of whether a company is artificially boosting sales, check the company's accounts receivable (listed in the asset section of the company's balance sheet). *Accounts receivable* refers to money that's owed to the company for goods that customers have purchased on credit. If you find out that sales went up by £10 million (great!) but accounts receivable went up by £20 million (uh-oh), then something just isn't right. This situation may be a sign that the financing terms were too easy, and the company may have a problem collecting payment (especially in a recession).

Expenses

What a company spends has a direct effect on its profitability. If spending isn't controlled or held at a sustainable level, it may spell trouble.

REMEMBER

When you look at a company's expense items, consider the following:

>> **Compare expense items to the previous period.** Are expenses higher, lower or about the same as those from the previous period? If the difference is significant, you should see commensurate benefits elsewhere. In other words, if overall expenses are 10 per cent higher compared to the previous period, are sales at least 10 per cent more during the same period?

>> **Are some expenses too high?** Look at the individual expense items. Are they significantly higher than the year before? If so, why?

>> **Have any unusual items been listed as expenses?** Sometimes an unusual expense isn't necessarily a negative. Expenses may be higher than usual if a company writes off uncollectible accounts receivable as bad debt expense. Doing so inflates the total expenses and subsequently results in lower earnings. Pay attention to non-recurring charges that show up on the P&L and determine whether they make sense.

Profit

Profit or earnings is the single most important item on the P&L and also the one that receives the most attention in the financial media. When a company makes a profit, this profit is usually reported as earnings per share (EPS). If you hear that XYZ Ltd beat last year's earnings by a penny, here's how to translate that news. Suppose that the company made £1 per share this year and 99 pence per share last year. If that company had 100 million shares outstanding, then its profit this quarter is £100 million (the EPS times the number of shares outstanding), which is £1 million more than it made in the previous year (£1 million is 1 pence per share times 100 million shares).

TIP

Don't simply look at current profit as an isolated figure. Always compare current profit to profit in past periods (usually a year). For example, if you're looking at a retailer's interim results, you can't compare that with the retailer's finals from the previous year. Doing so is like comparing apples to oranges. What if the company usually does well during the summer holidays but poorly in the winter? Or the previous year was a pandemic? In that case, you don't get a fair comparison.

A strong company should show consistent earnings growth from the period (such as the year or the same quarter from the previous year) before, and you should check the period before that, too, so that you can determine whether earnings are consistently rising over time. Earnings growth is an important barometer of the company's potential growth and bodes well for the share price.

When you look at earnings, here are a few things to consider:

>> **Total profit:** This item is the one to watch most closely. Total profit should grow year on year by at least 10 per cent.

>> **Operating profit:** Break down the total earnings and look at a key subset – that portion of earnings derived from the company's core activity. Is the company continuing to make money from its primary goods and services?

>> **Nonrecurring items:** Is profit higher (or lower) than usual or than expected and why? Frequently, the difference results from items such as the sale of an asset or a large depreciation write-off.

We like to keep percentages as simple as possible. To reiterate, 10 per cent is a good number – easy to calculate and a good benchmark. However, 5 per cent isn't unacceptable if you're talking about tough times, such as a recession. Obviously, if sales, earnings and/or net worth are hitting or passing 15 per cent, that's great news.

Playing around with ratios

A *ratio* is a helpful numerical tool that you can use to identify the relationship between two or more figures found in the company's financial data. A ratio can add meaning to a number or put it in perspective. Ratios sound complicated, but they're easier to understand than you think.

Say that you're considering a share investment and the company you're looking at has earnings of £1 million this year. You may think that's a tidy sum, but in order for this amount to be meaningful, you have to compare it to something. What if you find out that the other companies in the industry (of similar size and scope) had earnings of £500 million? Does that change your thinking? Or what if you find out that the same company had earnings of £75 million in the previous period? Does that change your mind?

Two key ratios to be aware of are

>> Price-to-earnings ratio (P/E)

>> Price-to-sales ratio (PSR or P/R)

TIP

Every investor wants to find shares that have a 20 per cent average growth rate over the past five years and have a low P/E ratio (sounds like a dream). Use share-screening tools available for free on the Internet to do your research. Some brokers have them on their websites (such as The Share Centre at www.share.co.uk). Some excellent screening tools are also available from websites such as Stockopedia.com and SharePad.co.uk. You can also buy some wonderful computer software programs that do all the hard work for you; the best is probably Sharescope, available at www.sharescope.co.uk. A *share-screening tool* like Sharescope lets you plug in numbers such as sales or earnings and ratios such as the P/E ratio or the dividend yield and then click! Up come shares that fit your criteria. This is a good starting point for serious investors. Check out Appendix B for even more on ratios.

Running into the P/E ratio

The *price-to-earnings (P/E) ratio* is important in analysing a potential share investment because this ratio is one of the most widely regarded barometers of a company's value and is usually reported along with the company's share price in the financial pages. The major significance of the P/E ratio is that it establishes a direct relationship between the bottom line of a company's operations – the earnings – and the share price.

The *P* in P/E stands for the share's current price. The *E* is for earnings per share (typically the most recent 12 months of earnings). The P/E ratio is also referred to as the *earnings multiple* or just *multiple.*

REMEMBER

You calculate the P/E ratio by dividing the price of the share by the earnings per share. If the price of a single share of a company is £10 and the earnings (on a per-share basis) are £1, then the P/E is 10. If the share price goes to £35 per share and the earnings are unchanged, then the P/E is 35. Basically, the higher the P/E, the more you pay for the company's earnings.

Why would you buy shares in one company with a relatively high P/E ratio instead of investing in another company with a lower P/E ratio? Keep in mind that investors buy shares based on expectations. They may bid up the price of the share (subsequently raising its P/E ratio) because they feel that the company's earnings are going to increase in the near future. Perhaps they feel that the company has great potential (a pending new invention or lucrative business deal) that will eventually make the company more profitable. More profitability in turn has a beneficial impact on the company's share price. The danger with a high P/E is that, if the company doesn't achieve the hoped-for results, the share price may fall.

GETTING A BALANCED PICTURE OF A COMPANY

You should look at two types of P/E ratios to get a balanced picture of the company's value:

>> **Trailing P/E:** This P/E is the most frequently quoted because it deals with existing data. The trailing P/E uses the most recent 12 months of earnings in its calculation.

>> **Forward P/E:** This P/E is based on projections or expectations of earnings in the coming 12-month period. Although this P/E may seem preferable because it looks into the near future, forward P/E is still considered an estimate that may or may not prove to be accurate.

The following example illustrates the importance of the P/E ratio. Say that you want to buy a business and we're selling a business. If you come to us and say, 'What do you have to offer?', we may say, 'Have we got a deal for you! We operate a retail business in the centre of town that sells spatulas. The business nets a cool £2,000 profit per year.' You reluctantly say, 'Uh, okay, what's the asking price for the business?' We reply, 'You can have it for only £1 million! What do you say?'

If you're sane, odds are that you politely turn down that offer. Even though the business is profitable (a cool £2,000 a year), you'd be crazy to pay a million quid for it. In other words, the business is way overvalued (too expensive for what you're getting in return for your investment cash). The million pounds would generate a better rate of return elsewhere and probably with less risk. As for the business, the P/E ratio (£1 million divided by £2,000 = a P/E of 500) is outrageous. This example is definitely a case of an overvalued company – and a lousy investment.

What if we offered the business for £12,000? Does that price make more sense? Yes. The P/E ratio is a more reasonable 6 (£12,000 divided by £2,000). In other words, the business pays for itself in about six years (versus 500 years in the prior example).

EVALUATING P/E RATIOS

Looking at the P/E ratio offers a shortcut for investors asking the question, 'Is this company overvalued?' As a general rule, the lower the P/E, the safer (or more conservative) the shares are. The reverse is more noteworthy: the higher the P/E, the greater the risk.

REMEMBER

When someone refers to a P/E as high or low, you have to ask the question, 'Compared to what?' A P/E of 30 is considered high for a large-cap electricity supplier but quite reasonable for a small-cap technology firm. Keep in mind that phrases such as 'large-cap' and 'small-cap' are just a reference to the company's relative market value or size. 'Cap' is short for capitalisation (the total number of shares outstanding times the share price). See Chapter 3 for more on market cap.

TIP

The following basic points can help you evaluate P/E ratios:

>> **Compare a company's P/E ratio with its industry.** Electricity industry shares generally have a P/E that hovers in the 10 to 20 range. Therefore, if you're considering an electricity supplier with a P/E of 45, then something is wrong with that company.

>> **Cross-reference a company's P/E with the general market.** If you're looking at a small-cap share on the Alternative Investment Market (AIM) that has a P/E of 100 but the average P/E for established companies on the AIM is 40, find out why. You should also compare the share's P/E ratio with the P/E ratio for major indices such as the FTSE 100, the FTSE 250 and maybe even the Dow Jones Industrial Average (DJIA) (for more on market indices, see Chapter 5).

>> **Check a company's current P/E against recent periods (such as this year versus last year).** If it currently has a P/E ratio of 20 and it previously had a P/E ratio of 30, you know that the share price has declined or that earnings have risen. In the latter case, the share is less likely to fall. That bodes well for the company.

>> **Remember low P/E ratios aren't necessarily the sign of a bargain.** However, if you're looking at a company for many other reasons that seem positive (solid sales, strong industry and so on) and it also has a low P/E, that's a good sign.

>> **Remember high P/E ratios aren't necessarily bad, but they do mean that you should investigate further.** If a company is weak and the industry is shaky, heed the high P/E as a warning sign. Frequently, a high P/E ratio means that investors have bid up a share price, anticipating future income. The problem is that, if the anticipated income doesn't materialise, the share price may fall.

WARNING

>> **Watch out for a share that doesn't have a P/E ratio.** In other words, it may have a price (the P), but it doesn't have earnings (the E). No earnings mean no P/E, meaning that you're better off avoiding it. Can you still make money buying a company with no earnings? You can, but you aren't investing; you're speculating.

Discovering PSR

The *price-to-sales ratio (PSR or P/S)* is the company's share price divided by its sales. Because the sales number is rarely expressed as a per-share figure, it's easier to divide a company's total market value (see the 'Market value' section earlier in this chapter to find out what this term means) by its total sales for the last 12 months.

TIP

As a general rule, shares trading at a PSR of 1 or less are reasonably priced and worthy of your attention. For example, say that a company has sales of £1 billion and the stock has a total market value of £950 million. In that case, the PSR is 0.95. In other words, you can buy £1 of the company's sales for only 95 cents. All things being equal, that share may be a bargain.

Analysts frequently use the PSR as an evaluation tool in the following circumstances:

>> In tandem with other ratios to get a more well-rounded picture of the company and its shares.

>> When you want an alternate way to value a company that doesn't have earnings.

>> By analysts who want a true picture of the company's financial health, because sales are tougher for companies to manipulate than earnings.

>> When you're considering a company offering products (versus services). PSR is more suitable for companies that sell items that are easily counted (such as products). Companies that make their money through loans, such as banks, aren't usually valued with a PSR because deriving a usable PSR for them is more difficult.

REMEMBER

Compare the company's PSR with other companies in the same industry, along with the industry average, so that you get a better idea of the company's relative value.

3 Picking Winners

Know how to identify the key indications that a particular share's price is going to rise.

Understand some general economic and political factors that can have a huge effect on your shares.

Focus on key financial information and important company documents and then interpret the information you find.

Investigate big picture themes that build on key global trends to help make your investments more resilient.

Chapter **11**

Decoding Company Documents

Good grief. Financial documents. Some people would rather suck a hospital mop than read a dry corporate or government report. Yet, if you're serious about choosing shares, you should be serious about your research. Fortunately, research is not as bad as you think (put away that disgusting mop!). When you see that basic research helps you build wealth, it gets easier.

In this chapter, we discuss the basic documents that you come across (or should come across) most often in your investing life. These documents include essential information that all investors need to know, not only at the time of the initial investment decision, but also for as long as those shares remain in their portfolio. Oh, and one bit of good news, for the planet and you: You can read all the documents we discuss in this chapter online using PDFs, thus avoiding having to print the reports and saving hundreds of trees from being chopped down.

TIP

If you plan to hold the shares for the long haul, reading the annual report and other reports covered in this chapter can only help you. If you intend to get rid of the shares soon or plan to hold them only for the short term, reading these reports diligently isn't that important.

Slices from the Big Cheese:
The Annual Report

When you're a regular shareholder, the company sends you its annual report. If you're not already a shareholder, contact the company's investor relations department for a hard copy.

TIP

You can often view a company's annual report on its website. Any major search engine can help you find this site. Downloading or printing the annual report should be easy. If in doubt, search online for the name of the company, go to the company website and then search for a menu option or tab that says Investors or Investor Centre. You'll usually then see an option for key documents.

You need to carefully analyse an annual report to find out the following:

>> **You want to know how well the company is doing.** Are earnings higher, lower or the same as the year before? How are sales doing? These numbers should be clearly presented in the financial section of the annual report.

>> **You want to find out whether the company is making more money than it's spending.** How does the balance sheet look? Are assets higher or lower than the year before? Is debt growing, shrinking or about the same as the year before? For more details on balance sheets, see Chapter 10.

>> **You want to get an idea of management's strategic plan for the coming year.** How are management planning to build on the company's success? This plan is usually covered in the beginning of the annual report – frequently in the letter from the chairman of the board.

REMEMBER

Your task boils down to working out where the company has been, where the company is now and where the company is going. As an investor, you don't need to read the annual report like a novel – from cover to cover. Instead, approach it like a newspaper and jump around to the relevant sections to get the answers you need in order to decide whether you should buy, or hold on to, the shares.

Analysing the annual report's anatomy

Not every company puts its annual report together in exactly the same way – the style of presentation varies. Some annual reports have gorgeous graphics or actual shareholder special offers for the company's products, whereas others are in a standard black-and-white typeface with no cosmetic frills at all. But every annual report does include common basic content, such as the profit and loss statement and the balance sheet.

The following sections present typical components of an average annual report. Keep in mind that every annual report may not have the sections in the same order.

Letter from the chairman of the board

The first thing you see is usually the letter from the chairman of the board or the chairman's statement. This is the 'Dear Shareholder' letter that communicates views from the head big cheese. The chairman's letter is designed to put the best possible perspective on the company's operations during the past year. Be aware of this bias. If the company is doing well, the letter certainly points it out. If the company is having hard times, the letter probably tries to put a positive spin on the company's difficulties. If the Big Bad Wolf had an annual report, odds are that the letter would have stated, 'Our little pig capturing ventures are being upgraded to cope with the increased sophistication of building materials used by porcine targets. And we have decided to discontinue our Red Riding Hood subsidiary as the risks far outweigh the potential rewards.' You get the point.

REMEMBER

To get a good idea of what issues the company's management team feels are important and what goals they want to accomplish, keep the following questions in mind:

>> What does the letter say about changing conditions in the company's business? How about changing conditions in the industry?

>> If any difficulties exist, does the letter communicate a clear and logical action plan (cutting costs, closing loss-making plants and so on) to get the company back on a positive track?

>> What is being highlighted and why? For example, is the company focusing on research and development for new products or on a new deal with China?

>> Does the letter offer apologies for anything the company did? If, for example, the company fell short of sales expectations, does it offer a reason for the shortcoming?

>> Did the company make (or will it make) new acquisitions or major developments (selling products to China or a new marketing agreement with a Fortune 500 company)?

The company's offerings

This section of an annual report can have various titles (such as 'Operating review'), but it covers what the company does to make its money. Whatever the company sells – products or services or both – understand what they are and why customers purchase them.

If you don't understand what the company offers, then understanding how the company earns money, which is the driving force behind the company's shares, is more difficult. Are the company's core or primary offerings selling well? If the earnings of McDonald's are holding steady, but earnings strictly from burgers and fries are fizzling, that's a cause for concern. If a company ceases making money from its speciality, you should become cautious. Here are other questions to ask yourself:

» How does the company distribute its offerings: through a website, shops, agents or other means? Does it sell only to the UK market or is its distribution international? The greater the distribution, the greater the sales and, ultimately, the higher the share price.

» Are most of the sales to a definable marketplace? If, for example, most of the company's sales are to a war-torn or politically unstable country, you should worry. If the company's customers aren't doing well, that has a direct impact on the company and, eventually, its shares.

» How are sales doing versus market standards? In other words, is the company doing better than the industry average? Is the company a market leader in what it offers? The company should be doing better than (or as well as) its peers in the industry. If the company is falling behind its competitors, that doesn't bode well for the shares in the long run.

» Does the report include information on the company's competitors and related matters? You should know who the company's competitors are because they have a direct effect on the company's success. If customers are choosing the competitor over your company, the slumping sales and earnings will ultimately hurt the share's price.

Financial statements

Look over the various financial statements and find the relevant numbers. Every annual report should have (at the least) a balance sheet and a profit and loss statement. Catching the important numbers on a financial statement isn't that difficult to do. However, it certainly helps when you pick up a little basic accounting knowledge. Chapter 10 can give you more details on evaluating financial statements.

First, review the *profit and loss statement* (called the *I* but also known as the *income statement*). The P&L gives you the company's sales, expenses and the result (net income or net loss).

Look at the balance sheet. The balance sheet provides a snapshot of a point in time (annual reports usually provide a year-end balance sheet) that tells you what the company owns (*assets*), what it owes (*liabilities*) and the end result (*net worth*). For a healthy company, assets should always be greater than liabilities.

Carefully read the footnotes to the financial statements. Sometimes big changes are communicated in small print.

Performance review

The performance review, which may also be called the summary of past financial figures, gives you a snapshot of the company's overall long-term progress. Most reports look at the company's performance over a five-year period and may even show a graph charting total shareholder return against the performance of the FTSE 100 Index (see Chapter 5 for more on indexes).

Management issues

The management issues section of an annual report includes a reporting of current trends and issues, such as new things happening in the industry, which affect the company. This section may be called the 'Chief Executive's report or review' or the 'Directors' statement'. See whether you agree with management's assessment of economic and market conditions that affect the company's prospects. What significant developments in society does management perceive as affecting the company's operations? Does the report include information on current or pending legal action?

The auditor's report

Annual reports typically include comments from the company's auditors – qualified and certified accountants. It may be an opinion letter or a simple paragraph with the auditors' views regarding the financial statements that were prepared.

The report normally says that the accounts are true and fair – an opinion about the accuracy of the financial data presented and how the statements were prepared. Check to see whether the report qualifies this phrase in any way or includes any footnotes regarding changes in certain numbers or how they were reported. For example, a company that wants to report higher earnings may show depreciation more conservatively, rather than a more aggressive method of depreciating. In most cases, the auditors' reports in annual accounts are similar because they stick to accounting standard practice.

The 'About us' section

Every annual report includes detailed information about the company and its subsidiaries (or lesser companies that it owns) and brands. Often, each part of the business is given its own pages to explain who runs that part of the business and exactly what it does and where.

Directors' shareholdings

This section can usually be found as a table near the back of the report alongside details of directors' earnings (called *remuneration*). This gives a good picture of which directors are increasing their stakes in the business and how the share price has to perform to trigger their next long-term incentive plan share option target. See Chapter 19 for more on directors' share ownership.

Share data

The share data section may include a history of the share price – usually over the last five years – along with information such as what exchange the share is listed on, the share code, the company's dividend reinvestment plan (if any) and so on. It also includes information on shareholder services and whom to contact for further information.

Going through the proxy materials

As a shareholder (or investor – same thing), you're entitled to vote at the annual shareholders' meeting called the *Annual General Meeting* (AGM). If you ever get the opportunity to attend one, do so. You get to meet other shareholders and to ask questions of management and other company representatives. Usually, the investor relations department provides you with complete details. At the meetings, shareholders vote on company matters, such as approving any new share options plans for senior executives or deciding whether the salaries for executives are acceptable.

Companies also have occasional special meetings called extraordinary general meetings (EGMs), which are held to vote on a particular issue such as whether a proposed merger with another company should go ahead.

If you can't attend (which is usually true for the majority of shareholders), you can vote by proxy. *Voting by proxy* means essentially that you vote by post. You indicate your vote on the proxy statement (or card) and authorise a representative to vote at the meeting on your behalf. The proxy statement is usually sent to all shareholders, along with the annual report, just before the meeting. If you hold your shares in a nominee account with your stockbroker, you may not get a vote automatically. Talk to your broker about this. See Chapter 7 for more on dealing with brokers.

Getting a Second Opinion

A wealth of valuable information is available for your investing pursuits. The resources in this section are just a representative few – a good representation, though. The information and research they provide can be expensive if you buy or subscribe on your own, but fortunately, most of the resources mentioned are usually available in the business reference section of a well-stocked public library or on the Internet. To get a more balanced view of the company and its prospects, take a look at several different sources of information for the shares you're researching.

Company documents filed with the RNS

The serious investor doesn't overlook the wealth of information that you can cull from documents filed with the regulated news services such as RNS (Regulatory News Service). Take the time and effort to review these documents because they offer great insight regarding the company's activities. Here's how to obtain the main documents that investors should be aware of:

» **Drop by the company itself.** Shareholder service or investor relations departments keep these publicly available documents on hand and usually give them at no cost to interested parties. Most companies put them on their websites.

» **Ask the Financial Conduct Authority, the UK's listings authority, by phone or online.** If you can't find the documents you want or the company doesn't want to let you see them, you can always ask the FCA whether there should be public access. You can find out more by contacting the Financial Conduct Authority, 12 Endeavour Square, London, E20 1JN.

» **Check out regulatory news services to search any public documents filed.** Companies in the UK have to publish their financial reports through authorised news services. Some are free to access and others charge a subscription. A list of the main ones is given in Chapter 6.

» **Check out the London Stock Exchange's free Annual Report Service** (www.londonstockexchange.com). The LSE provides free information on more than 1,300 listed companies.

» **Review the Annual Report Service** (www.annualreports.com/). This site maintains an extensive database of company annual reports.

Trading updates

As the name suggests, the *trading update* gives you an update on current trading. Trading updates – sometimes called *trading statements* – tend to be issued every quarter. They give a brief overview of the company's progress since the last formal report – probably the annual or half-year results.

Unlike the annual report that you get from the company, a trading update tends not to provide very much detailed financial information. It covers the general progress of the company and a little bit of information on each of the company's main divisions. Retailers tend to publish these updates shortly after the major seasons – for example, Christmas trading updates are common in the retail sector. The update may give an indication of how business is doing in terms of percentages but is unlikely to give figures in pounds and pence. It may say that growth of 10 per cent has been seen in sales, or that a division has had its best quarter for five years, but not say how much profit has been made. The meat is kept for the next results.

You can find trading updates reported in the press and on financial websites such as:

>> **Yahoo! Finance UK:** https://uk.finance.yahoo.com

>> **Google Finance:** www.google.com/finance

REMEMBER

Keep in mind that not every company has the same financial year or the same financial calendar. A company with a calendar year financial year (ending December 31) will probably file a trading update for the first quarter (January 1 to March 31) in May. Half-year results may be in August followed by a third-quarter trading update in November and final or full-year results in February.

Insider reports

Two types of insiders exist: those who work within the company and those outside the company who have a significant (10 per cent or more) ownership of company shares. Tracking insider activity is profitable for investors who want to follow in the footsteps of the people who are in the know. See Chapter 19 for information about monitoring and benefiting from insider activity.

Every time an insider (such as the CEO or financial director) buys or sells shares, the transaction has to be reported to the FSA. The insider has to report the trade soon after the transaction. These reports become publicly available documents – published on the regulated news services – that allow you to see what the insiders are doing. Hearing what they say in public is one thing, but seeing what they're actually doing with their share transactions can be more important.

Brokerage reports: The good, the bad and the ugly

Traditionally, brokerage reports have been a good source of information for investors seeking informed opinions about shares. And they still are, but in recent years some brokers have been criticised for biased reports. Brokers should never be the sole source of information.

The good

Research departments at brokerage firms provide share reports and make them available for their clients and investment publications. The firms' analysts and market strategists generally prepare these reports. Good research is critical, and brokerage reports can be valuable. What better source of guidance than full-time experts backed up by multimillion–pound research departments? Brokerage reports have the following strong points:

>> The analysts are professionals who should understand the value of a company and its shares. They analyse and compare company data every day.

>> They have at their disposal tremendous information and historical data that they can sift through to make informed decisions.

>> If you have an account with the firm, you can usually access the information at no cost.

>> They have regular meetings with company insiders and the ability to ask probing questions about the company's fortunes.

The bad

Brokerage reports may not be bad in every case, but at their worst, they're quite bad. Brokers make their money from commissions and investment banking fees (nothing bad here). However, they can find themselves in the awkward position of issuing brokerage reports on companies that are (or may be) customers for the brokerage firm that employs them (hmmm – could be bad). Frequently, this relationship can result in a brokerage report that paints a more positive picture of a company than it really merits (yes, that's bad).

REMEMBER

Sometimes, good research can be compromised by conflicts of interest.

Remember the Internet boom, or the 'Dot.com fiasco' as it's called by some writers and investors? During the late 1990s an overwhelming number of brokerage reports issued glowing praise of spiffy-sounding technology companies that were mediocre or dubious. Investors bought up those shares in tech start-ups and telecom superstars. The sheer demand pushed up share prices, which gave the appearance of genius to analysts' forecasts, yet the prices rose essentially as a self-fulfilling prophecy. The shares were highly overvalued and were cruisin' for a bruisin'. Analysts and investors were feeling lucky.

The ugly

Investors lost a stack of money (sounds ugly). Money that people had painstakingly accumulated over many years of work vanished in a matter of months as the bear market of 2000 hit (uglier). Retirees who had trusted the analysts saw nest eggs lose 40 to 70 per cent in value (blimey, very ugly). Not all investors had been reading the brokers' notes on these shares. Many novice investors gambled their savings because of the buzz in the media about tech shares.

During that bear market, a record number of lawsuits and complaints were filed against brokerage firms. Brokers and investors discovered a few tough facts. Regarding research reports from brokerage firms, the following points can help you avoid getting a bad case of the uglies:

>> Always ask yourself, 'Is the provider of the report a biased source?' In other words, is the broker getting business in any way from the company they're recommending?

>> Never, never, *never* rely on just one source of information, especially if this source is the same one that's selling you the shares or other investment.

>> Do your research first before you rely on a brokerage report.

>> Do your due diligence before you buy shares anyway. Look at the chapters in Part 1 and Part 2 to understand your need for diversification, risk tolerance and so on.

>> Verify the information provided to you with a trip to the library or websites (see Appendix A).

Although we generally don't rely on brokerage analysts, we do track a few independent investment analysts. You can find some of our favourites mentioned in Chapter 13.

Paid-for research

One last category of research is worth noting – *paid-for research*. The company in question pays for these detailed reports that are written about the company and published by specialists such as Edison Research. Before you throw your hands up in the air, be aware that these reports have to be detailed and factual. Of course, they're more positive about the future prospects for the company concerned. Nevertheless, they're still useful and detailed. Don't ignore them; just realise their bias.

Compiling Your Own Research Department

You don't need to spend an excessive amount of time or money, but you should maintain your own library of resources. You may only need one shelf (or a small amount of memory on your computer's hard drive). But why not have a few investment facts and resources at your fingertips? Paul maintains his own library loaded with books, magazines, newsletters and lots of great stuff downloaded on his computer for easy search and reference. When you start your own collection, keep the following in mind:

>> **Keep selected newspapers.** The *Financial Times* and the *Wall Street Journal* regularly have editions that are worth keeping.

>> **Subscribe to financial magazines.** Publications such as the *Investors Chronicle* magazine and *MoneyWeek* offer great research and regularly review shares, brokers and resources for investors.

>> **Keep annual reports.** Regarding the shares that are the core holdings in your portfolio, keep all the annual reports (at the least, the most recent three).

>> **Go to the library's business reference section.** Go periodically to stay updated. Hey, you pay the tax that maintains the public library – you may as well use it to stay informed.

>> **Use the Internet.** The web offers plenty of great sites to peruse, and we list some of the best in Appendix A.

TIP

Financial reports are important and easier to read than most people think. An investor can easily avoid a bad investment by simply noticing the data in what seems like a jumble of numbers. Figure out how to read them. For a great book to help you with reading financial reports (without needless technicality), check out *Interpreting Company Reports For Dummies* by Ken Langdon, Alan Bonham and Lita Epstein (John Wiley & Sons, Inc.).

Chapter **12**

Analysing Industries

S uppose that you have to bet your entire nest egg on a one-mile race. All you need to do is select a winning group. Your choices are the following:

Group A: A group of thoroughbred race horses

Group B: A group of overweight Elvis impersonators

Group C: A group of lethargic snails

This isn't a trick question, and you have one minute to answer. Notice that we didn't ask you to pick a single winner out of a giant mush of horses, Elvis Presleys and snails; we only asked you to pick the winning group in the race. The obvious answer is the thoroughbred race horses (and, no, they weren't ridden by the overweight Elvis impersonators because that would take away from the eloquent point being made). In this example, even the slowest member of group A easily outdistances the fastest member of groups B or C.

Industries aren't equal, and life isn't fair. After all, if life was fair, Elvis would be alive and the impersonators wouldn't exist. Fortunately, picking shares doesn't have to be as difficult as picking a winning racehorse. The basic point is that you can pick a successful company to invest in more easily from a group of winners (a growing, vibrant industry). Understanding industries only enhances your share-picking strategy.

A successful, long-term investor looks at the industry just as carefully as they look at the individual company. Luckily, choosing a winning industry to invest in is easier than choosing individual company shares. We know investors who can pick a winning company in a losing industry, and we also know investors who've chosen a losing company in a winning industry (the former investors are far outnumbered by the latter). Just think how well you do when you choose a great company in a great industry. Of course, if you repeatedly choose bad companies in bad industries, then you may as well get out of the stock market altogether (maybe your calling is to instead be a celebrity impersonator!).

This chapter dives a little deeper into the tricky subject of how to trawl through the Internet to find the right kind of information about how different sectors evolve over time.

Interrogating the Industries

Your common sense is an important tool in choosing industries with winning shares. The following sections explore some of the most important questions to ask yourself when you're choosing an industry. Keep in mind that an industry isn't the same as a sector. Even some market pros use the two words almost interchangeably. A *sector* is basically a 'mega-industry' or a group of interrelated industries. For example, pharmaceuticals and private hospital providers each constitute separate industries, but both of them are part of the healthcare sector. An *industry*, on the other hand, is typically a category of business that performs a precise activity (such as computer chips or trucking). Not all industries in a sector perform equally in the same market conditions.

Is the industry growing?

The question may seem too obvious, but you still need to ask it before you purchase shares. The saying 'the trend is your friend' applies when choosing an industry in which to invest, as long as the trend is an upward one. If you look at three different shares that are equal in every significant way but you find that share A is in an industry growing 15 per cent per year while the other two shares are in industries that have little growth or are shrinking, which share would you choose?

Sometimes, shares in a financially unsound or poorly run company go up dramatically because the industry the company is in is exciting to the public. The most obvious example in recent decades is the Internet industry, in which shares in both good and bad leading companies have shot up to incredible heights during the dotcom bubble in the late 1990s because investors thought the Internet was the place to be. It was, and some of today's most successful businesses were born in that era, notably Amazon – but plenty of others crashed and burned when the bubble burst. Sooner or later, the measure of a successful company is its ability to be profitable. Serious investors look at a company's fundamentals (see Chapter 10 to find out how to do this) and the prospects for the industry's growth before settling on a particular share.

TIP

To judge how well an industry is doing, various information sources monitor all the major industries and measure their progress. The more reliable sources include the following:

>> Confederation of British Industry (www.cbi.org.uk)

>> Standard & Poor's Industry Survey (www.spglobal.com)

>> Yahoo! Finance News (uk.finance.yahoo.com/news)

>> *Financial Times* (www.ft.com)

The preceding sources generally give you in-depth information about the major industries. Visit their websites to read their current research and articles along with links to relevant sites for more details. The *Financial Times*, for example, publishes indexes for all the major sectors and industries so that you can get a useful snapshot of how well an industry is doing (including information about whether shares are up or down and how they're performing year-to-date), and it updates its website regularly.

Are the industry's products or services in demand?

Look at the products and services that an industry provides. Do they look like things that society will continue to want? Are products and services on the horizon that may replace them? Does the industry face the danger of potential obsolescence?

When evaluating future demand, look for a *sunrise industry*, which is one that is new or emerging or has promising appeal for the future. Good examples in recent years have been biotech and Internet companies. In contrast, a *sunset industry* is one that's declining or has little potential for growth.

Current research unveils the following megatrends:

>> **The ageing population:** More senior citizens than ever before will be living in the UK. Because of this, financial and healthcare services are set to prosper.

>> **Advances in new technology:** Internet, telecoms, medical and biotechnology innovations will continue.

>> **Increasing need for basic materials:** As society advances here and in the rest of the world, building blocks such as metals and other precious commodities are sure to be in demand.

>> **Security concerns:** Terrorism and other international tensions mean more attention for defence, national security and related matters.

>> **Energy challenges:** Traditional and nontraditional sources of energy (such as solar, biofuels and so on) are sure to demand society's attention as it faces the prospect of life after oil.

What does the industry's growth rely on?

An industry doesn't exist in a vacuum. External factors weigh heavily on its ability to survive and thrive. Does the industry rely on an established megatrend, in which case it should be strong for a while, or on factors that are losing relevance? Technological and demographic changes are other factors that may contribute to an industry's growth.

Perhaps the industry offers great new medical products for senior citizens. What are the prospects for growth? Ageing population is an established megatrend. As more and more Britons live past the age of 60, profitable opportunities await companies that are prepared to cater for them.

Is this industry dependent on another industry?

This twist on the previous question is a reminder that industries frequently are intertwined and can become co-dependent. When one industry suffers, you may find it helpful to understand which industries will subsequently suffer. The reverse can also be true – when one industry is doing well, other industries may also reap the benefits.

In either case, if the shares you chose are in an industry that's highly dependent on other industries, you should know about it. If you're considering shares in holiday resort companies and you see the headlines blaring 'Airlines losing money as public stops flying', what do you do? This type of question forces you to think logically and consider cause and effect. Logic and common sense are powerful tools that frequently trump all the number-crunching activity performed by analysts.

Who are the leading companies in the industry?

After you've chosen the industry, what types of companies do you want to invest in? You can choose from two basic types of companies:

>> **Established leaders:** These companies are considered industry leaders or have a large share of the market. Investing in these companies is the safer way to go; what better investment for novice investors than companies that have already proven themselves?

>> **Innovators:** If the industry is hot and you want to be more aggressive in your approach, investigate companies that offer new products, patents or new technologies. These companies are probably smaller but have a greater potential for growth in a proven industry.

Is the industry a target of government action?

You need to know whether the government is targeting an industry because inter-vention by politicians and bureaucrats (rightly or wrongly) can have an impact on an industry's economic situation. For example, would you invest in a tobacco company now that smoking bans have been implemented in most restaurants, bars and workplaces across the country?

WARNING

Investors need to take heed when political 'noise' starts coming out about a par-ticular industry. An industry can be hurt by direct government intervention or by the threat of it. Intervention can take the form of lawsuits, investigations, taxes, regulations or sometimes an outright ban. In any case, being on the wrong end of government intervention is the greatest external threat to a company's survival.

REMEMBER

Sometimes, government action helps an industry. Generally, beneficial action takes two forms:

>> **Deregulation and/or tax decreases:** Governments sometimes reduce burdens on an industry. In 1986, Margaret Thatcher deregulated the bus industry in the UK and spawned dozens of successful companies that made millions for their founders and healthy sums for their workers, too. Companies such as Stagecoach, First Group, Arriva and Go-Ahead all had their origins in those initial changes to the restrictions on bus competition. Many of those bus firms started up by former bus drivers cut prices, increased passenger numbers and expanded routes into rural areas.

>> **Direct funding:** Governments have the power to steer taxpayers' money towards business as well. Recent UK governments have steered away from directly bailing out failing industries, but they've encouraged foreign companies to the UK using government grants. The tonnage tax for instance has brought more than 800 ships into the UK shipping industry by allowing companies to pay a flat rate fee on their tonnage rather than paying corporation tax on their profits.

Which category does the industry fall into?

Most industries can neatly be placed in one of two categories: cyclical and defensive. In a rough way, these categories, which we discuss in the following sections, generally translate into what society wants and what it needs. Society buys what it *needs* in both good and bad times. It buys what it *wants* when times are good and holds off when times are bad. A need is a 'must have' while a want is a 'like to have'.

Cyclical industries

Cyclical industries are industries whose fortunes rise and fall with the economy's rise and fall. In other words, if the economy is doing well and the stock market is doing well, cyclical industries tend to do well. When the economy is doing well, consumers and investors are confident and tend to spend and invest more money than usual. Mining, property and motoring are great examples of cyclical industries.

Your own situation offers you common-sense insight into the concept of cyclical industries. Think about your behaviour as a consumer, and you get a good idea about the thinking of millions of consumers. Think about the times you felt good about your career and your finances. When you (and millions of others) feel good about money and about the future, you have a greater tendency to buy more (and/or more expensive) stuff. When people feel financially strong, they're more likely to buy a new house or car or make another large financial commitment. Also, people take on more debt because they feel confident that they can pay it back. In light of this behaviour, which industries do you think would do well?

The same point also holds for business spending. When businesses think that economic times are good and foresee continuing good times, they tend to spend more money on large purchases such as new equipment or technology. They think that, when they're doing well and flush with financial success, they should reinvest that money to increase future success.

Defensive industries

Defensive industries are industries that produce the goods and services needed no matter what's happening in the economy. Your common sense kicks in here. What do you still buy even when times are tough? Think about what millions of people buy no matter how bad the economy gets. A good example is food. People still need to eat regardless of good or bad times. Other examples of defensive industries are utilities.

In bad economic times, defensive shares tend to do better than cyclical shares. However, when times are good, cyclical shares tend to do better than defensive shares. Defensive shares don't do as well in good times because people don't eat twice as much or use up more electricity.

So how do defensive shares grow? Their growth generally relies on two factors:

>> **Population growth:** As more and more consumers are born, more people become available to buy.

>> **New markets:** A company can grow by seeking out new groups of consumers who can buy their products and services. Coca-Cola, for example, found new markets in Asia during the 1990s and the first decade of this new century. As communist regimes fell from power and more societies embraced a free market and consumer goods, the company sold more beverages, and its shares soared.

One way investors can invest in a particular industry is to take advantage of Exchange Traded Funds (ETFs), which have become popular in recent years. If you find a winning industry but you can't find a winning share (or don't want to bother with the necessary research), then ETFs are a great consideration especially as many of the leading ETF issuers have 'sector'-based funds that let you invest in the biggest companies in each sector.

Outlining Key Industries

Not all industries go up and down in tandem. Indeed, at any given time, some industries are successful no matter what's happening with the general economy. In fact, investors have made a lot of money simply by choosing an industry that benefits from economic trends.

For example, the economy was in bad shape during the 1970s. It was a period of *stagflation* – low growth, high unemployment and high inflation. This decade was the worst time for the economy since the depression of the late 1920s; most industries (and therefore most shares) were having tough times. But some industries did well; in fact, they flourished. Property and precious metals, for example, performed well in this environment. Because the inflation rate soared into double digits, inflationary hedges such as gold and silver did well. During the 1970s, gold skyrocketed from $35 an ounce to $850 an ounce by the end of the decade. Silver went from under $2 to more than $50 in the same period. What do you think happened to shares in gold and silver mining companies? That's right. They skyrocketed as well. Gold shares gave investors spectacular returns.

In the 1980s, the economy became rejuvenated when taxes were cut, some industry red tape decreased and inflation fell. Most industries did well. But even in a growing economy, some industries struggled. Examples of industries that struggled during that time included precious metals and energy companies.

Fast-forward to 2021. Think about those industries that struggled and those that did well after the Covid pandemic. The leading e-commerce and Internet businesses have boomed. In the same time frame, industries such as airlines have had a rough time. Choosing the right industries (or avoiding the wrong ones) has always been a major factor in successful share picking.

For sale

Property is a key industry because property is a cyclical *bellwether industry* (one that has a great effect on many other industries that may be dependent on it). Property is looked at as a key component of economic health because so many other industries, including building materials, mortgages, household appliances and contract labour services, are tied to it. When the property industry is booming, that bodes well for much of the economy. Equally, when property prices are on their back – everyone feels a little gloomier!

Housing starts (new developments) are one way to measure property activity. This data is an important leading indicator of health in the industry. Housing starts indicate new construction, which means more business for related industries.

TIP

Keep an eye on the property industry for negative news that may be bearish for the economy and the stock market. Because property is purchased with mortgage money, investors and analysts watch the mortgage market for signs of trouble such as rising *defaults* (missed debt payments) and *foreclosures* (when banks insist on repayment of a debt earlier than planned). These statistics serve as a warning for general economic weakness.

Starting in 2002, the property industry started to grow fiercely, with much of that demand driven by free and easy credit. Almost every month new records were being set for housing, but some investors in 2005 and 2006 began to start exercising caution because they believed that they were seeing growing evidence of a mania. A *mania* is typically the final part of a mature bull market. In a mania, the prices of the assets experiencing the bull market (such as shares or property) are skyrocketing to extreme levels, which excite more and more investors as they jump in. More investors piling in causes the prices to rise even further. It gets to the point where seemingly everyone thinks that getting rich by buying this particular asset is easy, and almost no one notices that the market has become unsustainable. After prices are exhausted and start to level off, investor excitement dies down and then investors try to exit by selling their holdings to realise at least some profit. As more and more sell off their holdings, demand decreases while supply increases. The mania disappears and the bear market appears. Guess what happened next? Well, you probably don't need to guess as it would take a hermit in a deep, dark cave not to know what happened in 2007 and 2008 as first the US, then the UK property market dived! The rest, as they say, is history!

Baby, you can drive my car

The motor industry is another business that you want to watch carefully. When cars are selling well, you can generally interpret that as a positive indicator for the economy. People buy new cars when they're doing well. Cars are big-ticket items that are another barometer of people's economic well-being.

Conversely, trouble in the motor industry is a red flag for trouble in the general economy. Rising car repossessions and car loan defaults is a warning about general economic weakness.

Thanking Mr Roboto

In recent years, technology has become popular with investors. Indeed, technology is a great sector, and its impact on the economy's present and future success can't be underestimated.

The price of shares in technology companies can rise substantially because investors buy them based on expectations – today's untested, unproven companies may become the Microsofts and Apples of tomorrow. Despite the sector's potential, companies can still fail if customers don't embrace their products.

Even with technology shares, you must still apply the rules and guidelines that we discuss throughout this book for financially successful companies. Pick the best in a growing industry, and you're bound to succeed over the long haul.

Banking on it

Banking and financial services are an intrinsic part of any economy. Debt is the most telling sign of this industry for investors. If a company's debt is growing faster than the economy, you need to watch to see how the debt affects the company's shares and bonds. If debt gets out of control, it can be disastrous for the economy . . . as you may have noticed back in 2007 and 2008. One bank going bust is bad news; two is trouble; three is the end of the global economy as is known! Anyone who invested money in Lehman Brothers will know the sorry tale of picking the wrong bank. Yet banks can recover quickly, especially if they're bailed out by taxpayers. Bank shares crashed in 2008 but then bounced back in the second half of 2009 as investors realised, first, that the market wasn't heading into a new depression (or at least not for a few years), second, that the governments were going to rescue the banks, and third, that money could be made if the economy picked up again.

Chapter **13**

Being Prepared for a Changing World

Yes, you can do your own research (and you want to, don't you?), but we may as well make you privy to what our research tells us are the unfolding megatrends that offer the greatest potential rewards for investors in shares.

Making just a handful of changes in your portfolio over the past four decades would have made you tremendously rich. Had you put your money into natural resources (such as gold, silver and oil) at the beginning of the 1970s and stayed put until the end of the decade, you would have made a fortune. Then had you cashed in and switched to Japanese shares in 1980 and held them for the rest of the decade, you would have made another fortune. Then had you switched in 1990 to US shares for the entire decade, you would have made yet another fortune. What if you'd cashed in your shares in 2000? You could have reinvested in energy stocks a little after 2001 and then sat back and watched them rise alongside the price of oil. And then, in 2007, sensing that everything was looking a bit fragile, you could yet again have cashed in. At that point you'd have sat tight for a year and then started investing in technology stocks for most of the rest of the decade, by which point you'd be feeling very smug about your investment strategy.

Obviously with the benefit of hindsight we could be richer than we are today, but the really important thing to know is what might happen in the next decade. If we had to make a guess, we'd suggest that two sectors might be worth closer examination: technology and resource stocks. After a period of underperformance after 2010, the general realm of natural resources looks to be nicely set up for the coming decade. But not all resource stocks are well positioned with much of the energy complex looking fairly dodgy. Materials used in the coming green transition – especially involving batteries – look rather more promising. As for technology, well, look around you. The digital transformation is very clearly underway, and you'd have to have been living in a cave not notice that the world is changing at a phenomenal speed. Chapter 22 zeroes in on this broad spectrum of disruptive change.

However, the coming decade is likely to have its fair share of what we might euphemistically call 'challenges'. These include, in no particular order of importance:

>> Debt, debt and more debt. Even after the global financial crisis of 2007 to 2009 debts are still growing at an unaffordable level.

>> China and India are new economic superpowers.

>> There's still a huge mountain of derivatives sitting out there, many of them highly leveraged, waiting to explode.

>> Pension and healthcare liabilities. Everyone gets older – lots and lots of people, all at the same time.

This list isn't comprehensive (because of space limitations). These points are enough to make you understand that the investing environment has changed dramatically, so re-focus your overall game plan to keep your money growing.

By the way, you see two types of opportunities in this chapter: bullish and bearish. (See Chapter 15 for more information on bullish and bearish markets.) If we can't help you find the winning shares, at least we can show you the losers to stay away from.

Charging at Bullish Opportunities

Being bullish (or going *long*) is the natural inclination for most investors. It's an easy concept; buy low, sell high. No rocket science there. The following sections don't identify every bullish opportunity, but they do cover the most obvious ones (at least to us).

Globalisation and the need for commodities

What will have a mega-impact on the world can be boiled down to two words: China and India. In the past two decades, these two countries have put their economies on the fast track. Consider the following:

>> They have generally turned away from socialism and a *command economy* in which the state dictates the supply and prices of goods, and instead turned to a free market or more capitalist system.

>> Industrialisation, privatisation and profit incentives have ignited tremendous booms in those countries.

>> Both countries' populations have continued to grow. China has about 1.4 billion people while India recently surpassed 1.36 billion.

What do these facts mean for investors in shares?

Somebody's got to sell them what they need. China, for example, has a voracious appetite for natural resources such as building materials, energy, copper, grain and so on. Companies that have provided the goods and services China needed do well.

Of course, China and India are only a part of the world's emerging markets, but they're certainly the most important (in terms of economic impact). They are indeed 'megatrends' that help (or hurt) your portfolio. In the coming years, demand is likely to continue to be strong, and investors will see the obvious positive implications for solid companies that meet this demand.

The energy transition

For decades scientists have been warning about a potentially warming planet. Developing countries for decades also have had endless global conferences promising bold actions – but didn't follow up with any bold policies. The young Swedish activist Greta Thunberg and other activists have helped climate change emerge as a live-wire issue for tens of millions of people. In his own idiosyncratic way Elon Musk at Tesla has also helped galvanise investor interest. You may not want to buy a Tesla or accept his outlandish tweets, but you can't avoid the incredible hype he has generated around electric cars.

Their personal interventions – and those by many others – have helped make the coming energy transition real and tangible. They helped concentrate minds about which cars to drive, how many flights people take on airplanes, and the materials used in modern consumer society. Whatever your conclusion has been, the net impact on the economy and corporates has been huge. You can be as cynical as you like, but a real transition is underway. For example, there have now been many days where the UK's National Grid has used *no* coal-fired power stations and only a handful of gas-fired power stations. The rest of the energy supplied has come from renewable sources. Until just a few years ago, only a few thousand electric cars had been sold in the UK, whereas most analysts expect that by 2025, electric car sales will overtake diesels.

This transition has enormous implications, that aren't just restricted to funds with an environmental, social and (corporate) governance focus otherwise known as ESG funds. In no particular order the following list highlights some key trends:

>> Solar and wind generating ever more renewable power

>> Batteries being used more for cars and to store spare electricity

>> Minerals such as cobalt, nickel, lithium and rare earths being used more for electric motors

>> Hydrogen being used more, especially around developments such as synthetic fertilisers that use green hydrogen as an input

>> Humans consuming less meat and more plants

>> The parallel push to making the air cleaner in major cities, which isn't good news for diesel

>> Some energy sources such as coal and oil facing a less than certain future as regulations tighten and demand in the developed world begins to wane

TIP

Sometimes, it can make sense to be a bit contrarian and go against the grain and invest in 'sinful' stuff. Oil company shares have had a rough few years, but they're still selling oil to plenty of people and demand remains high. At some point, many investors think that oil company share valuations might get out of whack and become too cheap. There is a parallel for this in the tobacco sector. This was also regulated to within an inch of its life and faced an enormous backlash. Share prices collapsed, but the cashflows kept coming in. After a while, the share prices started creeping up and along the way investors picked up generous regular dividend payouts. So, sometimes, it pays to be a bit contrarian, even if that doesn't always equate with what's right for the planet.

TIP

As you read this chapter, you may not be sure about what particular company you should invest in for this green transition. If that's the case, why not consider a convenient way to invest in an entire industry or sector? A good consideration is an *exchange traded fund* (ETF). A great many ETFs exist, covering every conceivable sector, including those that focus on big oil companies as well as clean energy companies. (Chapter 21 also provides more details about ETFs.)

Inflation hedges

In the later section 'Central banks and monetary policy', we discuss how central bank policies have pushed interest rates close to zero. These central banks have also taken on huge debts via their quantitative easing (QE) programmes of bond buying. After the first few waves of the pandemic, central banks also stepped up their purchases of government bonds to unprecedented levels. All this monetary intervention has been designed to kick-start developed world economies.

Governments also, post pandemic, started spending freely, pushing up government debt in order to reflate their sickly economies. This extra state spending may all work a treat, by increasing employment, but it might also produce inflation. Some of that inflation is expected as economies simply bounce back and prices tick up again. But if economies start to run near full employment again, and *sticky prices* – that is the price of goods and services that rarely increase – start to nudge upwards, the big western economies could see measures of inflation start to creep past 2 and then 3 per cent, and then 4 per cent. That should be no problem at all, but if those inflation rates start to increase past 5 percent and stay there, the markets could be in for a turbulent ride. Interest rates might not go up as quickly, and central banks might be happy to let economies overheat for a few years. If that happens, inflation could become more persistent, at which point, investors will be looking for some protections against inflation.

Protection against inflationary forces in an economy are many and varied, some of which aren't easily bought by ordinary private investors. Most hedge funds for instance aren't interested in smaller, poorer private investors. But the good news is that there are some tried-and-tested inflation hedges out there that we can all buy into.

Gold

Over the ages, gold has come to be synonymous with wealth. In modern times it's become known as an inflation hedge and investment insurance, especially during times of inflation and geopolitical uncertainty. Lots and lots of investors are buying into gold as the most secure defensive asset in a time of great uncertainty.

Because gold does well in an inflationary environment, understanding inflation itself is important. *Inflation* isn't the price of things going up; it's the value of the currency itself going down. The reason it goes down in value is primarily the result of the increase in the money supply.

Gold analysts in the US reckon the gold price could hit $4,000 an ounce and possibly even $8,000 an ounce if the major western economies ever revert to the gold standard. It's an extreme scenario though not impossible. If it did happen, gold mining shares would perform fantastically well (not unlike their heyday in the late 1970s). For conservative investors, consider the large, established mining firms, while more daring investors may want to consider junior mining shares.

Silver

We may easily have lumped silver in with gold and just labelled the section 'precious metals', but we think that silver merits special attention. Out of all the precious metals (and base metals) that we've analysed, silver probably has the strongest potential. Why? Demand for silver is strong and growing stronger for various reasons (including investment, jewellery, industrial and so on). Yet the above-ground supply of silver has been shrinking for more than two decades. In fact, silver has been experiencing a chronic deficit for more than a decade.

Although some point out that silver's primary use in industry (photography) has declined as the result of digital photography, silver demand has been growing significantly in healthcare, electronics and military equipment. For these reasons, the supply and demand fundamentals are outstanding. As a matter of fact, silver is rarer than gold. As the market catches on, silver's current modest bull market could easily become a 'raging bull'.

The coming healthcare revolution

You've probably heard a lot about the 'grey pound'. This phrase obviously represents a firm megatrend in place. For investors, this megatrend is a purely demographic play, and the numbers are with you. The number of people who are older than 50, and especially those considered senior citizens, are the fastest growing segment of society. The same megatrend is in place in all corners of the world (especially Europe), bar Africa. As more and more people fall into this category, the idea that companies that serve this segment also prosper becomes a no-brainer. Well-managed companies that run nursing homes and services caring for the elderly should see their shares rise.

Beyond these direct services to an aging society a much bigger trend – or opportunity – is lurking. Over the last decades, the developed world has made huge advances in scientists' understanding of DNA and genomics. Scientists have developed amazing new machines – like CRISPR machines – and genomic research technologies that introduce the prospect of conquering many diseases. At the moment most effort is focusing on relatively rare, genetic diseases, but science continues its effort to conquer cancer, still one of the biggest killers in western society (though much less deadly than it used to be). But you don't only have to look at cancer treatments to see the potential. A broad range of new biotech-related businesses have been emerging, many of which are being snapped up in expensive mergers and acquisitions deals by mega large pharmaceutical companies that are looking for high margin, blockbuster new treatments.

WARNING

Be careful which healthcare firms you select because this sector can include shares that are defensive and also shares that are cyclical. Companies that sell expensive equipment (such as CAT scans or MRI technology) may not do that well in an economic downturn because hospitals and other healthcare facilities may not want to upgrade or replace their equipment. Therefore, healthcare companies that sell big-ticket items can be considered cyclical. On the other hand, companies that sell medicine (pharmaceuticals) can be considered defensive. People who need medicine (such as aspirin or antacids) buy it no matter how bad the economy is. In fact, people probably buy even more aspirin and antacids in bad economic times.

To find out more about healthcare opportunities, check out the industry and main companies using the resources in Appendix A.

An aging society

Most investors look at an aging society and tend to make the immediate mental leap to healthcare and pharmaceuticals (which we discuss in the previous section), but a society that is aging presents other opportunities. Perhaps the most obvious is increasing wealth. By and large, most older people have accumulated some wealth including nice homes – mortgage free – as well as savings plans and pensions. Much of this investment wealth needs to be carefully managed, which is why demand for wealth management services and private banks has increase. However, these pots of capital also tend to find their way into funds that have to be managed by said wealth advisers and, more importantly, fund managers (also called *asset managers*). Enormous businesses such as BlackRock (which owns the iShares ETF business), Vanguard and State Street have emerged in the fund management space, many of which are now very highly valued as shares. The impact of an aging society fans out even further into modern consumer society. Older consumers also like to spend more time travelling, which has led to a boom for upmarket travel businesses, especially in the cruise industry.

Figure 13-1 shows how different age groups are distributed throughout the population in the UK in 2021. You can see that the bulge towards the top – for older people – has grown over the last few decades. Lifespans have increased. That's great news, although there are some equally obvious implications around paying for all those pensions.

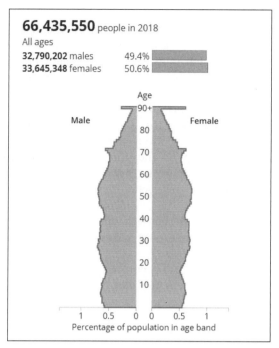

66,435,550 people in 2018
All ages
32,790,202 males   49.4%
33,645,348 females   50.6%

Age
90+
Male   80   Female
70
60
50
40
30
20
10

1   0.5   0   0   0.5   1
Percentage of population in age band

FIGURE 13-1:
The UK age
pyramid
for 2021.

Hugging Tight with a Bearish Outlook

Shares are versatile in that you can even make money when they go down in value. Techniques range from using put options to going short. (See Chapter 17 regarding going short.) For traditional investors, the more appropriate strategy is first and foremost to avoid or minimise losses. Making money betting that a stock is going to fall is closer to speculating than actual investing.

All we want is that you see the pitfalls and act accordingly. Choosing the right sector is critical for your share-investing success. The following sections offer cautionary alerts to keep you away from troubled areas in the economy (or to find speculative opportunities for short investments).

Central banks and monetary policy

Too much debt means that someone gets hurt. The great financial crisis of 2007 and 2008 caused a huge property crash as well as a financial crisis. In the immediate aftermath banks busily scaled back their lending and corporations have been busy building up record cash levels. But that doesn't mean that the great monster of debt has been conquered. Governments around the world are now racking up huge debts post Covid, and many individuals – consumers like you and us – are still struggling under an avalanche of debt. Debt weighs heavily on shares directly or indirectly. Because every type of debt is now at record levels, no one is truly immune. Say the shares you have are in a retailer that has no debt whatsoever. Are you immune? Not really, because consumer debt (credit cards, personal loans and so on) is still very high by historic standards. If consumer spending declines, then the retailer's sales go down, its profits shrink and – ultimately – its share price goes down.

Debt is also a major political issue. Banks and other lenders are under huge pressure to be responsible lenders. Regulation of mortgages and advertising of loans has become tougher in recent years as the Financial Conduct Authority flexes its muscles. The Treating Customers Fairly initiative has forced many lenders to think carefully about how they market their products and about the consumers they target. Intense interest from the media and MPs – particularly on the influential Treasury Select Committee – is making it harder for lenders to make a killing on credit. The credit monster can attack lenders in more ways than one.

REMEMBER

What's an investor in shares to do? Well, remember that first commandment to 'avoid or minimise losses'. Make sure that you review your portfolio and sell shares that may get pulverised by the credit monster. Make sure that the companies themselves have no, low or manageable debt. (Check their financial reports – Chapter 11 shows you how to do so.)

This credit machine has a flip side – near zero rates environment. As central banks have struggled to keep their economies afloat, interest rates have collapsed to near zero. Figure 13-2 shows historic interest rates for the last few hundred years. You'll immediately notice that until the first part of the new millennium – until the global financial crisis – interest rates tended to be above 4 per cent. Since then, rates have crashed to near zero and stayed there.

There has even been talk of negative interest rates – you'd be paid to borrow money (yes, that does happen in places such as Denmark for instance). These near zero rates have had a knock-on impact on the rates that big corporates can borrow at, which have crashed to the low single digit percentages. Many very large corporations can now borrow for more than 10 years at rates of less than 2 per cent per annum. Unsurprisingly, many large corporations have chosen to take advantage of these rates, by paying older, more expensive debt and taking on cheap new, long-term debt. Yes, debt can be dangerous, but it's also hugely more affordable than it used to be. That said, at some point there is a serious possibility that interest rates might rise again and at that point all that bingeing on cheap debt might come back to haunt future governments!

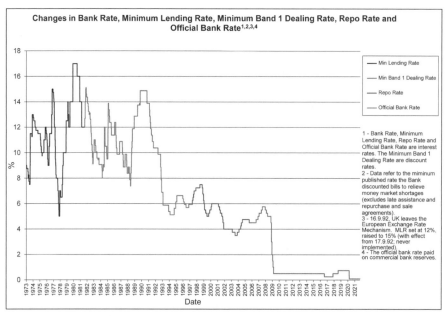

FIGURE 13-2:
UK interest rates over the very long term.

Source: www.bankofengland.co.uk/monetary-policy/the-interest-rate-bank-rate

Cyclical shares

Another group of shares that can be vulnerable in a downturn are *cyclical* shares. Heavy equipment, cars and technology tend to be cyclical and are highly susceptible to downturns in the general economy. Conversely, cyclical shares do well when the economy is growing or on an upswing (hence the label).

As individuals and corporations get squeezed with more debt and less disposable income, hard choices need to be made. Ultimately, the result is that people buy fewer big-ticket items. That means that a company selling these items ends up selling fewer of them and earning less profit. This loss of profit, in turn, makes that company's share price go down.

Companies that experience lagging sales often turn to aggressive discounting. Retailers have been known to turn to heavy discounting to clear out stock when they've failed to buy the right products for their customers. Companies including Next, Marks & Spencer and Selfridges have all turned to this tactic in the past when their buyers have failed to tempt consumers. The trouble is that even half-price tags don't make rails full of last season's fashions look appetising to discerning consumers.

In a struggling, recessionary economy, investing in cyclical shares is like sunbathing on an ant hill and using jam instead of sun cream. Not a pretty picture.

Discussing Important Info for Bulls and Bears

We just want to reiterate a few of the points that apply here. We don't presume that shares go straight up or that they zig-zag upward indefinitely. Your due diligence is necessary for success. Make sure that you're investing appropriately for your situation. If you're 35 and heading into your peak earnings years and want to ride a rocket all the way to retirement – and you understand the risks – then go ahead and speculate with those small-cap gold mining shares or the solar power technology shares.

But if you're more risk averse or your situation is screaming out loud for you to be conservative, then don't speculate. Go instead with a more diversified portfolio of blue chip shares or get the ETF for that particular sector.

For those people who want to make money by going short in those sectors that look bearish, again take a deep breath and remember what's appropriate. Conservative investors should simply avoid the risky areas. Aggressive investors or speculators may want to deploy profitable bearish strategies (with a *portion* of their investible funds). Here are some highlights for all of you.

Conservative and bullish

After you choose a promising sector, just select large-cap companies that are financially strong, are earning a profit, have low debt and are market leaders. This entire book shows you how to do just that. However, you may not like the idea of buying shares directly. Consider sector unit trusts or ETFs. That way, you can choose the industry and be able to effectively buy a basket of the top shares in that area. ETFs have been a hot item lately, and we think that they're a great idea for most investors because they offer some advantages over unit trusts. For example, you can put stop-loss orders on them or borrow against them in your share portfolio. Check with your financial advisor to see whether ETFs are appropriate for you.

Being conservative and bullish makes sense when you're retired (or are nearly at that point), have a family to support or live in a large shoe with so many kids that you don't know what to do.

Aggressive and bullish

If you're aggressive and bullish, you want to buy the shares directly. For real growth potential, look at mid-caps or small-caps. Remember that you're speculating, so you understand the risk that the price is going to fall but are willing to tolerate this risk because the potential reward may be handsome. Few things in the investment world give you a better gain than a super-charged share in a hot sector.

Conservative and bearish

For many (if not most) investors, making money on a falling market isn't generally a good idea. Doing so takes a lot of expertise and risk tolerance. Really, for conservative investors, the key word is 'safety'. Analyse your portfolio with an advisor you trust and sell the potentially troubled shares. If you're not sure what to do on a particular share, then (at the very least) put in stop-loss orders and make them GTC (good till cancelled). (See Chapter 17 for details.) As odd as it sounds, sometimes losing less than others makes you come out ahead if you play it right.

Aggressive and bearish

Being aggressive in a bearish market isn't for the faint of heart. However, it's where some of history's greatest investors have made the quickest fortunes. Going short can make you great money when the market is bearish, but it can sink you if you're wrong. Put options are a way to make money with limited risk when you essentially make a bet on an investment (such as shares) that will go down. Obviously, options go beyond the scope of this book, but at least let us give you some direction, because an appropriate options strategy exists for most share portfolios. You should be aware that trading options is more readily available in the US but you can trade US options if you open a dollar trading account in the UK.

Diversification

This point is self-explanatory, right? If you take a portfolio approach and spread your capital across three to five sectors, then you're making a safer bet. And don't forget the trailing stop-loss strategy (see Chapter 17 for more on this). That makes your investing approach safer still.

IN THIS CHAPTER

» Investing in actively managed
investment trusts is a great way of
backing smart fund managers

» Thinking about alternatives as a way
of diversifying your portfolio

» Making sense of investing in real
assets such as infrastructure or real
estate funds

Chapter **14**

Getting Active and Alternative with Investment Funds

Most investors instinctively think that when buying a share listed on a stock exchange, they're buying directly into a company. But you can also buy shares in funds, run by managers who do all the heavy lifting for you by buying shares in different companies. In effect, you're employing a fund manager to do all the heavy lifting of share selection.

As you discover in this chapter that information can come in handy when you're investing in more alternative investment areas where the need for an experienced stock-picking fund manager comes into its own. Which is where the world of investment trusts, a very British type of investing, comes into its own. In this chapter we' investigate how these actively managed stock market–listed funds with shares can really help private investors build a diversified portfolio.

Understanding Investment Trusts

An alternative type of fund to passive funds that we discuss in Chapter 13 are called *active funds,* and they're listed as shares on the stock market just like exchange traded funds. What makes them unique is they feature an active manager who jumps around declaring, "Hey, I reckon I can predict which way the markets might be going, and I intend to buy this smaller bunch of shares." This stock-picking approach is very different than the passive approach. On paper it might be riskier, less diversified – you're not buying everything in the market – but it might also produce outperformance. Or at least that's the theory anyway!

In essence, an *investment trust* is a closed-end investment company listed on the London Stock Exchange. Lots of technicalities are lurking behind that simple, bland statement, including the following:

» The company is listed as the result of issuing shares on the market, which makes it a *closed-end fund;* that is, it only issues a limited number of shares at inception and doesn't continually issue new shares. It can, however, list additional shares every once in a while via a placing. This idea of closed fund is a key concept because it means you give your fund manager a fixed sum of money that they must go to the market to invest. The value of that fund may move up and down as will the value of your shares in that fund, but a discrepancy can emerge between the total value of the fund's assets and the value put on fund by the market. This 'discrepancy' – either a discount or premium – can be both an opportunity and a hindrance.

» The company has a board of directors, who then offer the contract to run the fund to a fund management outfit.

» That contract may be terminated or revised over time if the fund managers make a hash of running the fund.

» The fund managers make a charge to the company, which is passed on to the trust investors.

Why bother with yet another fund structure? Investment trusts tend to have a number of things going for them. Their most important feature is that large institutions like using them as part of their own investment process. That means that the fund managers have to offer competitive rates, which makes many investment trusts very cost-effective as a way of accessing key asset classes, with total expense ratios well below 1 per cent per annum as standard.

Institutions also like the clear corporate governance of a trust and particularly the possibility of sacking an underperforming fund manager. Such a focus on performance also extends to a willingness on the part of investment trust boards to actually wind up the fund if the original purpose of the trust becomes redundant.

Add these features up and the advantages of an investment trust are obvious:

>> They charge lower fees than most equivalent unit trusts.

>> Lots of choice is available, especially in more complex asset classes. Institutional investors tend to prefer an investment trust, which means that an active fund manager is given a real investment niche in which they can prove their skills (or not, as the case may be!).

>> Corporate governance is generally very good, with a focus on pushing the active fund manager to excel – either that or they're out!

>> They're easy to trade via a stockbroker.

A LOOK BACK AT HOW INVESTMENT TRUSTS CAME TO BE

Investment trusts are the archetypal listed actively managed funds listed on the UK market. Hundreds and hundreds of them are available, and they've been around for a very long time. The first investment company, called the Foreign & Colonial Investment Trust, was set up in 1868. By 1873 another long-standing trust had been launched – Robert Fleming launched the Scottish American Investment Trust (now called Dunedin Income Growth) to finance the building of the railway network that would ultimately link the United States. The late 1800s also saw the launch of two investment trusts now managed by Janus Henderson: The Bankers Investment Trust in 1888 and City of London Investment Trust in 1891. By the outbreak of the First World War in 1914, 90 investment trusts had been established. Of those, 26 are still in existence today.

The Foreign and Colonial Investment trust is a venerable British institution. Philip Rose founded the F&C Investment Trust alongside barrister Samuel Laing, and Laing's business partner James Thompson Mackenzie, who was also Deputy Chairman of the East Bengal Railway. With the backing of influential politician Lord Westbury, F&C Investment Trust was launched in 1868. Initially the fund invested in an exotic range of global businesses (not shares as such), as well as bonds (during World War 1 it invested in war bonds). F&C Investment Trust's first recorded purchase of an ordinary share was Shell Transport & Trading in 1925. Ninety years later, this company is still in the portfolio as Royal Dutch Shell. Other early equity investments included Peninsular & Oriental (P&O) and Liebig's Extract of Meat (?), followed by Debenhams, ICI, and General Electric.

(continued)

(continued)

> Over the last century, investment trusts have had their ups (after WW2) and downs (in the 1970s), but they have gone from strength to strength. For example, at the end of 2019, the total assets under management with UK investment trusts was in the region of £200 billion, whereas the assets within the UK investment industry as a whole was about £9.1 trillion. By 2021 total assets had grown again to £239 billion, up from bp90 billion in just ten years.

Exploring the Rise of Alternatives and Investment Trusts

Traditionally investment trusts since WW2 have been seen as simple, easy-to-access investment vehicles for putting money to work in equities (usually in the FTSE All Share index or the S&P 500). In recent years though more and more investment trusts have started emerging that invest in more alternative ideas. Nowadays only half of all funds invest directly in equities, with an almost equally large chunk of money invested in more exotic, alternative strategies such as property or private equity.

For example, there are now just less than 200 mainstream funds investing in equities, with the largest segment focused on UK equities (around 60 in total) and then global equities (around 40). By contrast a little less than 200 funds invest in alternatives with property funds and infrastructure funds the biggest slug.

Another way of viewing the same trend is to look at new money invested in these funds. New fund launches or IPOS have dropped sharply. In 2014 £6 billion was raised plus another £3.7 billion in secondary fund raising, with funds investing in equities playing a leading role. By 2020 that number for IPOs was down to £1 billion plus £6.25 billion in secondary fund raising, the vast majority of which was for alternative funds.

The cynic might wonder why anyone needs 'alternatives' – what's the point? The thinking here is straightforward and is widely used by many big institutional investors. Why not invest in funds that might move in different ways to conventional equities (BP or Amazon) or bonds (government or corporate). The following introduces the useful idea of diversifying your sources of return, all done via easy to access stock-market–listed funds.

Recognising the main categories of alternatives

These alternative funds fall into five main categories:

>> **Property funds or real estate investment trusts (REITs):** These listed closed-end funds invest (mostly) in directly owned commercial (and to a lesser degree residential) property. That could mean everything from a huge office block in central London through to an industrial unit in Leeds. These REITs are very much focused on generating an income for shareholders alongside some steady capital gains. The income yield varies enormously, but a sensible range is usually between 2 and 6 per cent per annum. Because these funds pay out more than 90 per cent of their net income as dividends, the funds don't have to pay any tax on gains (capital or income). That leaves the investor to pay any income tax or capital gains tax on their account via their tax return.

>> **Private equity funds:** Another fast-growing segment, private equity funds invest in a range of early- to late-stage private businesses. A subsector called *venture capital funds* are more focused on early-stage businesses whereas most big private equity funds are concentrated on late-stage, profitable businesses in fast growing but well-developed markets. The listed private equity funds allow ordinary private investors to invest in these institutional structures using an investment trust. They're rather less focused on an income and rather more interested in generating long term capital gains.

>> **Infrastructure funds:** Like REITs, these types of funds are mostly focused on generating an income alongside some capital gains. They invest in . . .you guessed it, infrastructure. That could be anything from a public private partnership that owns a toll road through to a windfarm in the middle of the North Sea. Most funds involve some government participation, either running the service or providing subsides.

>> **Debt funds:** This category of funds has grown very popular in the last few years. These invest in some form of private sector debt, ranging from corporate bonds through to direct lending to a business. Again, like REITs, they're more income focused and yields vary between 4 and 10 per cent. They're riskier than infrastructure funds and REITs, but on average the income level is much higher.

>> **Specialist sector funds:** These types of funds are usually investing in a specialist part of the stock market such as biotech stocks or mining shares. They tend to compete more with ETFs.

If you're interested in generating long-term capital gains, you're probably best focusing on equity funds, whereas income investors tend to prefer REITs, and infrastructure funds. But don't assume that just because your fund is paying an income, that the share price can't go down drastically. Some alternative funds have had a torrid time in the last few years and seen their share price crash down, for manner of mundane reasons – such as failure to repay loans or bad investment strategies.

Playing the discount game

One of the biggest challenges presented by investment trusts stems from their inherent structure. An investment company lists a limited number of shares on the London stock market, and the price of those shares moves up and down depending on market sentiment. Yet the investment company trust has within its structure a fund that also invests in shares and bonds. The value of the fund can move up or down and is expressed as the *net asset value (NAV)* – the sum total value of all the assets in the fund minus any liabilities.

Precisely because markets are so volatile, big differences can emerge between the NAV and the ordinary share price. If the NAV is more than the share price, the investment trust trades at a discount to its book value; in contrast, if the trust's shares trade above the value of the investment fund, a premium is earned. Investment trust shares can zigzag between discounts and premiums at an alarming rate; if confidence in shares is especially low, discounts of more than 30 per cent of the fund's book value aren't uncommon. In this case, as a shareholder you may feel especially hard done by! Big institutional investors may get anxious, sack the managers and then demand that the investment trust company start selling the fund assets and 'close' the discount gap. Everything can all get a bit messy; although the reverse can also be true – you may want to buy a fund with a big discount to make a capital gain as that margin is closed.

But the situation gets worse. As an investor you may focus on the discount, but what happens if the fund underperforms against the index it's measured against? You're now paying more for an active manager in terms of fund management fees (when measured against an ETF), and you've also got a discount on the shares versus the NAV. And even this isn't the end of the potential nightmare. Far from it. The next horror is that investment trusts can borrow money to boost the funds under management. That situation's great when the assets you're buying increase in value but can be cataclysmic if these assets are falling in value – you still need to make the loan repayments but your assets are declining in value.

Many investment trusts are also in more difficult-to-access markets and asset classes, which means that demand for the shares is patchy, at best. On an average day the turnover in the shares might be very low, which means that the market makers who manage the mechanics of the stock market start to increase the bid offer spread on the trust's shares – in some cases that bid offer spread can be as much as 10 per cent.

Add it all up and you can see that investment trusts can be tricky (which is an understatement) for the uninitiated. They can trade at a wide discount to the NAV, the managers can underperform against an ETF, they can charge more than an equivalent ETF manager and the bid offer spread can be huge. No wonder the pricing of investment trusts can be so volatile.

TIP

Most trusts tend to trade at a small discount and in aggregate that discount trends around the 5 to 10 per cent range. Not all trusts do trade at a discount though, and some funds – especially those very much in demand – have traded in the past at a premium of more than 20 per cent, although that's exceptional. That said many well-established infrastructure funds continue to trade at a premium of 10 per cent or more. By contrast many private equity funds trade at a big discount, some of which are above 30 per cent. As a rough and ready reckoner, a discount of more than 15 per cent is regarded as noteworthy whereas a premium of more than 20 per cent might concern some investors.

WARNING

The temptation is to regard a chunky 20 to 40 per cent discount as a 'bargain'. Maybe. Some funds trade at these cavernous discounts for a very good reason (for instance, bad management, a tight bunch of insider shareholders who are happy to tolerate poor performance, poor market dynamics). Nothing is guaranteed that a big discount will narrow and even those funds that work hard to narrow the discount – typical measures include buying back shares or improving communication with shareholders – fail sometimes simply because investors aren't interested.

Examining the infrastructure boom

As we discuss in the section, 'Recognising the main categories of alternatives', earlier in this chapter, infrastructure assets have become ever more mainstream and less alternative. Part of the reason that these infrastructure funds have proved hugely popular with risk-averse, defensive investor who want assets that pay out a steady cash flow and have some inflation protection. Income yields on these funds vary wildly, but a sensible range is between 3 and 7 per cent per annum.

When we first started researching these infrastructure funds in the first decade of the century, there were just a handful of funds, but now there are dozens. More importantly, the types of assets these funds invest in has dramatically broadened. Infrastructure funds have changed over the years. Here are the main categories on infrastructure funds:

>> **Pure play (PPP/PFI):** Twenty years back, infrastructure was meant very narrowly – for instance, a toll road or port. Then governments saw the light and got infrastructure funds to help finance public assets through public private partnerships (PPP). In the UK, one particularly popular scheme was the Private Finance Initiative (PFI), which helped fund dozens of schools and medical centres. But that scheme became less popular as governments of all hues realised that they were an expensive way of funding public services.

>> **Renewables:** Just as that traditional infrastructure space was looking a bit more constrained, up popped the energy transition and the need to decarbonise the electricity grid. Suddenly a whole gang of renewables funds emerged to finance wind turbines – offshore and onshore – and solar farms. These renewable funds are still hugely popular although there have been concerns voiced by analysts in the City of London about the variability of wholesale power prices, and many analysts are worried about the excess power generated by offshore wind turbines when demand isn't high.

>> **Healthcare:** As the renewables space was booming, another very lucrative segment appeared – funding medical surgeries. The UK has lots of general practitioner doctors (GPs), most of whom operate out of local medical centres. Someone needs to fund these centres. The same goes for state-of-the-art retirement homes and assisted living spaces for individuals with physical and mental challenges. This latter development – housing in essence – has opened yet another idea – investing in affordable housing and social (council) housing.

What the first three bullets share in common is a government backstop. At some point the government is either providing a cheque directly (through PFI), via government-regulated energy policies (renewables) or through local government (social housing). An extra layer of protection is provided by inflation linkage — for instance, the payments tend to increase if inflation increases. Add this all up, and you begin to glimpse the attractiveness of the model, which is that it's lower risk, which means that returns are also likely to be lower (in the sub 10 per cent per annum range).

>> **Digital:** In the last few years one final version of infrastructure investment has emerged that is subtly different — digital infrastructure. In practical terms that means data centres, fibre optic cables and mobile phone towers. This area is obviously huge for growth, but it has one unique feature – it's not really government backed and may be seen as a bit riskier. That said, given the ever-increasing demand for Internet data, it's hard to argue that these base stations and servers will struggle to find customers.

>> **Social:** This is another relatively new subsector that focuses on property, but this time residential property that is rented out to tenants. Most of these tenants are likely to be subsidised by the government through various social housing schemes. There's also another subset that rents out property to

private renters, mainly younger families or students. The attractions of this space are obvious as the UK has consistently pushed up the price of residential property. Rents have also risen consistently.

Table 14-1 maps out this varied and growing spectrum of infrastructure funds, all involving some form of real asset backing (frequently property).

TABLE 14-1   **Pros and Cons to Infrastructure Spectrum**

Niche	Pure play (PFI/PPP)	Renewables	Healthcare	Digital	Social
Thoughts	A traditional source of finance and relatively low risk, assured revenues. These tend to generate a lower stream of dividend yields.	A growth area as renewables power output steadily increases. In the UK offshore wind is the dominant subsector.	A solid, boring business model funding GPs surgeries and care homes. This type is boring as you can get and highly sought after.	Servers, mobile phone masts and fibre networks. All solid, growth-oriented private sector backed.	Mainly housing of some shape or size, frequently paid for by government through housing associations or local councils.
Risks	Government policy can and does change	Government policies can change around subsidy regimes, and the costs of excess wind power generation at the wrong times of the day can be substantial.	Fairly low risk but the few funds in this space are very highly valued – in other words expensive.	Highly valued by many investors and thus expensive. Technologies come and go, and capex spending can sometimes cut back profits.	Vulnerable to changes in government policy. Some housing associations have had their challenges with poor service levels and worse finances.

WARNING

There is a general consensus amongst most big institutional investors that infrastructure assets are lower risk. That doesn't mean they're *no* risk. The share price of many of these funds has varied substantially although probably not quite as much as mainstream equities. The risks are varied. Government policy plays a major role. At one stage PFI was hugely popular, but now it's a no-no. The Labour party has also made threatening noises in the past about privatised public services. Governments can also cut back on energy subsidies as they did in Spain a few years ago when solar feed in tariffs were almost overnight abolished. But it's not all just government. Many of the renewable funds generate some of their revenues via wholesale markets for energy. These prices vary enormously, which can impact valuations. So low risk isn't no risk.

Investing in property

The predominant structure for investing in property in the UK is through a closed-end investment company, structured as a real estate investment trust or REIT. You can buy property through what's called an *open-ended unit trust* fund, but if investors rush looking to sell their units, these closed end funds can shut redemptions (payouts) for months on end. The fund manager is also forced to sell property into a weak market to help fund that avalanche of fund redemptions.

For that reason, most investors prefer a listed closed-end fund or investment trust whose shares trade in real time. If sellers try and sell all at once, the shares simply fall in price, opening a big discount. The fund by contrast can stick with its portfolio of properties through thick and thin.

Over time UK based investors have seen a steady growth in the number of UK listed REITs, and as with infrastructure funds, they've also seen a steady broadening out of niches and specialist spaces. What unites them all is a focus on income – nearly all profits are paid out as dividends – real asset backing and inflation protection (through upwards only inflation linked leases).

Here is a breakdown of the different types of REITs:

>> **Offices:** By and large the most popular sector within the REIT space has been those that focus on offices, mostly high quality in prime, city centre locations.

>> **Retail:** Shopping malls were also popular once although Amazon's remorseless rise and the pandemic have now massively knocked confidence.

>> **Industrial:** Industrial units – workshops for instance – as well as large logistics distribution warehouses are by contrast still hugely popular. The fastest growing segment is the big box logistics park, popular with e-commerce businesses.

>> **Residential housing:** The newest segment includes those funds investing in private rented housing, also known as the *private rental sector, or PRS.* Investing in flats and trailer parks is a long tradition in the US, but this area is relatively new in the UK.

Table 14-2 breaks down an overview of each and discusses risks for each type.

WARNING

Beware of leverage in real estate funds. Nearly all REITs use *leverage* – debt – in some shape or another. It's typically measured by what's called the *loan to value ratio.* If a development is worth £100m and there is £50m of debt, the LTV ratio is 0.5 or 50 per cent. Most LTVs are usually below 60. Debt is currently cheap, but if interest rates were to increase, that debt could become suffocating. And debt also has an impact on share prices. Because the equity returns are geared on the upside by all that debt, if stock markets become fearful, that leverage can turn nasty. Investors start to worry that their equity will be swamped by all the debt, and they start selling aggressively. Thus, many REITs suffer disproportionately in a market swoon.

TABLE 14-2   **Pros and Cons to the Property Spectrum**

Niche	Office	Retail	Industrial	Residential Housing
Thoughts	Prime city centre office developments, preferably as part of a big master planned development have stood the test of time best as have City of London/West End funds	Large city centre – and out of town – shopping developments prospered but have run into trouble. Some specialist funds investing in supermarkets have, by contrast, prospered.	Multi-let industrial units are very popular as are industrial estates and logistics parks.	Privately rented housing estates and developments are becoming more popular with institutional investors and through funds. They offer steady, reliable inflation-backed income and some hope of capital gain.
Risks	Most people start working from home.	Most people shop online.	Relatively low risk except in a deep recession. Valuations are also quite high.	Serving the private tenant can be difficult and challenging.

TIP

Those niches within property and real estate with low levels of market turbulence to date – such as medical centres – tend to be most in favour and are thus highly valued. In effect, they trade more like old-fashioned bonds. They have solid asset backing, steady cash flows and very low chance of default. That's great for defensive investors, but less exciting for the adventurous. By contrast, those niches where risk is perceived to higher tend to trade at lower valuations with higher income yields; they might even offer a discount to their net asset value.

Protecting inflation

All these property funds – and infrastructure assets for that matter – involve owning what are called real assets. That's property or land or some derivation to you and us. The great advantage of real assets is that for tenants or businesses to have access to them, they need to sign a lease. These leases tend to be legally backed contractual instruments that force a tenant to pay a regular cashflow for a number of years. Additionally, these contracts also usually come with some form of inflation review when the lease is due to renew. They tend to be measured against either the retail price index (RPI) or the less well known consumer price index (CPI). The RPI is more widely known and includes a much wider range of underlying price measures but is now out of favour with economists who prefer to use the narrower consumer price index.

This inflation protection isn't always automatic, and you may also have to wait for the next contract negotiation. Although these leases do offer inflation protection, it's not a simple "if RPI goes up 2 per cent every year, my lease income will go up exactly the same". It's more complicated than that, especially if the leases are very long term.

WARNING

Beware the difference between CPI and RPI. The CPI rate consistently under shoots the RPI measure, so ideally a real asset owner wants an RPI-related agreement but that's not always possible.

Investing for an income

Many funds are focused on income, and that's even true for some equity funds, where more than a few have a stated 'equity income' strategy, for instance, generating a steady income from equity dividends. Overall, across all investment trusts, the average income yield – dividend yield – for the whole funds market is around 4 per cent per annum, although that varies enormously.

Some sectors – REITs, infrastructure and lending funds – are very focused on generating an income. The yields on these funds tend to be higher than for many equity only funds, and you'll probably find most of these alternative income funds paying in a range of between 3.5 per cent to 7 per cent. Most equity income funds paying towards the lower end of that range.

Income is popular with investment trust investors for a number of obvious and less than obvious reasons:

>> **Yields:** The obvious reason is that most bonds in this low interest rate era pay meagre yields. Many big bond funds now struggle to generate yields of more than 2 per cent a year, if they're lucky. Nearly all the alternative income funds generate yields well in excess of these rates.

>> **Tax:** The less obvious reason is tax. Many of these funds are structured in a tax-efficient way so that the investment company can pay out the income free of tax direct to you the investor. If you aren't sheltering your investments in an ISA or SIPP tax wrapper, you'll still have to pay tax. Refer to Chapter 20 for more discussion about ways to reduce the amount of tax you pay.

WARNING

Keep a beady eye on what is called *dividend cover.* Say you have a £100 million fund, trading at par, that pays out a £5 million a year dividend. That equates to a yield of 5 per cent per annum. But if you dig around in the profit and loss statement, you discover that the actual cash earnings or profits that can be distributed are only £4 million. The other £1 million in dividends is being paid out of available cash and reserves. That means only £4 million of the £5 million is covered – in dividend *cover* terms the ratio is 0.80 (£4 million divided by £5 million). There's nothing necessarily wrong with this, especially in the early years of the fund, but after a few years by and large investors like that dividend cover number to be above 1.

TIP

A small, select bunch of long-established investment trusts have been steadily increasing their dividends year on year for a very long period of time. The key point to understand here is that unlike open-ended funds, investment companies don't have to pay out all the income they receive from their portfolios each year. They can save up to 15 per cent and tuck it away into what's called a *revenue reserve,* which means they can hold back some of the income they receive in good years and use it to boost dividends when businesses may be cutting theirs. This structural benefit has enabled many investment companies to pay consistently rising dividends through both good and bad years for decades, a record that's unrivalled by open-ended funds. As of 2021, 18 funds have increased their dividend every year for at least the last 20 years. Some, such as City of London Trust and Alliance Trust, have increased their dividend for more than 50 years in a row.

Deciding Whether Investment Trusts and Index Trackers Are Right for You

The complexity of investment trusts – as well index tracking funds, for that matter – will put off many readers. The idea of backing an active fund manager to invest in a basket of stocks sounds so complicated when compared to boring old blue chips. But be honest with yourself – if you want to increase your returns above the average, you need to take on more risk. You may also want to consider two additional concepts: diversification and the need to lower costs. Building a diversified portfolio of funds is essential, and that means hunting down both mainstream asset classes and more esoteric assets. ETFs and investment trusts offer you unprecedented choice, which is essential for a diversified portfolio.

Most importantly, index tracking funds and investment trusts offer that choice using structures that are easy to access and relatively inexpensive. If you don't like the structure of the investment trust or think the manager is useless, sell the shares and find a better manager – or stick with an index tracker. But whatever you do, keep costs to the minimum and think long and hard about the fund structures within your portfolio. Don't let the investment industry rip you off with unreasonable charges for managing your funds.

And that mantra of cutting costs and keeping fund managers on a tight leash is really important when it comes to alternative ideas, which are usually difficult to access and need lots of research. Careful selection of fund managers in the alternatives space is crucial, but the good news is that there's lots of interesting new niches opening up that can provide some real diversification benefits for your portfolio. As you discover in the next sections, more and more alternatives are starting to go a bit more 'mainstream'.

Proper, real alternatives

Today real alternatives are now much more esoteric and less common. These proper, real alternatives are less popular with big institutions and thus less common. That doesn't make them less useful, especially as sources of diversified income. If big institutions don't own these alternatives, that makes them less likely to sell them in a market rout. Thus, their diversification benefits – for instance, their prices – don't always correlate back to the wider stock market cycle. But over time, these proper, real alternatives have become more attractive, and clever institutions have found ways to structure them into accessible vehicles for investors.

Royalty funds

Every time you play a music track online through a streaming service, you trigger a payment to a music artist as well as the song writer (and producer) and record label. Those royalties can add up over time, and if one could design a fund to roll up various different music royalties, you'd have a valuable, diversified source of income. Not unexpectedly, some clever financiers have managed to do this and have listed music royalty funds on the stock exchange (two being Roundhill and Hipgnosis). They produce a steady income from royalties, which shouldn't (in theory at least) move up and down with the business cycle – for instance, the income might be uncorrelated with the wider business cycle.

The royalty model can also be applied to other industry. It works something like this. If I have a mine that needs funding to development, a new business product that needs developing, a new drug that needs marketing, I ask a financier to fund me in advance and in return they take a stream of royalties for many years. Call it an IOU structured as royalty. The stock market now has royalty funds that invest in music, films, new businesses, drugs, mines and precious metals. They all share the same basic idea, which is to produce a steadily increasing income over time.

WARNING

Music royalty funds have become very popular. The cash flows produced are real and valuable, but they're based on independent valuations of the underlying copyrights and intellectual property. That sounds a bit complicated, but in reality it means you need to get an expert to value those assets on a regular basis. They might use industry measures, metrics and statistics, but that asset value is only an estimate. That means those valuation estimates can be subjective, and thus they can change markedly especially if there is a big structural change no one predicted.

Crypto cometh

Hundreds of books have already been written about the various crypto assets including the currencies – bitcoin, ether and so on – blockchain structures, and even digital art (NFTs). We don't intend to add to this enormous wealth of knowledge except to add that all these digital assets have some evident value and funds can own them.

Here in the UK the structures come in two broad sizes:

>> If you want direct access to a crypto currency – say Blockchain – the most popular structure is through a 'tracker' of some sort. These are exchange traded products which track currencies just as they track commodity spot prices.

>> By contrast crypto art or NFTs as well as blockchain assets/businesses, tend to be structured as closed end investment funds, traded on the junior UK exchanges.

REMEMBER

Despite the best efforts of cynics to trash crypto currencies, they remain popular. But their pricing is highly volatile, and they go through long phases of despair followed by equally long phases of euphoria. But over time, more and more investors have become convinced that crypto assets might begin to rival precious metals as a store of long-term real value. If that becomes a consensus view – and it's far from that as we write – then it's possible that crypto-based assets might carry on increasing in value. Alternatively, if the cynics are right, crypto assets will crash in value. If we're honest, we have absolutely no idea what will happen, but if enough people believe in something, then that something tends to be more resilient.

Emotional assets

Emotional assets is a great catch-all term to describe all manner of collectible stuff ranging from art, stamps, and coins through to classic cars and wine. We use the term emotional because although many of these assets can be traded for huge sums in auctions, they also tend to have a very strong emotional input (they mean something to the buyer and presumably the seller). They're objects of passion and have an emotional value that can't always be summed up in numbers, no matter how big they are.

At varying times, some fund managers have attempted to turn these varying emotional investments into publicly accessible funds to be bought and sold on financial markets. But to date, to our knowledge, only one publicly listed fund has invested in coins. However, premium wines and whiskeys are traded through specialist private funds that aren't listed on the stock market. That might change in the coming years, especially as blockchain allows for the tokenisation of a single item.

Hedge funds

Way back when, the original, institutional alternative was the hedge fund. These masters of the universe managed huge funds that invested in all manner of exotic, hard-to-understand stuff and then charged huge fees for their expertise. Their core business model wasn't in truth that alternative. That was going both long *and* short equities and bonds. Chapter 17 explains what going short an asset such as a share means. Hedge funds simply systematised building long and short positions in one portfolio. Over time that strategy evolved and mutated, but the ability to be both bearish and bullish about an asset was a key to their success.

At one point dozens of hedge funds were listed as investment trusts on the London stock exchange. They were popular with investors looking to hedge their upside with downside protection. But then, the inevitable happened. The promise failed to materialise, the shine came off the marketing pitch and hedge funds were largely revealed to be a bit . . . pedestrian! Returns after fees were crushed, and many funds failed to deliver on what the promised.

Now there are just a handful of listed hedge fund investment trusts on the London stock market, and in truth, they do a pretty good job, meaning they do deliver absolute returns in both up and down markets).

Investigating the Rise of Crowdfunding

This alternative investment is arguably the newest in terms of structure. It's equity crowdfunding through an online platform, provided by the likes of Crowdcube, Seedrs or Syndicate Room plus a longer tail of smaller platforms.

The product here is actually deceptively simple.

Say I (David) am a smart, experienced entrepreneur who wants to get funding for my start up. I write a business plan, develop the basic outlines of a product, and perhaps get a minimum viable product (MVP) together. With all the accompanying paperwork and products, I then start a campaign online to raise finance for my business. I do this via selling shares in my business, which might also attract tax reliefs. As an extra incentive, many of these campaigns also offer investors valuable side benefits, such as a free product or first access to the product.

My campaign runs for 30 days, and if I hit my target – say £200,000 in funding – then I get funded. In return I issue shares in my business to the investors on this online platform. Over time as my business hopefully grows, I can then come back for extra funding, which is usually done via a structure that goes like this:

>> **Seed fund for the real start-up capital.** This is the very first step by which the founders get their start-up money from the first investors.

>> **Move up a gear to back Series A to C for the early stages of funding.** This next stage of funding helps early-stage businesses scale up, frequently with the help of institutional investors or venture capitalists.

>> **Fund the pre-IPO stage for more established businesses.** Many established businesses need extra capital before they make the leap on to the public stock markets.

>> **Invest in an IPO when I list on the stock market.** This last stage is the move on to the public stock markets.

The vast majority of crowdfunded businesses tend to be in the seed or Series A category. That should immediately alert you to a very obvious risk. Crowdfunding is risky stuff, investing in an early stage, young business. For every business that goes on to treble or quadruple your money, probably at least a dozen don't spark or go bust. A few may even be a bit dodgy and steal your cash!

So, crowdfunding isn't for the risk averse, and especially not widows and orphans.

But as crowdfunding has developed, some successes have emerged. Some investors have clocked up a 1000-fold return for an investment of say £1000. We think the best way of thinking about this kind of investing is to regard it as a kind of high-risk venture capital. Never put more than a tiny fraction of your wealth into this category and accept that most businesses will go wrong. But just as you might say put 5 or 10 per cent of your wealth into smaller listed companies, maybe put a tiny proportion of that into this form of venture capital. And have some fun while you're at it, backing bright young entrepreneurs.

Precisely because crowdfunding can be high risk you can invest a small sum of money in these businesses, minimums of £10 or £100 are common.

WHO'S INVESTING IN CROWDFUNDING?

One of the main platforms called Crowdcube reports some useful data on who invests on their platform. They reckon that 62 per cent of their investors are either high net worth or sophisticated investors, with the average age of this group in their 50s. Looking solely at these wealthier types, the average portfolio size is £15,000, the average number of investments is eight and the average investment per campaign or pitch is £1,800.

If we look at the wider investor base – let's call them the everyday investor - the average portfolio size is £2,093, average number of investments is five, and average investment size is £390. And for all types of investors, the average is a professional of some sort who lives in the South east or London. Looking at both categories – every day and wealthier – Crowdcube reports that in 2020 Fintech was their most popular sector, followed by mobility (guessing that's e-bikes and e-car related stuff), healthtech and cleantech.

TIP

Our advice is to stick to sectors and products you know very well. If craft brewed beers and ales are your speciality, for instance, then you're in luck with crowd-funding platforms. Plenty of craft breweries raise funding via these platforms.

Most but not all investments on equity crowdfunding platforms benefit from generous tax reliefs based on the EIS and SEIS scheme:

>> **EIS:** The Enterprise Investment Scheme or EIS scheme allows you to claim up to 30 per cent income tax relief on investments up to £1 million per tax year.

- Any gain is Capital Gains Tax (CGT) free if the shares are held for at least three years.

- Payment of CGT can be deferred when the gain is invested in shares of an EIS qualifying company.

- If you dispose of the shares at a loss, you can elect that the amount of loss be set against any income tax of that year or of the previous year.

>> **Seed EIS:** The Seed EIS (SEIS) is even more generous. Investors can receive initial income tax relief of 50 per cent on investments up to £100,000 per tax year in qualifying shares issued on or after 6 April 2012. A CGT exemption will offered in respect of gains realised on the disposal of assets in 2012/13 that are reinvested through SEIS in the same year.

4

Investment Strategies and Tactics

Understand the environment in which the market operates to help you choose a particular share.

Go beyond merely picking good shares and watching the financial news by implementing techniques and strategies that help you either minimise losses or maximise gains.

Discover some of the most effective investing techniques to help you profit from shares in a bull or a bear market.

Find out some smart ways to hold on to more of your profits when tax time rolls around.

Work with stock market–listed funds to build a more diversified portfolio using exchange traded funds and investment trusts.

Chapter **15**

Taking the Bull (or Bear) by the Horns

U nderstanding the general markets and their major directional trend may even be more important to your wealth-building success than choosing the right shares. Recent years – and a century of stock market history – bear (no pun intended) witness to this point.

Bull and bear markets have a tremendous effect on your share choices. Generally, bull markets tend to precede economic uptrends (also called *economic rebound*, *economic recovery* or *economic growth*), whereas bear markets tend to precede economic downtrends (also called *recession*, *depression* or *economic contraction*).

The stock market's movement is based on the fact that share prices go up (or down) in relation to people's buying or selling behaviour. If more people are buying shares (versus selling), then share prices rise. If more people are selling shares, then share prices fall. Why do people buy or sell a share? It can be explained in one word: expectations. People generally buy (or sell) shares in expectation of economic events. If they feel that times are getting bad and the economic statistics back them up (in the form of rising unemployment, shrinking corporate profits, cutbacks in consumer spending and so on), then they become more cautious, which can have a couple of results:

>> They sell shares that they currently own.

>> They don't buy shares because they feel that shares won't do well.

Of course, when the economy is doing well, the reverse is true.

Bulling Up

In the beginning, a bull market doesn't look like a bull market at all. It looks like anything but. Maybe that's why so few catch on early. Bull markets are marked by great optimism as the economy roars forward and shares go skyward. Everyone knows what a bull market should look like, and everyone can recognise it when the bull market has become a mature trend. The saying 'I don't know what it is, but I'll know it when I see it' certainly applies to a bull market. But if you can foresee it coming, you may be able to make a fortune by getting in just before the crowd sees it.

TIP

Just keep in mind that you personally want to behave like a contrarian. A *contrarian* is an investor who decides which securities to buy and sell by going against the crowd. To paraphrase the legendary billionaire J. Paul Getty, buy when people are selling and sell when people are buying. This approach is the essence of successful investing.

The following sections take a closer look at bull markets, including how you can spot them and ways you can steer clear of and approach them. Because bull markets usually start in the depths of a bear market, do research regarding bear markets; read the 'Identifying the beast' section later in this chapter.

Recognising the beast

In this book we concentrate on the modern era, starting in the early part of the 20th century, but bull markets in shares have shown themselves many times throughout the past few hundred years – plenty of time to have established a few recognisable traits, such as the following:

REMEMBER

>> **Bull markets tend to start in the depths of pessimism – the same way that dawn starts at the edge of darkness.** People have probably just been beaten up by a bear market. The phrase 'I'm into investing in shares' is about as welcome in polite conversation as 'I have a contagious disease'. If investors

are avoiding shares like the plague (or selling shares they already have), share prices drop to the point that much of the risk is wrung out of them. Value-orientated investors then can pick up solid companies at great prices. (See Chapter 10 for information on recognising a good share value.)

» **The major media mirrors this pessimism and amplifies it.** Usually, the mainstream media has greater value as a *counter indicator* because, by the time the major publications find out about the economic trend and report it, the major trend has already played itself out and is probably ready to change course.

» **Economic statistics stabilise.** After the economy has hit rock bottom, the economic statistics start to improve. The most-watched set of economic indicators is compiled by the Office for National Statistics. Investors want to make sure that the economy is getting back on its feet before it starts its next move upward. For example, in 1982, the economy was just starting to recover from the 1981 recession. The economic expansion (and accompanying bull market) became the longest in history.

» **Economic conditions for individuals and companies are stable and strong.** You know that's true if profits are stable or growing for companies in general and if consumers are seeing strong and increasing income growth. The logic holds up well: more money being made means more money to eventually spend and invest.

» **Industries producing large-ticket items hit rock bottom and begin their climb.** After consumers and companies have been pummelled by a tough economy, they're not apt to make major financial commitments to items such as new cars, houses, equipment and so on. Industries that produce these large, expensive items see sales fall to a low and slowly start to rebound as the economy picks up. In a growing economy, consumers and companies experience greater confidence (both psychologically and financially).

» **Demographics appear favourable.** Take a look at the census and government statistics on trends for population growth, as well as the growth in the number of business enterprises. The 1980s and 1990s, for example, saw the rise of the baby boomers, those born during the post-WW2 period of 1946 to 1964. Baby boomers wielded a great deal of financial clout, much of it in the stock market. Their investment money played a major role in propelling the stock market to new highs.

» **General peace and stability prevail.** A major war or international conflict may have just ended. Beyond death and destruction, war is also bad for the economy and presents uncertainty and anxiety for investors.

Avoiding the horns of a bull market

Believe it or not, a mature bull market poses problems for investors and stock market experts. In a mature bull market, just about any share – good, bad or indifferent – tends to go up. You can be a blind monkey throwing darts and pick a rising share. When everything goes up and everybody seems to be making a winning pick, human nature kicks in. Both beginners and serious investors believe that their good fortune can be chalked up to superior share-picking prowess and not simple luck or circumstance. Overconfidence is rampant at the top of the market and it becomes a prelude to disaster.

WARNING

When investors become convinced that they have the newfound ability to consistently choose winning shares, they grow more daring in their investment approach; they make riskier choices, using less discipline and relying on less diligence and research. Then . . . wham! They get knocked out by the market. Overconfidence lures the unsuspecting investor to more dangerous territory, invariably resulting in an expensive lesson. Overconfidence and money don't mix.

Let us tell you about a common phenomenon of human behaviour that Paul refers to as the Wile E. Coyote effect. Do you remember Wile E. Coyote from those great *Road Runner* cartoons? Of course, you do! You know the plot: Mr Coyote is chasing the Road Runner and seems to be gaining on him. He's confidently ready to pounce on the seemingly unsuspecting bird, but the Road Runner makes a quick turn and watches as Mr Coyote continues running over the cliff, ultimately plummeting into the ravine.

A mature bull market (also known as the 'mania' stage) does that to investors. Scores of true stories tell of investors lured to a game of easy riches (the dot.com fiasco, for example) only to watch their investments get pulverised. This phenomenon happened not only to beginners but also to experienced investors and many share investment experts. Crowd psychology, whether driven by fear or greed, is fascinating.

Toro! Approaching a bull market

Being fully invested in shares at the beginning of a bull market makes for spectacular success. But doing so takes courage. Then again, who says you have to go the whole hog? You can begin looking and get your first share now and slowly build your portfolio as the bull market emerges.

TIP

Choose the type of shares as well as the mix to fit into your unique situation and needs. When the bull market is in its infancy, start investing by using the following approach:

>> **Be a bargain hunter.** Frequently, at the tail end of a bear market, share prices have been sufficiently battered after going through an extended period of low demand and/or disproportionately more selling of the shares by nervous investors. Let the shopping begin! At the bottom of the bear market, you have a good chance of acquiring shares at share prices that are near (or in some cases below) the book value of the companies they represent. You also have less risk when you acquire the shares of a company that is generating positive growth in sales and earnings. Chapter 10 can help you better understand concepts such as book value.

>> **Look for strong fundamentals.** Is the company you're choosing exhibiting solid income and profit? Are income and profit rising compared to the previous year? How about from the same quarter last year? Conduct top-line and bottom-line analyses (which we discuss in Chapter 10). Do the company's products and services make sense to you? In other words, is it selling stuff that the public is starting to demand more of?

>> **Consider the share's class.** Remember that some shares are more aggressive choices than others. This choice reflects your risk tolerance as well. Figure out whether you want to invest in a small-cap with phenomenal growth prospects (and commensurate risk) or a blue chip that's a tried-and-true market leader.

All things being equal, small-cap shares exhibit the best growth performance in an emerging bull market. Small-caps are more appropriate for investors who have a higher risk tolerance. Of course, most shares do well in an emerging bull market (actually, that's what makes it a bull market!), so even risk-averse investors who put their money into larger companies gain. (For more information on growth shares such as small-caps, see Chapter 8.)

>> **Choose appropriate industries.** Look at industries that are poised to rebound as the economy picks up and individuals and organisations begin to spend again. In a rising market, cyclical shares such as those in the car, housing, industrial equipment and mining businesses resume growth. When the economy is doing well, individuals and organisations begin to spend more on items that meet their needs in an expanding economy. Companies upgrade their technology. Families get a new car or move to a bigger house. Construction firms need more and better equipment as residential and commercial building increases.

>> **Take stock of your portfolio.** As you start to add shares to your portfolio, first analyse your situation to make sure that you have diversification not only in different shares and/or unit trusts but also in non-share investments, such as savings bonds and bank accounts. You don't have to have 100 per cent of your investment in shares just because the market is bullish. Instead, you should consider putting as much as 100 per cent of the growth component of your investment money in shares.

One of the worst bear markets since the Great Depression started in 1973. The stock market in the UK was pummelled as the Dow Jones Industrial Average (DJIA) fell 45 per cent during an 18-month period ending in 1975. However, the DJIA didn't recover to its 1973 high until (you guessed it) 1982. The period from 1973 to 1982 had the hallmarks of tough times — high inflation, high unemployment, war (the Middle East conflict in 1973 and expansive Soviet aggression in Africa and Afghanistan), the energy crisis and high taxes. The 1970s were a tough decade for most companies in the UK and the US. The 1980s and 1990s were great decades for stock investors.

Say that you're investing for the long term. You're not that concerned with risk, and you want maximum growth from your investments. After setting aside money in an emergency fund, you decide that you want to devote your remaining funds of £25,000 to growth shares. In this case, 100 per cent of that sum becomes the *growth component* of your investment portfolio. If you decide to play it safer and split it 50/50 between bonds and shares, then £12,500 (or 50 per cent of your portfolio) is your growth component. The bonds are then your *income component*.

REMEMBER

» **Evaluate your personal goals.** No matter how good the market and the foreseeable prospects for growth are, investing in shares is a personal matter that should serve your unique needs. For example, how old are you, and how many years away is your retirement? All things being equal, a 35-year-old should have predominately growth shares, while a 65-year-old requires a more proven, stable performance with blue chip market leaders. The information in Chapter 2 can help you identify appropriate investment goals.

Some investors in a bull market may have little money in shares. Why? Maybe they have already reached their financial goals, so wealth preservation is more appropriate than growth. Perhaps they have a million-pound portfolio and are 70 years old and no longer working. In that case, having, say, 80 per cent of their investments in stable, income-producing investments and 20 per cent in proven (yet modestly) growing shares may make more sense for them.

Bearing Down

Alas, shares go down as well as up. Some ferocious bear markets have hit shares on several occasions since the Great Depression. The bear markets of 1973–1975 and 2000–2002 rank as the toughest in modern times, but the most savage bear market yet hit in 2007 and 2008, although the scare in spring 2020 was also fairly nerve tingling. Share prices in 2008 and 2009 plunged by more than 50 per cent in a matter of weeks and everyone sensed the market was near the edge of a financial catastrophe.

You don't need to worry about the occasional dips (referred to as *corrections*); however, be wary about *secular* (long-term) bear markets, which can last years. Discipline and a watchful eye can keep you and your money out of trouble.

The next sections walk you through the nightmare side of investing, namely when markets turn sour and the bears are on the rampage.

Identifying the beast

Bear markets can be foreseen and they've been most often seen starting during apparently bullish, jubilant times. Bear markets come immediately on the heels of market peaks (when share buying reaches 'mania' levels).

Emerging bear markets have tell-tale signs, including the following:

>> **Optimism abounds.** Everyone from London to Lerwick feels great. Financial reports declare that the business cycle has been conquered and a new economy or new paradigm has arrived. Good times are here for the foreseeable future! You start to see books with titles such as *The Footsie at 40,000* and *Easy Riches in the Stock Market* hit the bestseller lists. The *business cycle* refers to the economy's roller coaster-like behaviour when it expands (growth) and contracts (recession).

TRACKING THE BEARS

Anecdotal evidence about market peaks makes shrewd investors become cautious. Rumour has it that John D. Rockefeller (or was it Joe Kennedy?) got totally out of the stock market just before the 1929 crash when his shoeshine boy gave him a hot stock tip. Whether that story is true isn't the issue. The story is believable because you know similar moments have indeed happened in recent times.

In 2000, investors and tabloid share tippers were appearing on television giving stock market advice. In 2005, football players, glamour models and taxi drivers were building buy-to-let property empires on the side. Long-time professional observers have come to realise that once everybody and their uncle (and their aunt and their parrot) starts telling you about easy riches in a market, it's time to get out!

WHO NEEDS A PARTY-POOPER, RIGHT?

Sometimes, the financial experts believe that an economy is doing so well that it can continue to grow indefinitely. Examples of misguided exuberance abound in stock market history. In 1929, Irving Fisher, the best-known financial expert and share millionaire of his day, made the ill-fated declaration 'Stocks have reached a permanent plateau' as he predicted the bull market would continue for the foreseeable future.

A few weeks later, the infamous stock market crash occurred. Everyone who'd listened to Fisher got clobbered in the greatest bear market of the twentieth century. Even Fisher himself filed for bankruptcy. Not even Irving Fisher should've listened to Irving Fisher. In stark contrast, Ludwig von Mises warned about the oncoming depression throughout the late 1920s and was ignored.

>> **Debt levels hit new highs.** When optimism is high, people buy things and they pay for them on credit. That credit could be for houses, office blocks, cars or shares. By 2005 debt was ramping up in the West, but by 2007 it was obvious that something was going horribly wrong in one of the most indebted markets on earth, US housing. Prices started to fall and, before you knew it, banks started tumbling. The rest, as they say, is history, one we'd all probably rather forget. Those massive bad debts sadly are still working their way through the global economic system more than a decade later.

>> **Excessive speculation, credit and money supply expand.** Whenever a country's money supply grows beyond the economy's needs, huge problems can result. When the money supply expands, more money is circulated into the banking system. (Go to www.bankofengland.co.uk to find out more about the money supply.) The banks then lend or invest this excess money. The oversupply of money flows into investment projects, such as new issues and bond offerings. When too much money is available for too few worthy projects, invariably a lot of money is invested unwisely. This situation causes massive imbalances in the economic system, ultimately resulting in economic downturns that can take years to rectify.

History proves the truth of this economic situation. It happened to the US economy in the late 1920s, to Japan in the late 1980s, and to the US and the UK in 2006 through to 2008. Fortunately, statistics on credit and the money supply are easy to come by and readily available on the Internet. (See Appendix A for resources.)

>> **Government intervention increases.** Government has the power to do much good, but when it uses its power improperly, it can do a great deal of harm. Throughout history, every economy that collapsed ultimately did so

because of excessive government intervention. In progressive, free-market economies, this intervention usually occurs in the form of taxes, laws and regulations. Keep a watchful eye on the Chancellor and Parliament to monitor government intervention. Are they proposing policies that further burden the private economy? Are they advocating stringent new laws and regulations? We explain more about government's influence on the stock market and the general economy in Chapter 14.

>> **National and/or international conflict arises.** Nothing can have a more negative impact on the economy than war or political or civil unrest. (Perhaps war is a good example of 'excessive government intervention'.) Keep your eye on the news. Ask yourself what effect a particular conflict may have on the economy and the stock market. Sometimes the conflict isn't a violent one; sometimes it takes the form of a trade war when competing countries aggressively implement tariffs and boycotts that can devastate companies or even industries in one or both of the countries.

>> **Investors throw a taper tantrum.** Central banks have awesome power, if only because they get to control the printing presses. After the global financial crisis of 2008/2009 central banks waded into action to stabilize the financial system. They bought bonds like crazy and 'quantitatively eased' like no - one's business. (That means that the central banks expanded their balance sheets so they could buy oodles of corporate bonds to improve market liquidity.)

They pushed interest rates down and even bought government securities at unprecedented scale. But then, at some point, these central bankers started to worry a bit and turned hawkish. They worried about inflation and thought interest rates should go up. They stopped buying as many bonds. They restrained quantitative easing. Care to guess what reaction this *tapering* (where central banks start to ease off their balance sheet activities and reduce bond purchases) produced? You guessed it, concern, followed by nervousness and then finally panic. Or should we say *tantrums.* Investors started to worry that the party was over and that all this monetary intervention was winding down. Markets started to fall. In essence, the moral of the story is simple. Watch out for the taper tantrums by investors worried about central bank policy.

Heading into the woods: Approaching a bear market

Sticking to a *buy-and-hold strategy* (where you buy shares and hold on to them for better or worse) at the onset of a bear market is financial suicide. People have a tough time selling, and financial advisors have an even tougher time telling them to cut their losses because that's tantamount to saying, 'Sorry, I was wrong.' Admitting failure is hard for most people to do.

LOOKING FOR *TITANIC* TICKETS

In early 2008, the dapper pundits on TV told viewers to hang tight and hold on for the long haul. Shares then took a beating, prompting the pundits to say, 'It's a buying opportunity. Add to your portfolio.' Then what happened? The bear market took shares down again.

Investors would probably have avoided losing trillions during 2008 and the first part of 2009 – if they'd been more disciplined and if the pundits had been more careful in their pronouncements. When the economy is heading into treacherous waters, shares get the worst of it, yet experts continue to advise people to buy shares because shares are good for the long term. Hold on! Liking shares doesn't mean that you should always be in them. Just because you like boating doesn't mean that you'd take advantage of a free ticket on the *Titanic*.

Understand that investing should be a logical, practical and unemotional pursuit. You can't be married to shares – until death do you part – especially because bear markets can divorce you from your money.

In an emerging bear market, keep the following points in mind to maximise your gains (or just to minimise your losses).

Review your situation

Before you consider any move in or out of the market, review your overall financial situation to make sure that your money and financial condition are as secure as possible. Make sure that you have an emergency fund of three to six months' worth of gross living expenses. Keep your debt at a comfortably low level. Review your career, insurance and so on. Schedule a financial check-up with your financial planner.

Remember that cash is king

When the bear market is coming and economic storm clouds are rolling in, keep the bulk of your money in safe, interest-bearing vehicles such as bank and building society accounts, National Savings certificates and guaranteed income bonds. Doing so keeps your money safe. When shares are falling by 10 to 20 per cent or more, you're better off earning a low-percentage interest in a secure, stable investment. In addition, you can conduct research while your money is earning interest. Start shopping for undervalued shares with strong fundamentals.

Stick to necessities

In an economic downturn, defensive shares generally outperform the market. *Defensive shares* are shares in companies that sell goods and services that people need no matter how well or poorly the economy is doing. Good examples are food and drink, energy, utilities and certain healthcare shares.

Use trailing stops

Trailing stops are just the active use of stop-loss orders on a given share. (If a share is at £40, you have the stop loss at £36, if the stock moves to £46, then change the stop loss from £36 to £41, and so on. Chapter 17 provides a fuller explanation.) In the case of a bear market, you *tighten the trail* – set your stop losses closer to the share's market price.

Say, for example, that you once bought a share for £50 per share and this share is now at £110. Presume that you usually kept a trailing stop at 10 per cent below the current market price. If the bear market is becoming more evident to you, then change that 10 per cent to 5 per cent. Before, that trailing stop on the £110 stock was £99 (£110 minus 10 per cent, or £11), but now the trailing stop is at £104.50 (£110 minus 5 per cent, or £5.50). The trailing-stop strategy is one of our favourite ways to protect our shares' gains.

Straddling Bear and Bull: Uncertain Markets

Uncertain markets are . . . well . . . uncertain. Markets aren't always up or down. The end of a bear market doesn't automatically mean the beginning of a bull market and vice versa. Sometimes markets move only a little way until investors and participants in the economy figure out what's what as we discuss in these sections.

Pinpointing uncertainty is tough

Clashing points of view in the media tell you that even the experts aren't sure which way the market and the economy are going in the coming months. In uncertain markets, compelling evidence and loads of opinions evenly line up on both the pro and con sides of the economic debate – often in the same article. Bullish and bearish advisors and commentators may both seem persuasive, so you may be left scratching your head, wondering what to do. In this case, your patience and diligence should pay off.

Deciding whether you want to approach an uncertain market

The approach to take in uncertain markets is almost simplistic. If you think that a bull market is starting, you want to have 100 per cent of your growth portfolio invested in shares, and if a bear market is starting, you want the percentage to be 0. Therefore, in an uncertain market, 50 per cent in shares and 50 per cent in other investments is just right. Of course, these three scenarios need to be balanced by many non-share factors, such as your individual financial situation, age, debt level, career concerns and so on. However, all things being equal, those allocations aren't far off the mark.

REMEMBER

Treat uncertain markets as bear markets until your research starts to give you a clear idea of the market's direction. No matter how adventurous you are, the first rule of investing in shares is that you minimise or avoid losses. If no one can agree on the direction of the market, then you stand a 50 per cent chance of being wrong should you take the bullish stance. However, if you take a bearish stance and the market becomes decidedly bullish, no real harm is done except that you may miss an investment opportunity during a brief period of time. Just keep in mind that investing in shares is indeed a long-term pursuit. Jumping into a bullish market is easy, but recovering from losses may not be.

Chapter **16**

Choosing a Strategy That's Just Right for You

S hares are a means to an end. What end are you seeking? You should look at shares as tools for wealth building. Sometimes they're great tools, and sometimes they're awful. It depends on your approach. Some shares are appropriate for a conservative approach, while others are more suitable for an aggressive approach. Sometimes shares aren't a good idea at all. You what? A book about investing in shares that suggests that shares aren't always the answer! That's like a teenager saying, 'Dad, I respectfully decline your generous offer of money for my weekend trip, and I'd be glad to mow the lawn.'

Laying Out Your Plans

It's a common story. A respected investor or investment writer holds a seminar and is mobbed afterwards by private investors looking for ideas and inspiration. Imagine in this scenario a senior citizen who proclaims that he wants to be more aggressive with his portfolio; his stockbroker is more than happy to cater to his desire for growth shares. Of course, these kinds of shares get clobbered in volatile bear markets and guess what happened in 2008 during the GFC (remember that, the global financial crisis) . . . yes, he did lose lots of money. But imagine the surprise of our learned expert when he discovers that, even after the losses, this older investor still has a substantial shares portfolio valued at over £500,000. He had more than enough to ensure a comfortable retirement. He'd sought aggressive growth even though it was really unnecessary for his situation. If anything, the aggressive strategy may have put his portfolio (and hence his retirement) in jeopardy.

REMEMBER

Growth is desirable even in your twilight years because inflation can eat away at a fixed-income portfolio. But different rates of growth exist, and the type you choose should be commensurate with your unique situation and financial needs. Notice that we say 'needs', not 'wants'. These perspectives are entirely different. You may *want* to invest in aggressive shares regardless of their suitability (after all, it's your money), but your financial situation may dictate that you *need* to take another approach. Just understand the difference.

Shares can play a role in all sorts of investment strategies, but in this chapter, we discuss only a few well-known approaches. Keep in mind that a share investment strategy can change based on the major changes in your life and the lifestyle that you lead.

Living the bachelor life: Young, single, with no dependents

If you're young (age 20–40) and single, with no children or other dependents, being more aggressive with your share selection is fine (as long as you don't use your rent money for investments). The reasoning is that, if you do make riskier choices and they backfire, individuals who are dependent on you won't get hurt. In addition, if you're in this category, you can usually bounce back a lot easier over the long term even if you have financial challenges or if a bear market hits your shares. Chapter 15 can tell you more about bear and bull markets.

TIP

Consider a mix of small-cap, mid-cap and large-cap (see Chapter 1 for an explanation of each of these shares) shares in sectors with some growth potential. Either invest in funds that target this space (unit trusts or ETFs) or consider investing directly in five to seven shares and putting the remainder in funds that target growth in other parts of the world but especially in the emerging markets. You can revise your investment allocations along the way as the general economy changes and/or your personal situation (like when you finally say 'I do' to the love of your life) changes.

Going together like a horse and carriage: Married with children

Married couples with children must follow a more conservative investing strategy, regardless of whether one spouse works or both spouses do. Children change the picture drastically (believe us, we have them and the baggy eyes to prove it). You need more stable growth in your portfolio (and unbreakable furniture in your home).

TIP

Consider a mix of large-cap growth shares and dividend-paying defensive shares. (See Chapter 9 for more on defensive shares.) Think about investing in a mix of FTSE 100 tracker funds, some exciting large-cap stocks with growth potential, some smaller growth companies, plus a smattering of boring defensive companies and funds that target this form of investment. Of course, you can tweak your allocations along the way according to changes in the general economic conditions or to your personal situation. Consider setting aside money for university in a growth-orientated unit trust and in other vehicles such as annual ISAs or savings bonds (as early as possible).

Getting ready for retirement: Older than 40 and single or married

Whether you're older than 40 and single or you're older than 40 and married (whether one or both of you work), you should start to slowly convert your portfolio from aggressive growth to conservative growth. Shift more of your money out of individual shares and into less-volatile investments, such as investment trusts, unit trusts, guaranteed income bonds and National Savings certificates.

SAFETY FIRST: EXAMINING SAVINGS BONDS

A nice oasis in the valley of death known as Britain's debt load is National Savings and Investment (NS&I) issued savings bonds and certificates. They come in several types – including fixed and variable rate bonds. NS&I savings bonds are bonds that are issued on behalf of the Treasury. They can be purchased for as little as £25 but normally the minimum investment is around £100. New interest rates for the various issues of certificates or bonds can change every few months as needed to reflect changing interest rates. If rates go up, Her Majesty's Treasury usually updates the interest rates on your savings bonds if you aren't locked in to a fixed rate. Savings bonds are ultra-safe, convenient and inexpensive to buy, and they're usually tax free. Find out more at the NS&I website at www.nsandi.com.

Devote time and effort (with a financial planner, if necessary) to calculating your potential financial needs at retirement time. This step is critical in helping you decide what age to target for financial independence. (What's that? I can stop working? Whoo-hoo!)

TIP

Consider investing in more defensive industries, sectors and markets, as well as investment trusts and ETFs. Put the remainder of your investment money in guaranteed equity bonds and National Savings certificates, as well as unit trusts or mutual funds. Have a large portion of your money in savings bonds and savings accounts. Remember that you can revise your allocations in the future, as necessary.

Kicking back in the hammock: Already retired

If you're retired, you're probably in your sixties or older. Safe, reliable income and wealth preservation form the crux of your investment strategy. Growth-orientated investments are okay as long as they're conservative and don't jeopardise your need for income. At one time, financial planners told their retired clients to replace growth-orientated investments with safe income-orientated investments. However, times have changed as senior citizens live longer than ever before.

REMEMBER

Issues such as longevity and inflation (the steadily increasing cost of living) mean that today's (and tomorrow's) retirees need growth in their portfolios. To be safe, make sure that 5–20 per cent of retirement portfolios have a number of growth-orientated securities such as shares to make sure that you continue meeting your financial needs as the years pass. You should perform an annual review to see whether the shares allocation needs to be adjusted.

TIP

Consider a mix of boring large-cap companies with a defensive bias plus some index trackers with the remainder in mutual funds and short-term government bonds. Have a large portion of your money in savings bonds and savings accounts. You need to monitor and tweak your investment portfolio along the way to account for changes in the general economic environment or your lifestyle needs.

Allocating Your Assets – Diversification Is Key

Asset allocation is really an attempt to properly implement the concept of diversification – the key to safety and stability. *Diversification* is the inclusion in your portfolio of different investments to shield your wealth from most types of current risk while planning for future growth. To achieve proper diversification, you need to analyse your entire portfolio to look for glaring weaknesses or vulnerable areas. We don't discuss your total investment plan here, only the shares portion.

Investors frequently believe that having different shares in different industries constitutes proper diversification. Well . . . not quite. Shares in closely related industries tend to be affected (to differing degrees) by the same economic events, government policies and so on. Investing in shares across different sectors is best. As we mention in Chapter 12, a sector is essentially a group of related industries. Water, gas and electricity services are industries, but together they (plus a few other industries) make up the utilities sector. For more on analysing industries in order to pick winning shares, see Chapter 12.

In the following sections, we present typical amounts that most typical investors can (and should) devote to shares investing.

Investors with less than £10,000

If you have £10,000 or less to allocate to shares, you may want to consider a fund in a stocks and shares ISA rather than individual shares, because that sum of money may not be enough to properly diversify. But if you're going to invest a sum that small, consider allocating it equally into two to four shares in two different sectors that look strong for the foreseeable future.

TECHNICAL
STUFF

Because £10,000 or less is a small sum in the world of share investing, you may have to purchase fewer shares than you'd hoped. This situation may be a particular problem in a new issue or flotation, when you have to say how much you want to invest before you know the price the share is going to start trading at. So, you may find that, instead of getting say 2,000 shares at £5 each, you get an uneven number of shares – say, 1,872 shares at £5.34 each. Don't worry. You can build up the number of shares you own by reinvesting your dividends in the future. Find out whether the company has a dividend reinvestment plan (DRIP), and use the dividend money you earn to buy more shares. (We discuss DRIPs more fully in Chapter 18.)

WARNING

New issues can be a good entry into the stock market but they're risky – so be sure to do your research before you invest. Penny shares and other speculative issues are also a worry. Participation in them may cost little (penny shares often have penny prices), but the risk exposure is too high for inexperienced investors. (See Chapter 8 for more on new issues.)

Investors with £10,000–50,000

If you have between £10,000 and £50,000 to invest, you have more breathing space for diversification. Consider buying four to six shares in two or three different sectors plus a mixture of funds including unit trusts, investment trusts and ETFs. If you're the cautious type, defensive shares should do. For growth investors, seek the industries in those sectors that have proven growth. This approach gets you off to a good start, and the 'Knowing When to Sell' section later in this chapter can help you maintain your portfolio with changing strategy (if necessary).

Does diversification mean that you shouldn't in any circumstance have all your shares in one sector? It depends on you. For example, if you've worked all your life in a particular field and you're knowledgeable and comfortable with the sector, having a greater exposure is okay because your greater personal expertise offsets the risk. If you worked in retail for 20 years and know the industry inside and out, you probably know more about the good, the bad and the ugly of the retail sector than most City analysts. Use your insight for more profitability. You still shouldn't invest all your money in that single sector, however, because diversification is still vital.

Investors with £50,000 or more

If you have £50,000 or more to invest, have no more than five to ten shares in two or three different sectors plus a mixture of funds including unit trusts, investment trusts and ETFs. It's difficult to thoroughly track more than two or three sectors and do it successfully – best to keep it simple. For example, Warren Buffett, considered the greatest stock market investor of all time, didn't invest in website businesses when they were all the rage because he didn't understand them. He invests only in businesses that he understands. If that strategy works for billionaire investors, then, by golly, it can't be that bad for smaller investors.

TIP

Consider whether to employ a wealth manager (a person who manages investment portfolios for a fee). If you have more than £100,000 or more, doing so may make sense. Get a referral from a financial adviser and carefully weigh the benefits against the costs. Here are a few points to consider:

>> **Make sure that the wealth manager has a philosophy and an approach that you agree with.** Ask the wealth manager to give you a copy of their written investment philosophy. How do they feel about small-cap shares versus large-caps? Income versus growth?

>> **Find out whether you're comfortable with how the wealth manager selects shares.** Is this wealth manager a value investor or a growth investor?

Aggressive or conservative? Do they analyse a share because of its fundamentals (sales, earnings, book value and so on) or use share price charts?

>> **Ask the wealth manager to explain the strategy.** A good way to evaluate the success (or failure) of the strategy is to ask the wealth manager for past recommendations. Did they pick more winners than losers?

Knowing When to Sell

The act of buying shares is relatively easy. However, the act of selling shares can be an agonising decision for investors. But it's agonising only in two instances: when you've made money with your shares and when you've lost it. That about covers it. It sounds like a bad joke, but it's not that far from the truth.

REMEMBER

The idea of selling shares when they have appreciated (the share price has increased in value) comes with the following concerns:

>> **Tax implications:** This concern is a good reason to consider selling. See Chapter 20 for information about how selling shares under given circumstances can affect your tax.

>> **Emotional baggage:** 'Those shares were in our family for years.' Believe it or not, investors cite this personal reason (or one of a dozen other personal reasons) for agonising over the sale of an appreciated share.

REMEMBER

The following is a list of issues that investors want to be aware of when they're selling shares that have lost money:

>> **Tax benefits:** This issue is a good reason to consider selling shares. See Chapter 20 for more on timing your shares' sales to minimise your tax burden.

>> **Pride:** 'If I sell, I'll have to admit I was wrong' (followed by silent sobbing). So what? The best investors in history have made bad investments (some that have been quite embarrassing, in fact). Losing a little pride is cheaper than losing your money.

>> **Doubt:** 'If I sell my shares now, they may rebound later.' Frequently, when an investor buys shares at £5 and they go to £4, the investor believes that if they sell, the shares will make an immediate *rebound* – a recovery in value – and go to £6, and then the investor will be kicking themself. That may happen, but usually the share price goes lower.

>> **Separation anxiety:** 'But I've had this share so long that it's become a part of me.' People hang on to a losing share for all sorts of illogical reasons. Being married to a person is great; being married to a share is ludicrous. If a share isn't helping your goals, then it's hurting your goals.

People have plenty more reasons to agonise over the sale of a bad share. But you can find out how to handle the share sale in a disciplined manner.

You have only two reasons to consider selling a share regardless of whether the share price has gone up or down:

>> **You need the money.** Obviously, if you need the money for a genuine reason – such as paying off debt, wiping out a tax bill or buying a home – then you need the money. This reason is easy to see. After all, regardless of investment or tax considerations, shares are there to serve you. We hope that you engage in financial planning so that you don't need to sell your shares for these types of expenses, but you can't avoid unexpected expenditures.

>> **The shares ceased to perform as you desired.** If the share isn't serving your wealth-building goals or fulfilling your investment objectives, it's time to get rid of it and move on to the next share. Just as soon as you get a stiff upper lip and resolve to unload this losing share, a little voice saying 'If I sell my share now, it may rebound later' starts to haunt you. So, you hang on to the share, but then – bam! – before you know it, you lose more money.

Selling a share shouldn't require a psychologist. Here's where discipline steps in. This belief is why we're big proponents of trailing stops. (See Chapter 17 for more on stop orders.) Trailing stops take the agony out of selling shares. All else being equal, you shouldn't sell a winning share. If it's doing well, why sell it? Keep it as long as possible. But if it stops being a winning share, sell it. If you don't know how or when to sell it, then apply a stop-loss order at 5 or 10 per cent below the market value and let the market action take its course.

IN THIS CHAPTER

» Looking at different types of
brokerage orders

» Trading on margin to maximise
profits

» Making sense of going short

Chapter **17**

Using Your Broker and Trading Techniques

I nvestment success isn't just about picking rising shares; it's also about how you go about doing it. Frequently, investors think that good share picking means doing your homework and then making that buy (or sell). However, you can take it a step further to maximise profits (or minimise losses). As an investor in shares, you can take advantage of techniques and services available through your standard brokerage account. (Refer to Chapter 7 for more on brokerage accounts.)

This chapter presents a few of the best ways that you can use these powerful techniques – useful whether you're buying or selling shares. In fact, if you retain nothing more from this chapter than the concept of *trailing stops* (see the 'Trailing stops' section), you've had your money's worth.

Checking Out Brokerage Orders

Orders you place with your stockbroker neatly fit into two categories:

» Condition-related orders

» Time-related orders

Get familiar with both orders because they're easy to implement and invaluable tools for wealth building and (more importantly) wealth saving!

TIP

Using a combination of orders helps you fine-tune your strategy so that you can maintain greater control over your investments. Speak to your broker about the different types of orders you can use to maximise the gains (or minimise the losses) from your share investment activities. If you want to use all these orders you need to find a broker who can accommodate you. Read the broker's policies on these orders on the brokerage firm's website.

Condition-related orders

A *condition-related order* means that the order is executed only when a certain condition is met. Conditional orders enhance your ability to buy shares at a lower price, to sell at a better price or to minimise potential losses. When stock markets become bearish or uncertain, conditional orders are highly recommended. A good example of a conditional order is a *limit order*. A limit order may say, 'Buy Mojeski PLC at £45'. But if Mojeski isn't at £45 (this price is the condition), then the order isn't executed.

Market orders

When you buy shares, the simplest type of order is a *market order* or *at best* – an order to buy or sell a share at the market's current best available price. It doesn't get any more basic than that.

Here's an example: Kowalski PLC is available at the market price of £10. When you call up your broker and give the instruction to buy 100 shares 'at the market', the broker implements the order for your account, and you pay £1,000 plus commission.

We say 'current best available price' because the share's price is constantly moving, and catching the best price can be a function of the broker's ability to process the share purchase. For very active shares, the price change can happen within seconds. It's not unheard of to have three brokers simultaneously place orders for the same shares and get three different prices because of differences in the broker's capability. (Some computers are faster than others.)

The advantage of a market order is that the transaction is processed immediately, and you get your share without worrying about whether it hits a particular price. For example, if you buy Kowalski shares with a market order, you know that by the end of that phone call (or website visit), you're assured of getting the share. The disadvantage of a market order is that you can't control the price that you pay for the share. Whether you're buying or selling your shares, you may not realise the exact price you expect (especially if you're buying a volatile share).

REMEMBER

Market orders get finalised in the chronological order in which they're placed. Your price may change because the orders ahead of you in line caused the share price to rise or fall based on the latest news.

Stop orders (also known as stop-loss orders)

A *stop order* (or *stop-loss order* if you own the share) is a condition-related order that instructs the broker to sell a particular share only when the share reaches a particular price. It acts like a trigger, and the stop-loss order converts to a market order to sell the share immediately.

REMEMBER

The stop-loss order isn't designed to take advantage of small, short-term moves in the share's price. It's meant to help you protect the bulk of your money when the market turns against your share investment in a sudden manner.

Say that your Kowalski share rises to £20 per share and you seek to protect your investment against a possible future market decline. A stop-loss order at £18 triggers your broker to sell the share immediately if it falls to the £18 mark. In this example, if the share suddenly drops to £17, it still triggers the stop-loss order, but the finalised sale price is £17. In a volatile market, you may not be able to sell at your precise stop-loss price. However, because the order automatically gets converted into a market order, the sale is done, and you prevent further declines in the share.

The main benefit of a stop-loss order is that it prevents you from holding on and suffering a major decline in the value of a share that you own. It's a form of discipline that's important in investing in order to minimise potential losses. Investors can find selling a share that's fallen agonising. If they don't sell, however, the share often carries on plummeting as investors continue to hold on while hoping for a rebound in the price.

TIP

Most investors set a stop-loss amount at about 10 per cent below the market value of a share. This percentage gives the share room to fluctuate, which most shares tend to do on a day-to-day basis.

TRAILING STOPS

Trailing stops are an important technique in wealth preservation for seasoned share investors and can be one of your key strategies in using stop-loss orders. A *trailing stop* is a stop-loss order that the investor actively manages by moving it up along with the share's market price. The stop-loss order 'trails' the share price upward. As the stop-loss goes upward, it protects more and more of the share's value from declining.

A real-life example may be the best way to help you understand trailing stops. Say that in 2019 you bought Tesco (TSCO) at £3.50 per share. As soon as you finished buying it, you immediately told your broker to put a stop-loss order at £3 and make it a good-till-cancelled (GTC) order. Think of what you did. In effect, you placed an ongoing (GTC) safety net under your share. The share can go as high as the sky, but if it should fall, the share's price triggers a market order at £3. Your share is automatically sold, minimising your loss.

If Tesco goes to £4 per share in a few months, you can call your broker and cancel the former stop-loss order at £3 and replace it with a new (higher) stop-loss order. You simply say, 'Please put a new stop-loss order at £4.50 and make it a GTC order.) This higher stop-loss price protects not only your original investment of £3.50 but also a big chunk of your profit as well. As time goes by and the share price climbs, you can continue to raise the stop-loss price and add a GTC provision. Now you know why it's called a trailing stop. It trails the share price upward like a giant tail. All along the way, it protects more and more of your growing investment without limiting its upward movement.

Michael Walters, tipster and former *Daily Mail* market columnist, advocates setting a trailing stop of 20 per cent below your purchase price. That's his preference. He suggests that investors in highly volatile shares may put in trailing stops of 10 per cent.

REMEMBER

A trailing stop is a stop-loss order that you actively manage. The stop-loss order is good-till-cancelled (GTC), and it constantly trails the share's price as it moves up. To successfully implement trailing stops, keep the following points in mind:

>> **Remember that brokers usually don't place trailing stops for you automatically.** In fact, they won't (or shouldn't) place any type of order without your consent. Deciding on the type of order to place is your responsibility. You can raise, lower or cancel a trailing stop order at will, but you need to monitor your investment when substantial moves do occur to respond to the movement appropriately.

>> **Change the stop-loss order when the share price moves significantly.** You have to decide when to change the stop-loss and this decision differs depending on the cost of the share. If you're buying shares at 20 pence, then a 2 pence drop is significant. Say that you buy a share at £5 and place a stop-loss order at £4.50. Doing so shows that you're prepared to accept a loss of 50 pence and no more. As the share climbs you thus need to change your

order to match that wish. If the share hits £5.10, you want to set the stop-loss at £4.60 and so on. Some people set the stop based on percentages but that approach can be disappointing. If your share climbs to £10 and your stop-loss has trailed all the way up to sit at £9.50, you can still only lose 50 pence a share. If your stop-loss is set at 10 per cent, you can lose a £1 a share. The decision is yours.

>> **Understand your broker's policy on GTC orders.** If your broker usually has a GTC order expire after 30 days, you should be aware of it. You don't want to risk a sudden drop in your share's price without the stop-loss order protection. Make sure that you can renew the order for additional time.

If a share or a market goes into free fall, the price of your shares may fall through the stop-loss. This event can happen if the share is falling too fast for the broker to find a buyer at your price. Your broker finds you the best price available, which may be lower than you'd hoped.

>> **Monitor your share.** A trailing stop isn't a 'set it and forget it' technique. Monitoring your investment is critical. If shares fall, the stop-loss order you have prevents further loss. Should the share price rise substantially, remember to adjust your trailing stop accordingly. Part of monitoring the share is *knowing the beta*, which you can read more about in the next section.

USING BETA MEASUREMENT

To be a successful investor, you need to understand the volatility of the particular share you invest in. In share market parlance, this volatility is also called the *beta* of a share. *Beta* is a quantitative measure of the volatility of a given share (mutual funds and portfolios, too) relative to the overall market, usually the S&P 500 index, or the FTSE 100 index in the UK. (For more information on both indexes, refer to Chapter 5.) Beta specifically measures the performance movement of the share as the S&P or FTSE 100 moves 1 per cent up or down. A beta measurement above 1 is more volatile than the overall market, while a beta below 1 is less volatile. Some shares are relatively stable in the price movements; others jump around.

Because beta measures how volatile or unstable the share's price is, it tends to be uttered in the same breath as 'risk' – more volatility indicates more risk. Similarly, less volatility tends to mean less risk.

Table 17-1 shows sample betas of well-known companies (as of April 2021).

TIP

You can find a company's beta at websites providing a lot of financial information about companies, such as Yahoo! Finance (http://finance.yahoo.com/).

TABLE 17-1

Looking at Well-Known Betas

Company (Market Code)	Beta	Comments
Tesco (TSCO)	0.43	Less volatile than the market
Glencore (GLEN)	1.62	More volatile than the market

The beta is useful to know because it gives you a general idea of the share's trading range. If a share is currently priced at £50 and it typically trades in the £48–52 range, then a trailing stop at £49 doesn't make sense. Your share would probably be sold the same day you initiated the stop-loss order. If your share is a volatile growth share that can swing up and down by 10 per cent, you should more logically set your stop-loss at 15 per cent below that day's price.

REMEMBER

The share of a large-cap company in a mature industry tends to have a low beta – one close to the overall market. Small- and mid-cap shares in new or emerging industries tend to have greater volatility in their day-to-day price fluctuations; hence, they tend to have a high beta. (Chapter 1 has the lowdown on large-, small- and mid-cap shares.)

Limit orders

A *limit order* is a precise condition-related order, implying that a limit exists on the buy or the sell side of the transaction. You want to buy (or sell) only at a specified price or better. Limit orders work better for you if you're buying the share, but they may not be good for you if you're selling the share. Here's how it works in both instances:

» **When you're buying:** Just because you like a particular company and you want its share doesn't mean that you're willing to pay the current market price. Maybe you want to buy Kowalski, but the current market price of £20 per share isn't acceptable to you. You prefer to buy it at £16 because you think that price reflects its true market value. What do you do? You tell your broker, 'Buy Kowalski with a limit order at £16.' You have to specify whether it's a day order (good for the day) or a GTC order, which we discuss in its own section later in this chapter.

What happens if the share experiences great volatility? What if it drops to £16.01 and then suddenly drops to £15.95 on the next move? Actually, nothing, you may be dismayed to hear. Because your order was limited to £16, it can be transacted only at £16, no more or less. The only way for this particular trade to occur is if the share rises back to £16. However, if the price keeps dropping, then your limit order isn't transacted and may expire or be cancelled.

When you're buying a share, many brokers interpret the limit order as 'buy at this specific price or better'. Presumably, if your limit order is to buy the share at £10, you're just as happy if your broker buys that share for you at £9.95. This way, if you don't get exactly £10, because the share's price was volatile, you still get the share at a lower price. Speak to your particular broker to be clear on what they mean when talking about a limit order.

WARNING

» **When you're selling:** Limit orders are activated only when a share hits a specific price. If you buy Kowalski at £20 and you worry about a decline in the share price, you may decide to put in a limit order at £18. If you watch the news and hear that Kowalski's price is dropping, you may sigh and say, 'I sure am glad that I put in that limit order at £18!' However, in a volatile market, the share price may leapfrog over your specified price. It may go from £18.01 to £17.99 and then continue its descent. Because the share price never hit £18 on the nose, the share isn't sold. You may be sitting at home satisfied (mistakenly) that you played it smart, while your share plummets to £15 or £10 or worse! Having a stop-loss order in place is best.

Time-related orders

Time-related orders mean just that; the order has a time limit. Typically, investors use these orders in conjunction with conditional orders. They're often used by day traders – and some UK brokers only offer these orders on specialist trades such as spread betting and derivatives. The two most common time-related orders are day orders and good-till-cancelled (or GTC) orders.

Day order

A *day order* is an order to buy a share that expires at the end of that particular trading day. If you tell your broker, 'Buy BYOB Ltd at £37.50 and make it a day order', you mean that you want to purchase the share at £37.50. But if the share doesn't hit that price, your order expires at the end of the trading day unfilled. Why would you place such an order? Maybe BYOB is trading at £39, but you don't want to buy it at that price because you don't believe the share is worth it. Consequently, you have no problem not getting the share that day.

When would you use day orders? It depends on your preferences and personal circumstances. Few events really cause you to say, 'I know, I'll just try to buy or sell between now and the end of today's trading action'. However, you may feel that you don't want a specified order to linger beyond today's market action. Perhaps you want to test a price. ('I want to get rid of share A at £39 to make a quick profit, but it's currently trading at £37.50. However, I may change my mind tomorrow.') A day order is the perfect strategy to use in this case.

Unless you know that your broker's policy is to treat every order as a day order if not told otherwise, you need to specify when you want a day order.

Good-till-cancelled (GTC) order

A *good-till-cancelled* (GTC) order is the most commonly requested order by investors. Although GTC orders are time-related, they're always tied to a condition, such as when the share achieves a certain price. The GTC order means just what it says: the order stays in effect until it's transacted or until the investor cancels it. Although the order implies that it can run indefinitely, most brokers have a limit of 30 working days. By that time, the broker cancels the order or contacts you to see whether you want to extend it. Ask your broker about their particular policy.

A GTC order is usually coupled with conditional or condition-related orders. For example, say that you want to buy ASAP PLC shares but you don't want to buy them at the current price of £48 per share. You've done your homework on the share, including looking at the share's price-to-earnings (P/E) ratio, dividend cover and so on (see Appendix B for more on ratios), and you say, 'Hey, this share isn't worth £48 a share. I'd only buy it at £36 per share'. You think the share would make a good addition to your portfolio but not at the current market price. (It's overpriced or overvalued according to your analysis.) How should you proceed? Your best bet is to ask your broker to do a 'GTC order at £36'. This request means that your broker buys the shares if and when they hit the £36 mark (or until you cancel the order). Just make sure that your account has the funds available to complete the transaction.

GTC orders are useful, so you should become familiar with your broker's policy on them. While you're at it, ask whether any fees apply. Many brokers don't charge for GTC orders because, if they happen to result in a buy (or sell) order, they generate a normal commission just as any share transaction does. Other brokers may charge a small fee.

To be successful with GTC orders, you need to know the following:

>> **When you want to buy:** In recent years, people have had a tendency to rush into buying a share without giving thought to what they should do to get more for their money. Some investors don't realise that the stock market can be a place for bargain-hunting consumers. If you're ready to buy a quality pair of socks for £16 in a department store, but the sales assistant says that those same socks are going on sale tomorrow for only £8, what would you do – assuming that you're a cost-conscious consumer? Unless you're barefoot, you're probably better off waiting. The same point holds true with shares.

Say that you want to buy SOX PLC at £26, but it's currently trading at £30. You think that £30 is too expensive, but you're happy to buy the share at £26 or lower. However, you have no idea whether the share will move to your desired price today, tomorrow, next week or even next month (maybe never). In this case, a GTC order is appropriate.

>> **When you want to sell:** What if you bought a pair of socks at a department store, and you discovered that they have holes (darn it!)? Wouldn't you want to get rid of them? Of course, you would. If a share's price starts to unravel, you want to be able to get rid of it as well.

Perhaps you already own SOX (at £25, for instance) but are concerned that market conditions may drive the price lower. You're not certain which way the share may move in the coming days and weeks. In this case, a GTC order to sell the share at a specified price is a suitable strategy. Because the share price is £25, you may want to place a GTC order to sell it if it falls to £22.50, to prevent further losses. Again, in this example, GTC is the time frame, and it accompanies a condition (sell when the share hits £22.50).

Buying on Margin

Buying on margin means buying securities, such as shares, by using funds you borrow from your broker. This type of service isn't generally available through UK high street or online brokers. Specialist brokers who look after high net-worth clients should be able to offer the service, but don't expect your online broker to do the same. Buying shares on margin is similar to buying a house with a mortgage. If you buy a house at a purchase price of £100,000 and put 10 per cent down as a deposit, your equity (the part you own) is £10,000, and you borrow the remaining £90,000 with a mortgage. If the value of the house rises to £120,000 and you sell (for the sake of simplicity, we don't include closing costs in this example), you make a profit of 200 per cent. How is that? The £20,000 gain on the property represents a gain of 20 per cent on the purchase price of £100,000, but because your real investment is £10,000 (the down payment), your gain works out to 200 per cent (a gain of £20,000 on your initial investment of £10,000).

WARNING

Buying on margin is an example of using leverage to maximise your gain when prices rise. *Leverage* is simply using borrowed money when you make an asset purchase in order to increase your potential profit. This type of leverage is great in a favourable (bull) market, but it works against you in an unfavourable (bear) market. Say that a £100,000 house you purchase with a £90,000 mortgage falls in value to £80,000 (and property values can decrease during economic hard times). Your outstanding debt of £90,000 exceeds the value of the property. Because you owe more than you own, you're left with a negative net worth. We don't recommend inexperience investors to borrowing to buy shares, and although you may use other debt to fund your investments, reputable brokers caution against it.

Examining marginal outcomes

Suppose that you think that the share for the company Mergatroid PLC, currently at £40 per share, will go up in value. You want to buy 100 shares, but you have only £2,000. What can you do? If you're intent on buying 100 shares (versus simply buying the 50 shares that you have cash for), you can borrow the additional £2,000 from your bank. If you do that, what are the potential outcomes?

If the share price goes up

This outcome is obviously best for you. If Mergatroid goes to £50 per share, your investment is worth £5,000, and your outstanding loan is £2,000. If you sell, the total proceeds pay off the loan and leave you with £3,000. Because your initial investment was £2,000, your profit is a solid 50 per cent because ultimately your £2,000 principal amount generated a £1,000 profit. (For the sake of this example, we leave out any charges, such as commissions and interest paid on the loan.)

Leverage, when used properly, is profitable. However, it's still debt, so understand that you must pay it off eventually, regardless of the share's performance.

If the share price fails to rise

If the share goes nowhere, you still have to pay interest on the loan. If the share pays dividends, this money can offset some of the cost of the loan. In other words, dividends can help you pay off what you've borrowed from the bank.

Having the share neither rise nor fall may seem like a neutral situation, but you pay interest on your loan with each passing day. For conservative investors who invest in shares with high dividends, borrowing to buy shares may appear to make more sense because the dividend can pay off the interest. But the dividend may not be enough to cover all the interest and the point of investing is to get the income (the dividend), not shell it out on interest.

The big problem with borrowing to buy shares becomes apparent when the share price goes down. What if Mergatroid goes to £38 per share? The market value of 100 shares is then £3,800, but your equity shrinks to only £1,800 because you have to pay off your £2,000 loan. You're not exactly looking at a disaster at this point, but you'd better be careful because the loan exceeds 50 per cent of your share investment. If it goes any lower, you'd be considering selling. In fact, you'd probably have a stop-loss (see the section, 'Stop orders (also known as stop-loss orders)', earlier in this chapter) set at £45 or £40. Your broker would be selling your shares to cut your losses and you'd be left with a £2,000 loan to repay. See the next section for information about appropriate debt to equity ratios.

Contracts for difference (CFDs)

One area of stockbroking where trading shares on margin is often encouraged is in *contracts for difference* (CFDs). A CFD is a contract between two parties (you and your stockbroker, for example) to exchange the difference between the opening and closing price of a share, an index, a fund or just about anything that can be traded on a market. You can specify when the contract starts and ends and you never actually own the underlying investment you are (really) gambling on.

Some stockbrokers allow you to trade in CFDs with only 10 per cent of your investment paid upfront. However, you can lose much more than your original investment and may have to pay up at short notice. All reputable stockbrokers should warn you that trading in CFDs in this way isn't an endeavour for novice investors.

With CFDs, you're predicting whether a share price or other tradable investment will go up (*go long*) or go down (*go short*). If you get it right you make a profit, if you get it wrong you can make substantial losses.

Say you wanted to buy a CFD for a rise in the price of Mergatroid, which is currently at £10 a share. You buy 1,000 shares at £10, paying just 10 per cent (£1,000) upfront to give you a £10,000 position. Then Mergatroid announces a big deal that day and the shares jump to £50. Your position is now worth £50,000. You are quick to close the contract, selling at £50. You've made £40,000 in a day – and you only had to put down £1,000 upfront (plus a bit of commission on the purchase and sale). Sounds fab – so why isn't everyone doing it?

Imagine that you thought that Mergatroid shares were expensive at £10 each and due for a correction. You buy a CFD for a fall in the share price (1,000 shares at £10 each, paying 10 per cent, £1,000, upfront) and go on holiday for a couple of days. When Mergatroid announces its big deal and the shares jump to £50 you're whale watching in the Outer Hebrides and even your broker can't get hold of you on your mobile. The next day the shares climb again as the government announces restrictions that hit Mergatroid's competitors. The shares are £100 when you eventually check in with your (distraught) broker. Your broker insists that you close the contract and cover your losses and you have to sell your contract at £100 a share (100 × 1,000 = £100,000). You need to find £90,000 plus commission to pay off your debt. You also have to pay interest on the margin loan because (remember) you've been speculating with the broker's money. Sounds awful – that's why people aren't doing it.

In the UK, CFDs now account for more than 20 per cent of trading on the London Stock Exchange. You can typically trade CFDs in most larger UK companies as well as many European and American shares. You can also buy CFDs for the world's major indexes (refer to Chapter 5 for more on indexes).

Trading on margin, as you can see, can escalate your profits on the up side but magnify your losses on the down side. If your share plummets drastically, or your CFD heads in the wrong direction, you can end up with a margin loan that exceeds the market value of the share you used the loan to purchase.

Borrowing to buy shares isn't a good idea. But if you do, whether on margin or with other loans, use a disciplined approach. Be extra careful when using leverage, such as a margin loan, because it can backfire. Keep the following points in mind:

>> **Have ample reserves of cash or other liquid assets in your account.** Try not to invest more than you can actually afford to pay out.

>> **If you're a beginner, you shouldn't be borrowing to buy shares at all. If you do, make sure that you invest in large companies with a relatively stable price and a good dividend record.** Some people buy income shares that have dividend yields that exceed the interest rate charged on their loans, meaning that the shares end up paying for the loan. Just remember those stop-loss orders.

>> **Constantly monitor your shares.** If the market turns against you, the result is especially painful if you use debt to fund your investment.

>> **Have a payback plan for your debt.** Loans aren't free money; if you borrow to fund your investments, you have to pay interest. Your ultimate goal is to make money, and paying interest eats into your profit.

Going Short and Coming Out Ahead

The vast majority of investors are familiar with buying shares, holding onto them for a while, and hoping their value goes up. This kind of thinking is called *going long*, and investors who go long are considered to be *long on shares*. Going long essentially means that you're bullish and seeking your profit from rising prices. However, astute investors also profit in the market when share prices fall. *Going short* (also called *shorting a share*, *selling short* or *doing a short sale*) on a share is a common technique for profiting from a share price decline. Investors have made big profits during bear markets by going short. A short sale is a bet that a particular share price is going to fall.

Going short isn't generally available on ordinary share trades in the UK, but has become available on specialist trading such as spread betting and contracts for difference (see the section, 'Contracts for difference [CFDs]', earlier in this chapter for more on these).

Your broker has to be sure that you're creditworthy before agreeing to any shorting. Speak to your broker (or check for this information on the broker's website) about limitations on your account regarding going short.

Because going short on shares involves greater risks than going long, we strongly advise new investors to avoid shorting shares until they become more experienced.

Most people easily understand making money by going long. It boils down to 'buy low and sell high'. Piece of cake. Going short means making money by selling high and then buying low. Eh? Thinking in reverse isn't a piece of cake. Although thinking of this share adage in reverse may be challenging, the mechanics of going short are really simple. Consider an example that uses a fictitious company called DOA PLC. As a share, DOA (£5 per share) is looking pretty sickly. It has lots of debt and plummeting sales and earnings, and the news is out that DOA's industry is facing hard times for the foreseeable future. This situation describes a share that's an ideal candidate for shorting. The future may be bleak for DOA, but promising for savvy investors.

You must understand brokerage rules before you conduct short selling. The broker must approve you for it (see Chapter 7 for information on working with brokers), and you must meet the minimum collateral requirement, which is typically an agreed percentage of the shorted share's market value. If the share generates dividends, those dividends are paid to the owner of the share, not to the person who's borrowing it to go short. (See the next section, 'Setting up a short sale', to see how this technique works.) Check with your broker for complete details and review the resources in Appendix A.

Setting up a short sale

This section explains how to go short. Say that you believe that DOA is the right share to short – you're pretty sure that its price is going to fall. With DOA at £5, you instruct your broker to 'go short 100 shares on DOA'. (This amount doesn't have to be 100 shares; we're just using that as an example.) Now, here's what happens next:

1. **Your broker borrows 100 shares of DOA, from their own account or from another client or broker.**

   That's right. The share can be borrowed from a client, no permission necessary. The broker guarantees the transaction, and the client, the owner of the share, never has to be informed about it, because they never lose legal and beneficial rights to the share. You borrow 100 shares, and you return 100 shares when it's time to complete the transaction.

2. Your broker then sells the share and puts the money in your account.

Your account is credited with £500 (100 shares at £5) in cash – the money gained from selling the borrowed share. This cash acts like a loan on which you're going to have to pay interest.

3. You buy the share back and return it to its rightful owner.

When it's time to close the transaction (you want to close it, or the owner of the shares wants to sell them so you have to give them back), you must return the number of shares you borrowed (in this case, 100 shares). If you buy back the 100 shares at £4 per share (remember that you shorted this particular share because you were sure that its price was going to fall) and these 100 shares are returned to their owner, you make a £100 profit. (To keep the example tidy, we don't include brokerage commissions.)

Oops! Going short when prices grow taller

You guessed it: the wonderful profitability of selling short has a flip side. Presume that you were wrong about DOA and that the share price rises from the ashes as it goes from £5 to £8.70. Now what? You still have to return the 100 shares you borrowed. With the share's price at £8.70, that means that you have to buy the shares for £870 (100 shares at the new, higher price of £8.70). Ouch! How do you pay for it? Well, you have that original £500 in your account from when you initially went short on the share. But where do you get the other £370 (£870 less the original £500)? You guessed it – your pocket! You have to cough up the difference. If the share continues to rise, that's a lot of coughing.

How much money do you lose if the share goes to £10 or more? A sack full! As a matter of fact, there's no limit to how much you can lose. That's why going short can be riskier than going long. With going long, the most you can lose is 100 per cent of your money. With going short, you can lose more than 100 per cent of the money you invest. Whoops!

Because the potential for loss is unlimited when you short a share, we suggest that you use a stop order (also called a *buy-stop order*) to minimise the damage. Better yet, make it a GTC order, which we discuss in the section 'Good-till-cancelled (GTC) order', earlier in this chapter. You can set the stop order at a given price, and if the share hits that price, you buy the share back so that you can return it to its owner before the price rises even higher. You still lose money, but you limit your losses.

Feeling the squeeze

If you go short on a share, remember that, sooner or later, you have to buy that share back so that you can return it to its owner. What happens when a lot of people are short on a particular share and its price starts to rise? All those short sellers are scrambling to buy the shares back so that they can close their transactions before they lose too much money. This mass buying quickens the pace of the share's ascent and puts a squeeze (called a *short squeeze*) on the investors who had been shorting the share.

In the section 'Going Short and Coming Out Ahead', earlier in this chapter, we explain that your broker can borrow shares from another client so that you can go short on it. What happens when that client wants to sell the shares in his account – the shares that you borrowed and so are no longer in the account? When that happens, your broker asks you to return the borrowed shares. That's when you feel the squeeze – you have to buy the shares back at the current price. Contracts for difference (see the section on these earlier in this chapter) give you more flexibility to decide when to sell if you're going short.

REMEMBER

Going short can be a great manoeuvre in a declining (bear) market, but it can be brutal if the share price goes up. If you're a beginner, stay away from short selling until you have enough experience (and money) to risk it.

Understanding Leveraged Shares

This section is about another relatively recent form of investing that involves leverage, shares, indices and going long and short. The *leveraged share* first emerged in the US a few years back and is a simple variation on the index tracking fund or exchange traded fund (ETF) that we discuss in Chapter 21.

The first versions of leveraged shares emerged a few years ago based on an index such as the S&P 500. Basically, these leveraged shares came with two distinguishing features:

>> **They tracked the direction of an index on a daily basis long and short.**
The long version of a leveraged share would make money on the upside, for example, if the index went up in value. The short version made money in the reverse direction, for example if the index was falling in value.

>> **Crucially, the returns from tracking an index could be leveraged up, or boosted, by a significant multiple.** Early versions were just one time the daily returns, but very quickly that leverage moved up to three and then five times the daily returns.

To give an example, say the S&P 500, the US benchmark equity index, went up 5 per cent in one day, a three times long/bull leveraged share would rise – you guessed it – 15 per cent. If you were unlucky enough to hold the bearish/short version, it would go down 15 per cent in one day. Over time these leveraged shares expanded beyond main indices into specialist sub sectors – say biotech or energy – and then into tracking major commodity spot prices. In recent years single stock leveraged shares have also emerged on to the market – so you can go three times long or short a major blue-chip stock like Barclays Bank for instance.

You may be thinking that what we're describing looks a lot like other options and CFD-based products, but with one difference: Your loss is limited to your initial investment. You'd be right. In other words, if the leveraged share goes to zero, all you lose is your original investment. You won't be called out and forced to provide extra funding for the trade, as you might with CFDs. Another useful feature is that these leveraged shares – also sometimes called *short and leveraged trackers* – can be traded in real time on exchanges like other shares and ETFs. Leveraged shares are exchange traded products to be precise, and you can trade in them through any major online broking platform.

REMEMBER

Leveraged shares are always based on underlying moves in the share on a daily basis – for instance, your share moves in response to the daily price of the underlying security or index. That point is extremely important because you're trading the daily leveraged returns. Over a few weeks, lots of up and down movement in the underlying security and index can play havoc with the pricing of the leveraged share. Our general advice is not to stay invested in a leveraged share for many weeks and months at end. All that daily variation or volatility can eat into your returns for the share.

TIP

Leveraged shares are a useful way of hedging returns in a diversified portfolio. If, for instance, you have a portfolio jam-packed full of risky high growth tech stocks, you may want to insure yourself against a sharp, short-term fall in prices. These leveraged shares can be very useful over short periods.

Chapter **18**

Getting a Handle on DRIPs and PCA ... ASAP

What happens if we said to you that there was a simple, cheap way of making sure you bought shares in the companies you loved? And what's even better is that you don't even necessarily have to have a broker account, although in reality it's probably best you do have an account anyway.

The concept here is something of a hidden secret in the world of finance – a mechanism that allows for the direct purchase of shares in companies via reinvestment plans. They're offered by many of the biggest companies, and these share purchases are funded by the regular payment of dividends. These schemes are a great way of slowly, steadily building your wealth over many years. They go by a dreadful acronym called a DRIP – dividend reinvestment plans.

We also investigate another dreadful sounding acronym, PCA or pound cost averaging. As awful as it sounds, it's a brilliant way to make sure that you don't overpay for an investment and keep investing at a steady pace. And that's really the not-so-subtle message of this whole chapter. Simple, methodical ideas can make big profits in the long term as we explain now.

Dipping into DRIPs

A *dividend reinvestment plans (DRIP)* is a programme that a company may offer to allow investors to easily accumulate more of its shares. Sometimes the company doesn't charge commission, but increasingly companies are asking their registrars (who are also large stockbrokers) to handle the DRIPs, and the brokers do charge (small) dealing fees.

REMEMBER

To qualify for the DRIP, you must be on the shareholders' register with the company's registrar. A *shareholders' register* is simply the database that the company uses to track every single outstanding share and the owner of those shares. The *registrar* is the person (usually a company) responsible for maintaining the database. Whenever shares are bought or sold, the registrar must implement the change and update the records on share ownership. In the past, the broker would have issued a share certificate in your name after you owned the shares. Paper share certificates are dying out, and many investors hold their shares in nominee accounts (see Chapter 7 for more on different types of accounts). Having your name on a share certificate is still the most common way to get your name on the register, but you should still be able to qualify for the DRIP if your shares are held in a nominee account.

To be in a DRIP, here are the requirements:

>> You must already be a shareholder for that particular company.

>> You must already have a dividend reinvestment plan set up.

>> The shares must be paying dividends. (You had to guess this one!)

The following sections delve deeper in DRIPs and what you need to know before investing.

Getting a clue about compounding

Dividends are reinvested, offering a form of *compounding* for the small investor. Dividends buy more of the shares, in turn generating more dividends. Sometimes the dividends generated don't buy entire shares, so they are carried over in the DRIP account until you have enough to buy whole shares.

Say, for example, that you own 20 shares of Fraction PLC at £10 per share for a total value of £200. Fraction's annual dividend is £1, and it pays this dividend as a quarterly dividend of 25 pence every three months. What happens if you have a DRIP with Fraction? The 20 shares generate a £5 dividend payout in the first quarter, and this amount is applied to the shares purchase as soon as the amount is credited to the DRIP account. If you presume for this example that the shares' price hasn't changed, the dividend payout wasn't enough to buy an entire share, so it stays credited to the account until the next payment.

Say that, in the preceding example, three months have passed and that you have acquired no other shares since your previous dividend payout. Fraction issues another quarterly dividend for 25 pence per share. Now what?

>> The original 20 shares of Fraction PLC generate a £5 dividend payout.

>> You have £5 credited to your DRIP account from the previous dividend.

>> The two dividend payouts are added together to make £10 and this amount is used to buy one new share in Fraction PLC. This means you now have 21 shares and get dividends from 21 shares at the next dividend payout.

REMEMBER

To illustrate our point, the preceding example uses a price that doesn't fluctuate. Shares in a DRIP act like any other shares; the price changes constantly. Every time the DRIP makes a share purchase, whether this purchase is monthly or quarterly, the purchase price is probably going to change each time.

Checking out the cost advantages

Despite the fact that more and more DRIPs are charging service fees, DRIPs are still an economical way to invest, especially for small investors. The big savings come from not paying commissions. Although many DRIPs do have charges, they tend to be relatively small (but do keep track of them because the costs can add up).

Some DRIPs actually offer a discount of between 2 and 5 per cent (a few are higher) when buying shares through the plan. Still others offer special programmes and discounts on the company's products and services. Some companies offer the service of debiting your current account or salary to invest in the DRIP. One company offered its shareholders significant discounts for its restaurant subsidiary. In any case, ask the plan administrator because any plus is . . . well . . . a plus.

Weighing the pros and the cons

When you're in a DRIP, you reap all the benefits of shares investing (along with the risks and responsibilities). You get an annual report, and you qualify for share splits, dividend increases and so on.

A DRIP has two primary advantages:

>> **Compounding:** The dividends get reinvested and give you the opportunity to buy more shares.

>> **Optional cash purchases:** Some DRIPs give participants the ability to invest through the plan to purchase more shares, occasionally with no commission.

Before you start to salivate over all the goodies that come with DRIPs, be clear-eyed about some of the negative aspects to them as well. Negative aspects include the following:

>> You need to get that first share. But you knew that.

>> Even small fees cut into your profits.

>> Many DRIPs may not be eligible to be wrapped in tax-efficient savings, such as Individual Savings Accounts (ISAs). (See Chapter 20 for more information on ISAs.)

>> DRIPs are designed for long-term investing. Although getting in and out of the plan is easy, the transactions may take weeks to process because share purchases and sales are typically done all at once on a certain day during the month (or quarter).

>> Read the prospectus to avoid nasty surprises. You may not consider doing so a negative point, but for some people, reading a prospectus is not unlike giving blood by using leeches. Even if that is your opinion, you need to read the prospectus to avoid any surprises, such as hidden fees or unreasonable terms.

>> Understand the tax issues and don't land yourself with an unexpected tax bill. There, you see? We knew that we'd ruin it for you. The point is that you should understand the tax consequences. Chapter 20 goes into greater detail. Just know that dividends, whether or not they occur in a DRIP, are usually taxable (unless the DRIP is in an ISA, which is a different matter).

>> Perhaps the biggest headache of DRIPs is the need to keep good records. Keep all your statements together and use a good spreadsheet or accounting program if you plan on doing a lot of DRIP investing. These records become especially important at self-assessment time, when you have to report any subsequent gains or losses from share sales. Because capital gains tax can be complicated as you sort out short term versus long term, DRIP calculations can be a nightmare without good record-keeping.

DRIPs offer a great way to accumulate a large shareholding over an extended period of time. However, think about what you can do with these shares. Say that you accumulate 110 company shares, valued at £50 per share, in your DRIP. You can, for example, take out £5,000 worth of shares (100 shares at £50 per share) and place those 100 shares in your brokerage account. The remaining 10 shares can stay in your account to keep the DRIP and continue with dividend reinvestment to keep your wealth growing. Why remove those shares?

All things being equal, you're better off keeping the shares in the DRIP, but what if you have £2,500 in credit card debt and don't have extra cash to pay off that debt? Brokerage accounts still have plenty of advantages, such as, in this example, the use of margin (a topic we discuss in detail in Chapter 17). One way to reduce your debt would be to borrow against the £5,000 as a margin loan and use this amount, for example, to pay off £2,500 worth of credit card debt. Replacing unsecured debt (credit card debt that may be charging 15 per cent, 18 per cent, or more) with secured debt can save you money. However, think about moving your credit card debt to a cheaper card – some charge 0 per cent interest for up to a year on balance transfers. Or, if you're getting less than 15 per cent on your investment but paying that in interest, it makes sense to pay off the debt rather than keep your money invested.

The One-Two Punch: Pound Cost Averaging and DRIPs

Pound cost averaging (PCA) is a splendid technique for buying shares and lowering your cost for doing so. The example illustrated in Table 18-1 shows that investors in Acme Lifts Ltd (AL) don't find seeing a total cost that reflects a discount off the market value uncommon. PCA works especially well with DRIPs.

TABLE 18-1   **Pound Cost Averaging (AL)**

Month	Investment Amount (£)	Purchase Price (pence)	Shares Bought	Accumulated Shares
1	25	250	10	10
2	25	200	12	22
3	25	175	14	36
4	25	150	16	52
5	25	175	14	66
6	25	200	13	79
Totals	150	N/A	79	79

REMEMBER

PCA is a simple method for acquiring shares. It rests on the idea that you invest a fixed amount of money at regular intervals (monthly, usually) over a long period of time in that particular share. Because a fixed amount (say, £50 per month) is going into a fluctuating investment, you end up buying less of that investment when it goes up in price and more of it when it goes down in price. As Table 18-1 illustrates, your average cost per share is usually lower than if you buy all the shares at once.

PCA is best presented with an example. Presume that you decide to get into the DRIP of Acme Lifts Ltd (AL). On your first day in the DRIP, AL's shares are at £2.50, and the plan allows you to invest a minimum of £25 through its optional cash purchase programme. You decide to invest £25 per month and assess how well (hopefully) you're doing six months from now. Table 18-1 shows how this technique works. (*Note:* Cash left over after purchasing shares each month is added to the next month's investment.)

TIP

To assess the wisdom of your decision to invest in the DRIP, ask yourself questions:

>> **How much did you invest over the entire six months?**

Your total investment is £150. So far, so good.

>> **What is the first share price for AL, and what is the last share price?**

The first share price is £2.50, but the last share price is £2.

>> **What is the market value of your investment at the end of six months?**

You can easily calculate the value of your investment. Just multiply the number of shares you now own (79 shares) by the most recent share price (£2). The total value of your investment is £158. (And you have about 66 pence left in your account for next month.)

>> **What is the average share price you bought at?**

The average share price is also easy to calculate. Take the total amount of your purchases (£150) and divide it by the number of shares that you acquired (79 shares). Your average cost per share price becomes £1.89.

>> **Is that your final answer?** (Do your best Jeremy Clarkson voice from *Who Wants to Be a Millionaire*.)

Yes, these are my final answers (no need to ask the audience!), but you should take note of the following:

- Even though the last share price (£2) is lower than the original share price (£2.50), your total investment's market value is still higher than your purchase amount (£158 compared to £150)! How can that be? PCA is the culprit here. Your disciplined approach by using PCA was able to overcome the fluctuations in the shares' price to help you gain more shares at the lower prices of £1.75 and £1.50.

- Your average cost per share is only £1.89. The PCA method helps you buy more shares at a lower cost, which ultimately helped you make money when the share price made a modest rebound.

- PCA helps you invest with small sums, all the while helping you smooth out the volatility in share prices. This process helps you make more money in your wealth-building programme over the long haul. Can you visualise that retirement hammock yet?

The bottom line for long-term investors is that PCA is a solid investing technique and DRIPs are a great share investment vehicle for building wealth.

WARNING

PCA is a fantastic technique in a bull market and an okay technique in a flat or sideways market, but you probably shouldn't consider it during bear markets because the shares you're buying are going down in price and the market value can easily be lower than your total investment. If you plan on holding onto the shares long term, then simply cease your PCA approach until times improve for the shares (and their industry and the economy in general). Discover more about bear markets in Chapter 15.

Chapter **19**

Looking at What the Insiders Do: Corporate Capers

magine that you're boarding a cruise ship, ready to enjoy a hard-earned holiday. As you merrily walk up the plank, you notice that the ship's captain and crew are charging out of the vessel, flailing their arms, and screaming at the top of their lungs – some are even jumping into the water below. Quiz: Would you get on that ship? You get double credit if you can also explain why (or why not). What does this scenario have to do with investing in shares? Plenty, actually. The behaviour of the people running the boat gives you important clues about the near-term prospects for the boat. Similarly, the actions of company insiders can provide important clues regarding the near-term prospects for their company.

Company *insiders* are individuals who are key managers or investors in the company. Insiders may be the chairperson of the company, the treasurer or another managing officer. An insider can be someone who owns a large stake in the company or someone on the board of directors. In any case, insiders usually have a bird's-eye view of what's going on with the company. They have a good idea of how well (or how poorly) the company is doing.

REMEMBER

Keep tabs on what insiders are doing, because their buy/sell transactions do have a strong correlation to the near-term movement of their company's shares. However, don't buy or sell shares only because you heard that an insider did so. Use the information on insider trading to confirm your own good sense in buying or selling shares. Insider trading sometimes can be a great precursor to a significant move that you can profit from if you know what to look for. Many shrewd investors have made their profits (or avoided losses) by tracking the activity of the insiders.

Tracking Insider Trading

Fortunately, we live in an age of disclosure. Any trading by insiders has to be reported to the UK Listing Authority (UKLA), which is now part of the Financial Conduct Authority (FCA). Insiders who buy or sell shares must also file reports that document their trading activity with a *regulated news service* (RNS), which makes key corporate documents available to the public. A number of other similar services publish these documents, too – companies can choose which one to use. You have to subscribe to most of the services available if you want to see these announcements as soon as they're made.

Some of the most useful documents you can view on RNS include the following:

» **Transactions in shares:** When companies buy or sell their own shares they have to inform the various stock exchanges on which their shares are listed. Companies do this by issuing a *transaction in shares* announcement. This announcement gives the details of the transaction, including how many shares were bought and at what price. It also states the total shareholding following the transaction.

» **Director/PDMR shareholding:** This is the document that shows the insider's activity. It has to be published whenever a director or a 'person discharging managerial responsibilities' – a PDMR – buys or sells company shares. It gives the name of the person involved, the date and type of transaction, the number of shares involved and the price that was paid for them. Any purchase or sale must be reported as soon as possible and no later than the end of the business day on which the insider informed the company of the transaction. Insiders are required to inform their companies of transactions within four days.

- **Major interest in shares:** These statements are published when a large shareholding changes. Changes involving 3 per cent or more of the company's shares need to be notified. So if a fund manager buys or sells 3 per cent or more of a company's shares, the company has to make an announcement about it.

- **Grant of options:** Most company directors are given shares in the company as part of a long-term incentive plan. In most cases, the bonus scheme is set up as a series of options to buy shares at a certain fixed price. So a director joining a company with shares priced at £1 each could be given 100,000 options at 90 pence which he can exercise after three years. The directors have an interest in working to push the share price higher so that when they do take up their options to buy at 90 pence, they're buying shares that are worth much more. If the shares climb to £1.90, they pocket £100,000. When directors are given options or exercise them, the company has to publish the details.

TIP

Companies are required to make public the documents that track their trading activity. The LSE's website offers limited access to these documents, but for greater access, check out www.uk-wire.com, which offers free access to all RNS announcements.

THE SARBANES–OXLEY ACT

Often, a market that reaches a mania stage sees abuse reach extreme levels, too. Abuse by insiders is a good example. In the stock market mania of 1997–2000, this abuse wasn't just limited to insider buying and selling of shares; it also covered the related abuse of accounting fraud. Because insiders were primarily the top management, when they deceived investors about the financial conditions of the company they subsequently were able to increase the perceived value of the company's shares. The shares could then be sold at a price that was higher than market value.

In the US, Congress took notice of these activities and, in 2002, passed the Sarbanes-Oxley Act (SOX). Congress designed this Act to protect investors from fraudulent accounting activities by corporations. SOX established a public accounting oversight board and also tightened the rules on corporate financial reporting. Its reach is not restricted to the US as any UK company with listings in the US must comply. And similar accounting governance, at least for banks and financial companies, have already arrived in Europe and the UK with the latest big set of rules contained within something called Basel III which attempt to manage risk for the big international banks.

TECHNICAL STUFF

The part of a company that looks after all the regulatory stuff is called *investor relations* (IR). The financial governance of a company is tightly controlled by the IR department. Well-run companies never issue any figures that have not first been agreed with their IR director. And the best run companies now have their own IR websites to explain the financial figures that have been made public to shareholders. Even if the investor relations department doesn't have a website of its own, you can usually find a telephone number for it on the company's main website or in the annual report. You can always try phoning if you don't understand the figures.

Looking at Insider Transactions

The classic phrase 'Actions speak louder than words' was probably coined for insider trading. Insiders are in the know, and keeping a watchful eye on their transactions – both buying and selling their company's shares – can provide you with useful investing information. Analysing insider buying versus insider selling can be as different as day and night. Insider buying is simple, while insider selling can be complicated. In the following sections, we present both sides of insider trading.

Getting info from insider buying

Insider buying is usually an unambiguous signal about how an insider feels about the company. After all, the primary reason that all investors buy shares is that they expect them to do well. If one insider is buying shares, that's generally not a monumental event. But if several or more insiders are buying, those purchases should certainly catch your attention.

REMEMBER

Insider buying is generally a positive omen and beneficial for the share's price. Also, when insiders buy shares, fewer shares are available to the public. If the investing public meets this decreased supply with increased demand, then the share price rises. Keep these factors in mind when analysing insider buying:

>> **Identify who's buying the share.** The CEO is buying 5,000 shares. Is that reason enough for you to jump in? Maybe. After all, the CEO certainly knows how well the company is doing. But what if that CEO is new to the job? What if before this purchase the CEO had no shares in the company at all? Maybe the shares are part of the employment package.

REMEMBER

The fact that a new company executive is making a first share purchase isn't as strong a signal urging you to buy as the fact that a long-time CEO is doubling holdings. Also, if large numbers of insiders are buying, that sends a stronger signal than if a single insider is buying.

» **See how much is being bought.** Say the CEO bought 5,000 shares, which is a lot of shares no matter how you count it. But is it enough for you to base an investment decision on? Maybe, but a closer look may reveal more. If the CEO already owned 1 million shares at the time of the purchase, then buying 5,000 additional shares wouldn't be such an exciting indicator of a pending share rise. In this case, 5,000 shares is a small incremental move and doesn't offer much to get excited about.

However, what if this particular insider has owned only 5,000 shares for the past three years and is now buying 1 million shares? Now that should arouse your interest! Usually, a massive purchase tells you that that particular insider has strong feelings about the company's prospects and is hugely increasing their share ownership. Still, a purchase of 1 million shares by the CEO isn't as strong a signal as ten insiders buying 100,000 shares each. Again, if only one person is buying, that may or may not be a strong indication of an impending rise. However, if lots of people are buying, consider it a fantastic indication.

An insider purchase of any kind is a positive sign. But the sign is always more significant when a greater number of insiders are making purchases. 'The more the merrier!' is a good rule for judging insider buying. All these individuals have their own, unique perspectives on the company and its prospects for the foreseeable future. Mass buying indicates mass optimism for the company's future. If the treasurer, the chairperson, the sales director and several other key players are putting their wealth on the line and investing it in a company that they know intimately, that's a good sign for your share investment as well.

» **Insiders are acting on information that's already out there.** Cashing in on 'insider information' by directors, and other people in the know, is illegal. Strict rules exist about when directors can and can't trade in their company's shares. If directors are buying, or selling, their decision is based on information that has already been made public. You just have to look for it.

Picking up tips from insider selling

Insider buying bodes well for the company or is a neutral event at worst. Insider share buying is rarely a negative event. But how about insider selling? When an insider sells shares, the event can be neutral or negative. Insider selling is usually a little tougher to figure out because insiders may have many different motivations to sell shares that have nothing to do with the company's future prospects.

(See the next paragraph for a list of common reasons.) Just because the chairperson of the company is selling 5,000 shares from a personal portfolio, that doesn't necessarily mean that you should sell, too.

REMEMBER

Insiders may sell their shares for a number of reasons: they may think that the company won't be doing well in the near future – a negative sign for you – or they may simply need the money for a variety of personal reasons that have nothing to do with the company's potential. Some typical reasons why insiders may sell shares include the following:

>> **To diversify their holdings:** If an insider's portfolio is heavily weighted with one company's shares, a financial advisor may suggest balancing the portfolio by selling some of that company's shares and purchasing other securities.

>> **To finance personal emergencies:** Sometimes an insider needs money for medical, legal or family reasons.

>> **To buy a home or make another major purchase:** An insider may need the money to make a deposit on a house or perhaps to buy something outright without having to take out a loan.

How do you find out about the details regarding insider share selling? Although insiders must report their pertinent share sales and purchases to the UKLA, the information isn't always revealing. As a general rule, consider the following questions when analysing insider selling:

>> **How many insiders are selling?** If only one insider is selling, that single transaction doesn't give you enough information to act on. However, if many insiders are selling, you should see a red flag. Check out any news or information that's currently available. Websites such as www.ft.com and www.bloomberg.com can help you get that information (along with other sources in Appendix A).

>> **Are the sales showing a pattern of unusual activity?** If one insider sold shares last month, that sale alone isn't that significant an event. However, if ten insiders have each made multiple sales in the past few months, those sales are cause for concern. See whether any new developments at the company are potentially negative. If massive insider selling has recently occurred and you don't know why, consider putting a stop-loss order on your shares immediately. (Chapter 17 covers stop-loss orders.)

>> **How many shares are being sold?** If a CEO sells 5,000 shares but still retains 100,000 shares, that's not a big deal. But if the CEO sells all or most of their holdings, that's a possible negative. Check to see whether other company executives have also sold shares.

>> **Do outside events or analyst reports seem coincidental with the sale of the share?** Sometimes, an influential analyst may issue a report warning about a company's prospects. If the company's management pooh-poohs the report but most of them are bailing out anyway (selling their shares), you may want to do the same.

REMEMBER

Some insider dealing is illegal. Insiders who know damaging information is coming before it's in the public domain and sell their shares in advance of the information being made public can expect a call from the Serious Fraud Office (SFO).

Similarly, if the company's management issues positive public statements or reports that are contradictory to their own behaviour (they're selling their shareholdings), the FCA may investigate to see whether the company is doing anything that may require a penalty. The FCA regularly tracks insider sales.

Observing Corporate Share Buybacks

When you read the financial pages or watch the financial shows on television, you sometimes hear that a company is buying its own shares. The announcement may be something like, 'SuperQuids PLC has announced that it is spending £2 billion to buy back its own shares'. Why would a company do that, and what does that mean for you if you own the share or are considering buying it?

When companies buy back their own shares, they're generally indicating that they believe their shares are undervalued and that they have the potential to rise. If a company shows strong fundamentals (for example, good financial condition and increasing sales and earnings) and is buying more of its own shares, investigate – these shares may make a great addition to your portfolio.

REMEMBER

Just because a company announces a share buyback doesn't always mean that one will happen. The announcement itself is meant to stir interest in the shares and cause the price to rise. The share buyback may be only an opportunity for insiders to sell shares, or it may be needed for executive compensation – recruiting and retaining competent management is a positive use of money.

WARNING

If you see that a company is buying back its shares while most of the insiders are selling their personal shares, this is not a good sign. It may not necessarily be a bad sign, but it is not a positive sign. Play it safe and invest elsewhere.

The following sections present common reasons why a company may buy back its shares from investors as well as ideas on the negative effects of share buybacks.

Boosting earnings per share

By simply buying back its own shares from shareholders, a company can increase its earnings per share (refer back to Chapter 10 and see Appendix B for more on earnings per share) without actually earning extra money. Sound like a magician's trick? Well, yes, kind of. A corporate share buyback is a financial sleight of hand that investors should be aware of. Here's how it works: Nomore Earnings Ltd (NEL) has 10 million shares outstanding, and is expected to net earnings of £10 million for the fourth quarter. NEL's earnings per share (EPS) would be £1 per share. So far, so good. But what happens if NEL buys 2 million of its own shares? Total shares outstanding shrink to 8 million. The new EPS becomes £1.25 – the share buyback artificially boosts the earnings per share by 25 per cent!

REMEMBER

The important point to remember about share buybacks is that actual company earnings don't change – no fundamental changes occur in company management or operations – so the increase in EPS can be misleading. But the marketplace can be obsessive about earnings, and because earnings are the lifeblood of any company, an earnings boost, even if cosmetic, can also boost the share price.

If you watch a company's price-to-earnings (P/E) ratio (refer to Chapter 10), you know that increased earnings usually mean an eventual increase in the share price. Additionally, a share buyback affects supply and demand. With fewer available shares in the market, demand necessarily sends the share price upward.

REMEMBER

Whenever a company makes a major purchase, such as buying back its own shares, think about how the company is paying for it and whether it seems like a good use of the company's purchasing power. In general, companies buy their shares for the same reasons that any investor buys shares – they believe that the share is a good investment and will appreciate in time. Companies generally pay for a share buyback in one of two ways: funds from operations or borrowed money. Both methods have a downside. For more details, see the section 'Exploring the downside of buybacks', later in this chapter.

Beating back a takeover bid

Suppose that you read in the financial pages that Company X is attempting a hostile takeover of Company Z. A hostile takeover doesn't mean that Company X sent storm troopers armed with pepper spray to Company Z's headquarters to trounce its management. All a *hostile takeover* means is that X wants to buy enough shares of Z to effectively control Z (and Z is unhappy about being owned or controlled by X). Because the buying and selling of shares is done in a public market or exchange, companies can buy each other's shares. Sometimes the target company prefers not to be acquired; in which case it may buy back some of its own shares to give it a measure of protection against unwanted moves by interested companies.

In some cases, the company attempting the takeover already owns some of the target company's shares. In this case, the targeted company may offer to buy those shares back from the aggressor at a premium to thwart the takeover bid.

REMEMBER

Takeover concerns generally attract the investing public's interest, driving the share price upward and benefiting current shareholders.

Exploring the downside of buybacks

As beneficial as share buybacks can be, they have to be paid for, and this expense has consequences. If a company pays for the shares with funds from operations, it may have a negative effect on the company's ability to finance current and prospective operations. When a company uses funds from operations for the share buyback, less money is available for other activities, such as upgrading technology or research and development. In general, any misuse of money, such as using debt to buy back shares, affects a company's ability to grow its sales and earnings – two measures that need to maintain upward mobility in order to keep share prices rising.

A company faces even greater dangers when it uses debt to finance a share buyback. If the company uses borrowed funds, it has less borrowing power for other uses (such as upgrading technology or making other improvements). In addition, the company has to pay back the borrowed funds with interest, thus lowering earnings figures.

Say that NEL (a fictional company introduced in the section 'Boosting earnings per share', earlier in this chapter) typically pays an annual dividend of 25 pence per share and wants to buy back shares with borrowed money at a 9 per cent interest rate. If NEL buys back 2 million shares, it won't have to pay out £500,000 in dividends. That's money saved. However, NEL is going to have to pay interest on the £20 million it borrowed to buy back the shares over that same time frame to the tune of £1,800,000 (9 per cent of £20,000,000). The net result from this rudimentary example is that NEL sees an outflow of £1,300,000 (the difference between the interest paid out and the dividends savings). Using debt to finance a share buyback needs to make economic sense – it needs to strengthen the company's financial position. Perhaps NEL could have used the share buyback money for a better purpose, such as modernising equipment or paying for a new marketing campaign. Because debt interest ultimately decreases earnings, companies must be careful when using debt to buy back their shares.

Staging a Comeback with Share Scrips

Frequently, management teams decide to do a *share scrip*. A share scrip is the exchange of existing shares for new shares from the same company. Share scrips don't increase or decrease the capitalisation of the company. They just change the number of shares available in the market and the per-share price.

In a typical scenario, a company may announce that it's doing a 2-for-1 share scrip. For example, a company may have 10 million shares outstanding, with a market price of £40 each. In a 2-for-1 scrip, the company then has 20 million shares (the share total doubles), but the market price is adjusted to £20 (the share price is halved). Companies do other scrips, such as a 3-for-2 or 4-for-1, but 2-for-1 is the most common. This is known as a *share split* in the US and is sometimes called a *capitalisation issue* or *bonus issue* in the UK.

Why do companies carry out share scrips? Usually, management believes that the share's price is too high, thus possibly discouraging investors from purchasing it. The share scrip is a strategy to stir interest in the share, and this increased interest frequently results in a rise in the share's price.

Qualifying for a share scrip is similar to qualifying to receive a dividend – you must be listed as a shareholder as of the date of record. (For information on the date of record, see Chapter 6.)

REMEMBER

A share scrip is technically a neutral event because the ultimate market value of the company's shares doesn't change as a result of it. The following sections present the two most basic types of scrips: ordinary and reverse share scrips.

Ordinary share scrips

Ordinary share scrips – when the number of shares increases – are the ones we usually hear about. (For example, a 2-for-1 share scrip doubles the number of shares.) If you own 100 shares of Dublin Ltd (at £60 per share), and the company announces a share scrip, what happens? If you own the shares in certificate form, you receive a new share certificate for 200 shares of Dublin Ltd. Now, before you cheer over how your money just doubled, check the share's new price. Each share is adjusted to a £30 value.

Not all shares are in certificate form. Shares held in a brokerage account are recorded by registrars. Most shares, in fact, are held in nominee accounts. A company only issues share certificates when necessary or when the investor requests it. If you keep the shares in your broker account – called a nominee account – check with your broker for the new share total to make sure that you're credited with the new number of shares after the scrip issue.

REMEMBER

A scrip issue is primarily a neutral event, so why does a company bother to do it? The most common reason is that management believes that the shares are too expensive, so it wants to lower the share price to make individual shares more affordable and therefore more attractive to new investors. Studies have shown that share scrips frequently precede a rise in the share price. Although share scrips are considered a non-event in and of themselves, many share experts see them as bullish signals because of the interest they generate among the investing public.

Reverse share scrips

A *reverse share scrip* or *consolidation* usually occurs when a company's management wants to raise the price of its shares. Just as ordinary scrips can occur when management believes that the price is too expensive, a reverse share scrip means that the company feels that the share's price is too cheap. If a share's price looks too low, that may discourage the interest of individuals or institutional investors (such as mutual funds). Management wants to drum up more interest in the share for the benefit of shareholders (some of whom are probably insiders).

A reverse split can best be explained with an example. TuCheep Ltd (TCL) is selling at 2 pence per share on AIM. At that rock-bottom price, the investing public may ignore it. So TCL announces a 10-for-1 reverse share scrip. Now what? If an existing shareholder had 100 shares at 2 pence each (the old shares), the shareholder now owns 10 shares at 20 pence each.

Technically, a reverse scrip is considered a neutral event. However, just as investors may infer positive expectations from an ordinary share scrip, they may have negative expectations from a reverse scrip, because a reverse scrip tends to occur for negative reasons.

TECHNICAL STUFF

If, in the event of a share scrip, you have an odd number of shares, the company doesn't produce a 'fractional share'. Instead, you get a cheque for the cash equivalent or the company gets the money. For example, if you have 51 shares and the company announces a 2-for-1 reverse scrip, the odds are that they'll give you 25 shares and a cash payout for the odd share (or fractional share). Some companies ask you to donate the money to charity rather than ask for a cheque to be issued.

TIP

Keep good records regarding your share scrips in case you need to calculate capital gains for tax purposes. (See Chapter 20 for more information on tax issues.)

Chapter **20**

Considering Tax Benefits and Liabilities

After conquering the world of making money with shares, now you have another hurdle – keeping your money. Some people may tell you that tax is brutal, complicated and counterproductive. Other people may tell you that taxes are a form of legalised theft, whereas others still say that taxes a necessary evil. And then there are the pessimists. In any case, this chapter shows you how to keep more of the fruits of your hard-earned labour.

Keep in mind that this chapter isn't meant to be comprehensive. For a fuller treatment of personal taxation, refer to the latest edition of *Paying Less Tax For Dummies* by Tony Levene (John Wiley & Sons, Ltd.). However, in this chapter, we cover the most relevant points for share market investors. As a stock market investor, you need to know the tax treatment for dividends and capital gains and losses, along with common tax deductions for investors and some simple tax-reducing strategies.

You must take tax planning seriously because tax can be the single biggest expense during your lifetime. The average taxpayer pays more in tax than for food, clothing and shelter combined!

Paying through the Nose

This section tells you what you need to know about the tax implications you'll face when you start investing in shares. Knowing the basics in advance is a good move as it will matter to your investing strategy. If you're the type of investor who likes to cash in on a profitable share quickly, then realise that you'll probably pay more in tax than if you're more patient. Sometimes the difference can be just a matter of days. What if you're about to sell a share that you've held for 35 months and 28 days? Well, waiting just a few more days could mean less tax, which means more money in your pocket.

Understanding income and capital gains tax

Profit you make from your share investments can be taxed in one of two ways, depending on the type of profit. If you're a taxpayer, if you earn more than your personal tax allowance, you'll either pay income tax or capital gains tax:

>> **Income tax:** For the purposes of tax, dividends are treated as income. All investors who receive UK dividends pay income tax after receiving £2,000 tax free – after that sum, the amount you pay depends on your income tax band. Basic rate taxpayers pay 7.5 percent on dividend income over and above the £2,000 allowance. But if you're a higher rate taxpayer (taking into account your dividend income as well as any other income), you have to pay 32.5 per cent on dividends. On any income between £37,701 and £150,000 has to pay 32.5 per cent. This extra charge is worked out when you complete your tax return (if you pay the additional top tax rate of 45 per cent, you'll have to pay even more – 38.1 per cent!). Two types of investment profits get taxed as ordinary income:

- **Dividends:** When you receive dividends from your shares (either in cash or shares), these dividends get taxed as ordinary income. This is also true if those dividends are in a dividend reinvestment plan. (See Chapter 18 if you want to know more about dividend reinvestment plans, or DRIPs.) If, however, those dividends occur in a tax-sheltered savings scheme, such as an ISA, then they're exempt from tax for as long as they're in the scheme. We cover retirement plans in the section 'Taking Advantage of Tax Advantages', later in this chapter. At the end of March each year, investors who've joined DRIPs are sent a *consolidated tax voucher* (CTV) from the issuer of the dividends that includes information on the amount of dividends earned in the tax year.

- **Short-term capital gains:** If you sell a share for a gain, you may have to pay capital gains tax at the full rate. However, if these gains occur in a tax-sheltered savings scheme, such as an ISA, no tax payment is triggered.

» **Capital gains tax:** Back in the good old days, lots of loopholes existed, which meant that investors could use what was called 'taper relief' to control their total capital gains tax bill. *Taper relief* has now been replaced by a lower flat rate of 10 per cent for basic rate taxpayers and 20 per cent for higher rate taxpayers. You still get the annual £12,300 exemption – that means you can make £12,300 in profits before paying any tax – but many of the loopholes have vanished.

REMEMBER

Managing the tax burden from your investment profits is something that you can control. Gains are taxable only if the gain is *realised* – in other words, only if a sale actually takes place. If your shares in GazillionBucks PLC go from £5 to £87 per share, that £82 appreciation isn't subject to taxation unless you actually sell the share. Until you sell, that gain is *unrealised.* Time your share sales carefully to make full use of your annual allowances where practical.

TIP

When you buy shares, record the date of purchase and the *cost basis* (the purchase price of the share plus any ancillary charges, such as commissions). This information is very important when you have to fill in your tax return – especially if you've sold some shares. Say that you buy 100 shares of GazillionBucks PLC at £5 each and pay a commission of £18. Your cost basis is £518 (100 shares times £5 plus £18 commission). If you sell at £87 per share and pay a £24 commission, the total sale amount is £8,676 (100 shares times £87 less £24 commission).

TECHNICAL STUFF

Every individual has an annual *capital gains allowance* – an amount up to which profits can be made on the sales of assets, including shares, without triggering a tax charge. The allowance is set once a year by the Chancellor of the Exchequer in his Budget speech. As of April 2021, this allowance is £12,300.

Coping with capital losses

Ever think that having the value of your shares fall could be a good thing? Perhaps the only real positive regarding losses in your portfolio is that they can reduce your tax liability. A *capital loss* means that you lose money on your investments. This amount is generally deductible on your tax return, and you can claim a loss on either long-term or short-term share holdings. This loss can go against your other income and lower your overall tax bill.

Say that you bought Worth Zilch Co. shares for a total purchase price of £3,500 and sold them later at a sale price of £800. Your capital loss would be £2,700. This loss is tax deductible.

REMEMBER

You don't always have to realise the loss to claim it as a capital gains loss. If the asset has fallen to a negligible value, it can be counted for this purpose. And, any excess loss isn't really lost – you can carry it forward to the next year. However, most of the time you need to realise a loss to claim it and there are times when investors sell up to do just that. Sort of cutting your losses to get the benefit of your losses – if that makes sense. (See the section, 'Playing by the rules No B&B', later in this chapter for information on a practice called bed-and-breakfasting.)

Before you can deduct losses, you'll be expected to use capital losses from your investments to offset any capital gains. If you realise long-term capital gains of £7,000 in share A and £6,000 of realised long-term capital losses in share B, then you have a net long-term capital gain of £1,000 (£7,000 gain less the offset of £6,000 loss). Whenever possible, see whether losses in your portfolio can be realised to offset capital gains to reduce your potential tax liability.

Sharing Your Gains with the Tax Inspector

Of course, you don't want to pay more tax than you have to; however, as the old cliché goes, 'Don't let the tax tail wag the investment dog'. You should buy or sell a share because it makes economic sense first, and consider the tax implications as secondary issues. After all, tax consumes a relatively small portion of your gain. As long as you experience a *net gain* (gain after all transaction costs, including tax, the broker's fees and other related fees), consider yourself a successful investor – even if you have to give away some of your gain in tax.

REMEMBER

Hold on to shares over the long term to keep transaction costs and tax down. Remember that you don't pay tax on a share's profit until you sell the share.

Try to make tax planning second nature in your day-to-day activities. No, you don't have to consume yourself with a blizzard of paperwork and tax projections. We simply mean that, when you make a share transaction, keep the receipt and maintain good records. When you make a large purchase or sale, pause for a moment and ask yourself whether you'll have to face any tax consequences. (Refer to the section, 'Paying through the Nose', earlier in this chapter to review various tax scenarios.) Speak to a tax consultant beforehand to discuss the ramifications.

Filling out forms

Most investors report their investment-related activities on their individual tax returns (the self-assessment forms that can be completed online or on hard copy. The reports that you'll probably receive from brokers and other investment sources include the following:

>> **Brokerage and bank statements:** Monthly statements that you receive

>> **Trade confirmations:** Documents to confirm that you bought or sold shares

>> **Dividend vouchers:** Reporting dividends paid to you

>> **Consolidated tax voucher:** Reporting the total tax deducted on income paid to you, including interest and dividends

You may receive other, more obscure forms that aren't listed here, but you should retain all documents related to your share investments.

TIP

If you plan to work out your own tax liability, consider using the latest tax software products, which have become inexpensive and are easy to use. These programs usually have a question-and-answer feature to help you do your tax step-by-step, and they include all the necessary forms. Consider getting either TaxCalc (`www.taxcalc.com`) or Gosimpletax.com (`www.gosimpletax.com`); both have been successfully tested by HMRC's online service and can support all tax return supplementary pages.

Playing by the rules – No B&B

Some people get the smart idea of 'Hey! Why not sell my losing shares by April 5 and just buy back the shares on April 6 in the new tax year so that I can say I haven't really made a change to my investment?' Not so fast. The HMRC (at the time it was still called the Inland Revenue) put the kibosh on manoeuvres such as that when a practice called *bed-and-breakfasting* (B&B) was outlawed back in the 1998 Budget. B&B allowed investors to sell a share one day and buy it back the next. Their investment portfolio didn't change, but they were able to crystallise a gain or loss that could be offset against other gains or losses that had already been made in that tax year. You can still use bed-and-breakfasting but not as an overnight ploy. You have to wait 30 days to repurchase the share or the tax inspector won't view the sale as having taken place and you lose the tax advantage.

Understanding There's No Such Thing as a Free Share

Every so often investors find themselves getting a little bonus – some extra shares free from one of the companies they've invested in. This isn't generosity on the part of the company; rather, it's usually the result of a particular corporate action. Now you may think, and a lot of people do – or did, until the tax inspector put them right – that if a share is free, it has no value and therefore can't be taxed. Wrong! Some people say that if you can count it, then it's taxable. But that doesn't mean that the taxation of free shares is always the same, as we explain. Four main categories of 'free shares' exist:

» **Loyalty bonus shares:** In most privatisations – when the government sells off a state-owned business – shareholders who buy shares from the government and hold them for a specific time may be entitled to an issue of extra shares. For taxation purposes, these shares are treated as if they were purchased at their market value. If you get 50 free shares from an electricity company when the company's shares are worth £3 each and you sell them later at £5 each, you'll be taxed on a gain of £2 a share – even though you appear to have walked away with a £5 a share profit. This type of bonus may also be paid in the case of a conversion – when a *mutually owned business* (one owned by its customers) converts to a publicly listed company owned by shareholders.

» **Scrips:** A share *scrip,* or *split,* isn't really free shares; it's an exchange of shares usually to make a share more saleable. For example, if the share price of Dodo Holding PLC has hit £10 a share and the company wants to encourage more shareholders to invest, it might prefer to have a share price of £1 a share. To do this, it would exchange current shareholdings in a 10-for-1 scrip. If you had one share worth £10 before, you now have 10 shares worth £1 each, still a total holding of £10. As far as tax is concerned, you may have more shares, but the value of your holding hasn't changed – although it might if more shareholders pile in. You shouldn't pay any more tax from selling these shares than if you'd sold the £10 ones. But keeping all the paperwork about any scrips that come along is important so that your accountant can work out the real profit or loss when you do sell.

» **Conversion shares:** Firms that are mutually owned are still a big feature of UK corporate life, but they're getting fewer. Building societies, co-operative societies, friendly societies and some life and pension companies are owned by their customers or members rather than by shareholders. In recent decades a number of big demutualisations have occurred whereby mutually owned companies (or *mutuals)* have converted to companies listed on the stock market. Examples include Halifax Building Society (now part of the Lloyds Banking group), Standard Life (now Aberdeen Standard) and Woolwich (now part of Barclays). When these companies changed status from mutual to PLC, they paid their members compensation for loss of membership rights. These demutualisation shares – also called *windfall shares* – were issued to members who qualify under certain criteria. Members don't have to pay for their shares and are issued varying amounts depending on the conversion rules. Some mutuals give all members the same amount; others dish out more shares to members with larger interests, such as bigger savings balances in the building society. Whichever way the shares are issued, the taxation is pretty clear. If you get free shares worth £1,000 and sell them immediately, you've realised a capital gain of £1,000 and could be taxed on it if you've already used your capital gains allowance for the year. The shares are considered to have zero value when they were issued, so when you do sell, you'll have to pay tax on the total sale price – that will be the profit. See the section 'Understanding income and capital gains tax', earlier in this chapter.

Millions of unclaimed conversion shares are waiting to be collected. Many have been allocated to customers who failed to reply to letters telling them about the proposed demutualisation. Most can still be claimed, but for some of the oldest only the cash equivalent can now be retrieved. Contact the Unclaimed Assets Register (www.uar.co.uk) or the company itself if you think any of the unclaimed shares might be rightfully yours.

>> **Incentive shares:** If you work for a company that's listed on a stock market, a chance exists that you'll be offered shares as part of a savings scheme or incentive plan. For senior executives, these plans (sometimes called *long-term incentive plans*, or L-TIPs) can get very complex, involving the award of share options over several years. Share options are just that, the option to buy a share at a given price but on a future date. For instance, you may work for a young company that has a low share price of 10 pence. To encourage you to work hard and boost the company's fortunes, you could be offered options to buy a certain number of shares at 20 pence in two years' time, 30 pence in three years' time and 50 pence in five years' time. These are pretty tough targets. But say the company discovers a blockbuster product and the shares hit £1 within two years, £2 in three years and £10 in five years. When your options mature on those dates, you can buy £1 shares for 20 pence (hurray!), £2 shares for 30 pence (double hurray!) and £10 shares for 50 pence (some-one crack open the bubbly!). Of course, you'll have to pay tax on any gains when you finally dispose of the shares.

Keep all your paperwork to do with buying, selling or being awarded shares or dividends. You'll need it when it comes to calculating how much tax you owe.

Givin' it away

What happens if you donate shares to your favourite (registered) charity? The donation doesn't give rise to a capital gain or loss, but you can claim income tax relief on the value of any shares donated to charity.

Say that last year you bought shares for £2,000 and they're worth £4,000 this year. If you donate them this year, you can deduct the market value from your income tax liability at the time of the contribution. In this case, you have a £4,000 deduction against your income tax liability. You can also deduct the costs involved in selling the shares, such as brokers' fees.

Not banking on tax deductions

In some countries you can offset some of the costs of investing against your gains to save on tax. Can you do that in the UK? Fat chance. You'll only save tax by:

>> Keeping excellent records of all your share dealings

>> Using tax-efficient investment vehicles where possible

Are you having fun yet? You're probably saying, 'Why read the rest of the chapter? Can't I just wait for the film version?' Yeah, we know, tax can be intimidating. So, write to your MP and complain. After all, it's your money!

Taking Advantage of Tax Advantages

If you're going to invest for the long term (such as your retirement or to pay for your toddler's school and university fees), then you may as well maximise your usage of tax-sheltered savings plans. More than one way exists to skin the tax-efficient cat, and here we touch on the most popular methods. Although savings plans may not seem relevant for investors who buy and sell shares directly (as opposed to a unit trust or investment trust), some plans, such as self-select ISAs and self-invested personal pensions, allow you to invest directly.

ISAs

Individual Savings Accounts (ISAs) are accounts that you can open with a financial institution, such as a bank, building society or fund management company. An ISA is available to almost anyone older than 16 who has earned income, and it allows you to set aside and invest money for short- or long-term savings. Opening an ISA is easy, and virtually any bank, building society or fund manager can guide you through the process.

Two main types of ISAs exist: cash ISAs and stocks and shares ISAs. You can save in two separate ISAs in any one tax year: one cash ISA and one stocks and shares ISA. However, you can't save in more than one cash ISA or more than one stocks and shares ISA in the same tax year.

You can invest up to £20,000 in an ISA every year.

Three specialist ISAs are relatively new. They're as follows:

>> **Junior ISA:** For children only

>> **Lifetime ISA:** For adults younger than 40 saving for retirement or for the purchase of their first home

>> **Innovative finance ISA:** Peer-to-peer savings accounts that use an ISA wrapper to make the returns tax free

WARNING

Everyone is entitled to have an ISA whether they're working or not. But ISAs are only available for those older than 16. When they were first introduced, the minimum age limit was 18, but this was lowered to 16 to encourage school leavers in their first jobs to save.

REMEMBER

You can only pay into one cash ISA, one stocks and shares ISA, and one innovative finance ISA in each tax year.

Pensions

Pension plans are investment vehicles that are designed to build a capital sum for an individual, payable on retirement. Investing in a pension plan has significant tax advantages. Here we discuss the two types of pensions.

Company pension plans

Company-sponsored pension plans are widely used and are very popular. In a company pension, employees set aside money from their monthly salary that is invested in a group fund for employees' retirement. In many cases, the employer at least matches the amount invested each month. No tax is payable on the growth of the fund, but the pension paid from it is taxable. The big advantage is that investing in a pension attracts tax relief from the government, which adds a serious sum to your investment.

Self-invested personal pensions

Self-invested personal pensions (SIPPs) are the latest big noise on the pension stage. Tens of thousands of them are now being sold and they've become mainstream.

SIPPs are much more than just stuffing money away for the future. As the name suggests, you get to choose the investments yourself. You can get a manager to help you, but you have more choice in the types of investments you can pick from. You can invest in individual shares, stock market and property funds and bonds, real estate investment trusts, unquoted shares, gilts, cash and commercial property.

You can also invest in commercial property – even investing in your own business by buying the premises in your SIPP. And you can even borrow half of the value of your SIPP to fund the purchase.

REMEMBER

Being able to put away as much as possible into a SIPP sounds great, but you still must follow some rules about how much you can contribute. You can pay up to 100 per cent of your earnings into your SIPP (subject to a maximum of the current annual allowance of £40,000 gross) and receive tax relief up to that level.

Pension tax relief is given at a rate of 20 per cent (higher rate taxpayers can claim higher levels of tax relief via self-assessment). Your employer can also make contributions to your SIPP as well as or instead of a workplace pension. These contributions count towards your annual allowance, but they aren't limited by your income. If you don't have any earnings in the tax year, you can still contribute up to £3,600 gross into your SIPP. If you have begun to draw down income from your SIPP, you can contribute up to £4,000 gross per tax year.

WARNING

If you're fortunate enough to be earning more than £240,000 a year, you have to consider some additional complications around contributions. Individuals with high incomes may have a tapered annual allowance. You're counted as a high-income individual if you have one of the two:

>> **A threshold income of more than £200,000 for the tax year:** Your *threshold income* is your annual income before tax, less any personal pension contributions and ignoring any employer contribution. If your threshold income is more than £200,000, you'll need to check your adjusted income.

>> **An adjusted income of more than £240,000:** Your *adjusted income* is worked out by taking all income that you are taxed on – including dividends, savings interest and rental income, before tax – plus the value of your own and any employer pension contributions. Your annual allowance will reduce by £1 for every £2 that your adjusted income exceeds £240,000. The maximum reduction is £36,000, which reduces the annual allowance to £4,000 but only after your adjusted income reaches £312,000.

Comparing ISAs and Pensions

ISAs and pensions represent the two main tax-based schemes to encourage long-term savings. Pensions-based schemes have been around for decades whereas the ISA was only introduced in its original form in 1999, although a version called a *Personal Equity Plan* or PE had been around since 1987. Both structures have their strengths and weaknesses, and it's worth investigating which one is right for you.

According to the government approximately 11 million adults have an ISA whereas around 10 million contribute towards a personal pension. The average annual contribution to a personal pension was £2,700 in 2018/19 while the average annual contribution towards an ISA was just over £6000.

Table 20-1 compares ISAs and pensions in greater detail.

TABLE 20-1   **Differentiating between ISAs and Pensions**

ISAs	Pensions
The government doesn't pay in extra via tax relief.	Investors get tax relief on personal payments into your pension for amounts up to £40,000 or 100 per cent of your annual earnings (whichever is less).
All investments in an ISA can increase in value free of all tax.	Usually the most that can be added to your pension in a year before you start paying tax on it is £40,000. This limit is reduced in certain circumstances.
No capital gains tax or income tax is payable when savings are accessed.	No capital gains tax is payable when savings are accessed. The accumulated savings fund grows tax free.
You can access your savings whenever you want.	You can't access any of your pension until you retire.
The earliest age you can make payments is age 16 for cash ISAs and 18 for stocks and shares ISAs (also called *investment ISAs*). There is no maximum age limit. Children under the age of 18 can have a junior ISA opened on their behalf from birth. The earliest you can access your savings is age 16 for cash ISAs and 18 for stocks and shares ISAs (also called investment ISAs).	Payments to your pension can be made from birth to age 75.
Investment is allowed in cash, shares, government and corporate bonds. In addition to direct investments, a wide range of funds are available that invest in cash, shares and bonds and other investments such as property. Direct investment in residential property isn't allowed.	Investment is allowed in cash, shares, and bonds. Direct investment in residential property isn't allowed.
The maximum annual allowance is £20,000 for the 2021/22 tax year. Unused annual allowance can't be carried forward. There is no lifetime allowance or maximum overall saving amount.	There is currently a lifetime allowance limit on the amount that you save in pensions. For most people, the limit is currently £1,073,100. Only people above this limit have to pay an extra tax charge on their pension savings.
Employers can't make payments on your behalf.	If you're employed and earn enough, your employer must enrol you into a pension scheme. If you have a workplace pension, your employer is likely to make contributions too, which could considerably boost your savings.

(continued)

TABLE 20-1 *(continued)*

ISAs	Pensions
In terms of inheritance taxes, your ISA savings are counted as part of your estate. That means they'll be added to your assets when you die and your beneficiaries may have to pay inheritance tax, which is currently levied on estates worth more than £325,000 and charged at 40 per cent. But this tax *doesn't* apply if you're passing your money on to your spouse or civil partner.	If you die before 75 and you have a defined contribution pension, your pension is held outside your estate and can be passed on to your beneficiaries tax-free. If you die after the age of 75, your beneficiaries will have to pay tax at their marginal rate of income tax on any pension that you've left them.
Previously, your ISA always lost its tax-free status when it was inherited, but under new rules you can pass your ISA on to your spouse or civil partner, and it will retain its tax benefits, giving your partner a temporary additional allowance.	Income tax is charged on the remaining amount when it's taken from the pension. Usually 25 per cent of your pension can be taken tax-free.
	You can only access your pension money when you reach 55, but this age requirement increases to 57 in 2028. When you're 55, you've got quite a few options: You can take up to 25 per cent as a lump sum tax free, you can leave your money invested and take cash sums out when you need them (via *drawdown*), and you can buy an annuity (a guaranteed income).

The table shows you advantages to both pensions and ISAs. Some people choose one over the other. Investing in both makes sense for some investors if you're keen on enjoying the tax benefits of a pension, but need some money that's accessible now (with an ISA).

Chapter **21**

Creating a Smarter Portfolio with Lower-Cost Funds and ETFs

You're sitting in the dentist's chair, secure in the knowledge that the odd-looking person with a mask over their face, staring into your mouth, exudes confidence. They're running through the things that need to be done to your poor, bedraggled mouth, and you're busily gulping at the long list of expensive procedures.

You're also desperate to ask whether any of it is strictly necessary and, more to the point, how much it'll all cost. You're thinking to yourself, 'maybe I'll only have one root canal and a filling rather than the 'full works'. But you feel uncomfortable about confronting this drill-wielding professional with 'awkward' questions that might make you look a skinflint and the dentist a dunce. So, you swallow and try to say yes and then sign the inordinately large bill at the end of the session.

What's true for dentists is also true for all the other professionals you'll probably encounter, including those with an investment bias. Questions about cost and their effect on you – largely of the impoverishing variety – are a bit tricky, especially because these people in suits seem to know a lot more about investing than you do. But don't be fooled. Investing isn't always as complex as dentistry, and you shouldn't be afraid to ask awkward questions about what your fund manager or financial adviser is doing for their princely charges.

Crucially, you need to be bold and look systematically at all the costs within your portfolio of stocks, funds and bonds and ask – is it really necessary for me to rack up huge costs for advice, dealing and fund management? As you're about to discover in this chapter, costs *really* matter. You need to reduce costs to boost your returns and that's especially true when it comes to funds. Look to use lower-cost funds where the man in the Hermès suit has been replaced by a clever computer that watches the market very closely.

Alternatively, you may still want the smart, well-dressed fund manager to work on your behalf but you want him to cut his costs and offer his expertise through something called an investment trust. Whatever you decide, though, keep those costs down and understand that excessive fund management fees are the one certainty in the volatile world of investment. Nobody knows with any certainty what will happen tomorrow on the markets, but investors do know for a fact that each extra 1 per cent of charges every year on their funds under management will reduce our long-term profits. *Fact.* Even if the nice person in a smart suit sporting a badge stating they're your advisor or fund manager tells you otherwise.

Understanding Why Costs Matter

This book is for ordinary folk – mere mortal investors – and it doesn't have to be nice or even fair to financial professionals. However, even we have to accept that over the last few decades the big guys have got a great deal better at being honest about their costs. Which is useful, as those costs aren't insignificant!

Stockbrokers, for instance, have largely done away with confusing dealing tariffs and have tried to simplify their charges to round numbers such as £10 per trade, or even less! Independent financial advisers have also wised up and gone to great lengths to provide copious pieces of paper that detail their costs. Some financial planners have even gone a step further and started adopting transparent charging structures centred around a per hour charge, just like your accountant. Even investment fund managers have embraced the new zeitgeist of openness and honesty. Whereas the investment industry used to suffer from awful with-profits funds for which no one knew the costs, now fund managers willingly discuss their annual management charges (AMCs) and initial purchase charges.

Sadly – bet you knew a caveat was coming – this rush to openness hasn't gone far enough. A great deal of trickery still goes on beneath the surface, which means that when a fund manager quotes the AMC for running the fund – usually between 1 and 2 per cent per annum – that doesn't mean this number (as a percentage) is the full cost of owning that fund. Not by a long stretch, dear investor. The reason for our scepticism is that behind the scenes lots of little costs and expenses add up. Consider the cost of all that trading activity in the fund. Next is the cost of the 'platforms' and 'fund supermarkets' that host the fund. In fact, a long list of costs exists that we won't bore you with. Suffice to say that the list is very extensive and in many cases the cost of running a portfolio of funds and stocks can easily add up to between 3 and 5 per cent per annum.

Frankly, even an extra 0.5 per cent per annum is a massive drain on your future wealth, let alone 3 or even 5 per cent per annum, especially as returns from holding risky stuff like equities have been so low over the last decade or so.

To understand why each and every percentage of cost matters, assume you have a £50,000 savings pot (your portfolio) and that you expected an annual return of 8 per cent per annum. The results of this simple exercise in modelling are shown in Table 21-1. The figures show how a small extra annual cost for trading charges or fund management can make a huge difference over the very long term. By looking at the data in the table, you can see that a difference of just 1 per cent per annum in charges over 30 years results in a reduction of more than £100,000 in final returns.

TABLE 21-1 ## Observing How Charges Mount Up Over the Years

Fees (%)	5 years	10 years	20 years	30 years
0.5	71,781	103,052	212,393	437,738
1	70.128	98,358	193,484	380,613
1.5	68,504	93,857	176,182	330,718

With a stockbroker, you might be able to contain these costs and maybe reduce them by shopping around. You can also understand, arguably, what you're getting for your money – a fancy IT platform that lets you buy and sell shares. With an adviser, you get lots of personal, one-to-one time, plus some nice projections. Whether that's worth more than 1 per cent or so per annum is a matter of much anguished debate. But with an investment fund manager, these costs can be huge and you need to know that you're getting your money's worth for the AMC. In brutally simple language, are they giving you sufficient returns to compensate for their annual management costs?

This question introduces a subject that many mainstream fund managers don't like talking about – whether they're worth their charges. Here, you need to make a decision – if you sensibly decide to focus mostly on using funds, who will manage that fund? Will it be achieved using an active fund manager in a unit trust or will you do away with all this 'active' management and simply 'track' the market by following an index? Clearly, the fund management industry would like you to believe that using a fund manager to actively manage is essential and that doing so delivers the goods in terms of returns. Sadly, the evidence suggests otherwise, and to understand this point, it's time to get a little academic.

Acting on the Advice of Academics

Investment is all about taking a risk (or two) to achieve some extra returns. You don't invest in Chinese technology companies, for instance, just because you liked Beijing the last time you were there on holiday. You invest in high growth companies because hopefully you'll make money by doing so. The same is true with a fund manager. You invest in a fund manager because they'll control downside risk and increase your upside, that is, your returns.

But how to prove a fund manager's worth? Well, obviously, the investment fund managers will churn out copious amounts of data that'll prove their returns over time, but what would you expect them to do! What you really need is some objective analysis of those results. Not just from last year, or the year before that, but over a long period of time. And that analysis can't be done by fund managers because they'll almost certainly talk up their game – as you would, if you were them. No, you need someone objective, who's probably a bit boring and loves looking at numbers and isn't a fund manager.

Step forward the professional investment economists' brigade. These utterly scintillating folk do a fine job of looking at the past data and then number crunching. They look at past trends and explore key ideas. And then they test their hypotheses, again and again until . . . oh . . . at least the summer holidays, when they test them one more time just to make sure they work. The final results ultimately appear in learned academic journals, at which point the conclusions are ripped to shreds by envious colleagues keen to make their mark by rubbishing the work of others.

This scenario is called the *academic peer review process* and, in investment, lots of it takes place, backed up by detailed analysis. You'll be glad to know, however, that despite the wrangling, these academics have looked at the track record of fund managers and come to some pretty striking conclusions. The good news for you and the bad news for fund managers is that nearly all academic economists agree that, on average, fund managers don't add much value. In fact, academic economists have been scrutinising the performance of active fund managers for decades now and, although some controversy still rumbles on, the majority of studies now conclude that actively managed funds, on average, underperform key benchmarks such as the FTSE 100 index.

Study after study has revealed a huge discrepancy between two simple models of investment. The first involves you paying an active fund manager to manage a fund and then measuring that performance against a benchmark like the FTSE All-Share index or the FTSE 100 index. The alternative method is to cut out the fund manager altogether and look at the returns from simply investing in the index itself, through something called an *index tracking fund.*

And what's the bottom line? Time and time again, the index tracking alternative wins out, even though the active fund manager levies a large charge for their expertise. And while we're on the subject of academic research, it's also worth pointing out a number of related observations from the research world: that the past isn't much use in forecasting the future, that by and large prices set by the market are sensible and 'efficient' on a day-to-day basis and that it's devilishly difficult for money managers to use that past data or those largely efficient markets to make any extra return. In fact, the academics have come to an even more incendiary conclusion: when managers do outperform the market, they largely do so by taking on extra risk. And that's exactly what most private investors don't realise they're doing when they think they're buying a nice, safe, diversified actively-managed fund.

Considering Tracking an Index

Imagine that you're in the business of running a large investment company. Your job is to make a profit through the charges made for running a fund. Your marketing people keep pestering you, suggesting that you set up a fund that lets private investors invest in the London stock market. Clearly, you're a bit slow off the mark but, better late than never, you decide that such a fund is a good idea. You set up Acme's UK fund. But how do you decide what to invest in? The obvious place to start when answering that question is to study an index, such as the FTSE 100, which pulls together the aggregate market by looking at the values of a load of companies listed on the London Stock Exchange (LSE).

You then hire a manager and tell them to build a portfolio of shares in companies that look a bit like those listed in the FTSE 100 – but obviously you expect your manager to add some extra value by not buying any over-priced or 'dodgy' shares and only focusing on quality companies. Quite how you define these company and share attributes in terms of an investment process is a matter for debate, but your manager must earn their keep, so they make lots of decisions to buy and sell stuff.

Those trading costs mount up, and a strong possibility exists that most decisions made by the manager will be poor ones. Hopefully, a few decisions will result in lots of profit but, over time, all those costs and all those poor decisions eat into your returns, especially when you measure the returns against your benchmark, the FTSE 100.

Eventually, someone in the marketing department comes up with another brilliant idea: 'Let's fire the manager and simply invest in that index, copying it or tracking it, because the market knows best . . . not our manager.' And then they add, 'and what's more, because we've done away with that manager, we can cut the costs on the fund and charge less'. At which point the CEO fires the person from marketing for suggesting that the company create a range of lower-cost, tracking funds. The last thing the marketing person hears before being escorted off the premises is the CEO booming, 'What do you think we are? A blooming supermarket! We need those fees to make a profit'.

Hopefully by now you see why most big fund management companies aren't keen on launching a range of funds that charge less in fees and track a major index. Turkeys don't tend to vote for Christmas! You, however, may see the attraction of these funds in the following circumstances:

>> You're looking to invest in or access a major investment idea such as British shares or market such as the FTSE 100, but you're doing so via an index which is being tracked, for instance, your fund invests in the companies that are the constituents of the index being tracked.

>> You want to cut your costs by tracking an index and not hiring an expensive fund manager to make lots of decisions. On paper, you could just get a computer to do all the hard work, but in reality you still need a human touch to monitor activity.

>> You're thinking of reducing the risk involved in using an active fund manager, who may make lots of mistakes.

Not using a fund manager and just tracking an index should all be looking quite attractive for some investors now and hopefully a new way of thinking might begin to emerge. Sit down with a blank sheet of paper and work out what you want to invest in. Then look for the best index to capture that 'asset class' or investment idea. After you find the index, look for a fund that tracks that index, working out fund's structure and also how it tracks the market. Then sit back and watch those asset classes move up and down, confident in the knowledge that you've minimised both your costs and your exposure to daft decisions by an active fund manager. The key to this approach, though, is understanding two things, which we discuss in the following sections: first, what index you want to track and, second, how you intend to track that index in a fund.

Investigating the weird and wonderful world of indexes

Turn on the *Today* programme on BBC Radio 4 every morning and at some point you'll probably hear a short report on how the benchmark FTSE 100 index has started the day. Tune in to every other news show during the day and you can chart the progress of that index. Frankly, everything else about the workings of the stock market is slightly mysterious to most ordinary people, but many millions will understand that the FTSE 100 is big, is really important and matters very much.

They might even know if it's going up or down and, astonishingly, be aware of the rough level of the index that day or week. In sum, the London stock market is defined by its indexes, and the index of choice is the FTSE 100.

Welcome to the weird and wonderful world of stock market indexes. These indexes aren't real as such – unlike the major exchanges that do exist in an electronic form, even if their trading floors have largely been consigned to the dustbin of history. In essence, they're mathematical constructs, which are then marketed as brands to both institutional and private investors. These indexes are a shorthand way of 'capturing' the changes in major markets. The number of these index 'brands' has increased exponentially in recent years with major providers like MSCI, S&P Dow Jones and even the FTSE Russell turning into research houses sporting every kind of niche index imaginable.

These global index brands are usually built around one of those famous core indexes that tracks a main market. In the UK, the actual market making bit is provided by the London Stock Exchange and the key indexes are the FTSE 100 (known as the Footsie) and its related sibling, the FTSE All-Share index, which comprises around 98 per cent, by value, of all stocks listed on the LSE (many very small listed companies based on market cap aren't included in the FTSE All-Share and thus this index isn't one that features all listed companies and funds despite the *All* in its title).

Table 21-2 lists the top ten companies in a big index fund run by iShares that tracks the FTSE 100 index with numbers from April 2021. Check out `www.ishares.com/uk/individual/en/products/251795/ishares-ftse-100-ucits-etf-inc-fund` for a complete list of the funds. In simple terms, the following points may be made about this 'benchmark' FTSE 100 index, including:

>> The list actually comprises more than 100 stocks. Currently there are 101 stocks in the FTSE 100. Many ETFs tracking this index have even more than 101 – this iShares ETF technically has more than 105 although the 100 top stocks comprise more than 99 per cent of the value of the fund.

THE FTSE 100 – SOME HANDY FACTS

The FTSE 100 is a market-capitalisation weighted index representing the performance of the 100 largest UK-listed large-cap or blue chip companies.

- All companies in the FTSE 100 must pass a test that looks at size in terms of market capitalisation and the availability or liquidity of their shares, that is, only easy to purchase shares or investable shares are included. Constituents also need to have a full listing on the London Stock Exchange with a sterling- or euro-dominated price on the Stock Exchange Electronic Trading Service (SETS). Most constituents must by law include the abbreviation 'PLC' at the end of their name, indicating their status as a publicly limited corporation.

- The index represents a little more than 80 per cent of the entire market value of the various London-based stock exchanges.

- The index began on 3 January 1984 with a base level of 1,000. The highest value reached to date is 7,877 on 22 May 2018.

- The FTSE 100 is calculated in real time and the level of the index is published every 15 seconds. Trading lasts from 08.00–16.29 (when the closing auction starts), and closing values are taken at 16.35.

- The constituents of the index are determined quarterly – the larger companies in the adjacent index, the FTSE 250, are pushed up or promoted to the FTSE 100 if they pass the tests described above and their market cap goes above a certain level. At time of writing, the market cap is approximately £4 billion.

The weighting of shares in the index is a relatively simple exercise – the index is built around the market capitalisation of the constituent companies (all 100 of them), so that the larger companies have a disproportionate impact on the value of the index, compared to a smaller (by market cap) company. So, if HSBC, for instance, comprises 10 per cent of the index and its shares rise by 10 per cent, all things being equal with the other constituent companies, the index should rise by 1 per cent. This approach is called the free-float method of constructing an index and the basic formula for any index is

Index level = (Price of stock × Number of shares) × Free-float factor / Index divisor.

The free-float adjustment factor represents the proportion of shares floated as a percentage of issued shares and then it is rounded up to the nearest multiple of 5 per cent for calculation purposes. To find the free-float capitalisation of a company, first find its market cap (number of outstanding shares x share price), then multiply its free-float factor. The free-float method, therefore, does not include restricted stocks, such as those held by company insiders.

>> All of the companies in the list are 'weighted' by their market capitalisation. The *market cap* of a company is simply how much the markets 'values' a company – in Table 21-2, Unilever is 'valued' at £107 billion, which makes it the largest company by market cap and, in the FTSE 100 index, its weighting is just under 5.5 per cent of the index.

>> The aggregate 100 companies in the index are valued at a total of more than £1.51 trillion.

>> The average market cap size is around £17 billion.

>> The smallest market cap for a stock in the index is £4 billion.

>> The top 10 stocks in the index comprise 39 per cent of the value of the total index.

>> The bottom stock in the list is an engineering business called Renishaw.

>> In 2020 the index lost 11.5 per cent in value, the largest loss in the previous ten years. In 2016 the index gained 19.1 per cent in value.

TABLE 21-2   ## Top Ten on the FTSE 100 ETFs

Issuer Ticker	Name	Weight (%)	Price	Sector
ULVR	UNILEVER PLC	5.49	40.52	Consumer Staples
AZN	ASTRAZENECA PLC	5.29	75.61	Health Care
HSBA	HSBC HOLDINGS PLC	4.78	4.4	Financials
DGE	DIAGEO PLC	3.95	32.3	Consumer Staples
RIO	RIO TINTO PLC	3.56	61.55	Materials
GSK	GLAXOSMITHKLINE PLC	3.51	13.37	Health Care
BATS	BRITISH AMERICAN TOBACCO PLC	3.28	26.98	Consumer Staples
BP	BP PLC	3.12	2.95	Energy
RDSA	ROYAL DUTCH SHELL PLC	2.96	13.55	Energy
RDSB	ROYAL DUTCH SHELL PLC CLASS B	2.56	12.93	Energy

Source: Data from iShares Core FTSE 100 UCITS ETF, BlackRock, Inc. Data retieved from: https://www.ishares. com/uk/individual/en/products/251795/ishares-ftse-100-ucits-etf-inc-fund (27-Apr-21).
*EPIC stands for Exchange Price Information Computer; it is a code for each company listed in the FTSE 100 to identify each one unambiguously.

You could, of course, go out and buy all the companies in this index and 'track' the FTSE 100 yourself. Good luck – your trading expenses will be huge and your poor stockbroker will spend most of the day running the transactions. And then, suddenly, the markets will move up or down the following day and the weighting on the index will change – you'll have to contact the broker up again and he'll have to run a whole load more transactions. Costs will escalate and you'll start to wonder what on earth you're doing. Step forward the sensible alternative to you tracking an index on your own, namely: you buy a fund that tracks the index.

Working out how to track your chosen index

One of the pioneers in the field of establishing funds that track an index is iShares, owned by a giant American investment group called Blackrock. Over the last few decades, iShares has grown at a phenomenal rate by offering one simple deal – they let you track many major indexes through their funds, many of which are traded on the London Stock Exchange.

Perhaps their most popular UK fund is called iShares FTSE 100, which boasts the *ticker* (an identifier) ISF. This ticker allows you to ring up a stockbroker and buy (or sell) the fund by muttering 'buy XXX ISF'; once the fund is safely in your portfolio, you're tracking the FTSE 100 index.

If you peer under the bonnet of the fund, you'll see that the constituents of the fund track almost exactly those of the index. Go to iShares' website, see what's in the different funds and even download a spreadsheet. They're also in the FTSE 100 iShares fund. If you go to the company's website, you can also see the charge they make for running the fund – in total, the expenses of this fund charged to the end investor are 0.07 per cent compared to at least 0.5 per cent per annum for most mainstream UK equity funds.

Crucially, you can be sure that every day the mix of companies in this tracking fund changes as the FTSE 100 index itself changes. If Unilever falls in price and its weighting drops to, say, 4 per cent, you can be sure that iShares' computers and managers will adjust their holdings slightly to account for this change. Also important is the fact that this ETF can be bought in real time via a stockbroker and the total market value of the fund can move up and down in real time.

REMEMBER

Obviously the exact mechanics of the tracking are a good deal more complex than we've let on! Lots of clever stuff is whirring away in the background making sure that the tracking is accurate and that a big difference between the returns from the index and the returns from the fund doesn't exist; this discrepancy is called the *tracking error.* On the iShares website you can even check on this tracking error – in 2020 for instance, the FTSE index lost 11.58 per cent whereas the iShares' fund lost 11.64 per cent. Why the 0.06 per cent difference? Remember that you also need to deduct the 0.07 per cent cost of managing the fund.

You're very accurately tracking a major index using one single fund at a cost of just 0.07 per cent per annum, or 7 basis points. And this iShares fund isn't even the cheapest index tracker on the market; competitor funds from the likes of French-owned Lyxor charge just 0.04 per cent per cent per annum for tracking the FTSE 100 index.

Understanding that not all trackers are created equal

On paper, all this index tracking sounds simple but lots of moving bits are operating inside the engine. Crucially, the manner in which an index is tracked varies enormously, which is reflected in a blizzard of acronyms used to describe the different types of funds (see the box below). In simple terms, two methods of tracking an index exist:

» You physically track an index by building a fund whereby the shares in it almost exactly match the companies in the underlying index. This fund actually holds lots and lots of different shares. The major fund management companies in this space consist of iShares, Vanguard, HSBC and Credit Suisse.

» You synthetically copy the index through what is in effect an IOU. In this scenario, a big investment bank promises to pay out the return on the index and offers some security so that the fund investors know they'll get their return. This 'collateral' could be any stocks or bonds the bank holds on the day and the IOU is effectively structured as something called a swap, which is an options contract. These synthetic funds have become less popular in recent years, but they still exist in less mainstream investment spaces.

Synthetic ETFs tend to boast lower charges (though not always) and the tracking error on the fund return (versus the index return) is lower because at the heart of the fund is a swap or IOU, which can simply be changed to reflect the return on the underlying index. But of course, there's a rub: as you're effectively taking an IOU from a major bank, that instantly introduces a new element of risk into the equation; that is, the bank might go bust and your basket of collateral could have dozens of useless stocks in it.

ACRONYM CITY – ETFs, ETPs AND BEYOND

An enormous multiplicity of different tracking structures exists out there, which allow you to invest in an index. The key distinction is between funds and notes. Funds are what they say they are – actual funds – whereas a *note* (also called a *certificate*) is in essence an IOU issued by a bank, which involves a promise to pay to you a return on an index.

Within the fund world, some key differences are also evident. Most of the major index tracking funds are actually listed on the London Stock Exchange, in which case they're Exchange Listed Funds, or ETFs. But some funds are also available as unit trusts, from the likes of Vanguard and Legal & General; these can be purchased by an adviser or through a fund's supermarket.

Beyond these simple distinctions, you may also encounter the following acronyms:

- **Exchange traded products (ETPs):** These cover all forms of funds and notes listed on a stock market.

- **Exchange traded funds (ETFs):** These are regulated as funds, which are in turn listed on the London Stock Exchange.

- **Exchange traded commodities (ETCs):** These track the future or spot price of major commodities, including oil and gas.

- **Exchanged traded notes (ETNs):** These are notes or IOUs issued by major banks to track the returns on an index. These aren't funds and are aimed at more experienced investors.

Many investors are rightly confused by all this choice and all those acronyms. They don't really understand what they're investing in and their ignorance tends to produce shortcuts – they look to track an index and simply plump for the tracker with the lowest cost. This approach could ultimately be a big mistake because you need to understand what's happening in an index tracking fund – the cheapest product isn't always the best product! We think you should construct a simple checklist, which you can use to examine the fund (s) via the manager's website:

- How does it track an index – physically or synthetically? Neither is good or bad, but you need to understand the risks involved.

- If the fund is in the form of a note, a certificate or a synthetic ETF, what is your counter-party risk with the bank? How happy do you feel about that bank and what proportion of your portfolio is now exposed to that bank?

- What happens inside the index? Understand the index and work out what makes it tick. Is it too narrow an index?

- What's the annualised tracking error on the fund versus the index? Is it too big? Is that because the fees charged on the fund are too substantial?

- How easy is it to trade into and out of the fund? What's the bid offer spread?

Differentiating between index funds and ETFs

When most investors start to look at index tracking funds, they tend to quickly think about ETFs. But there is an alternative structure that is also worth exploring: the *index tracking mutual fund*, or *unit trust*. If we strip away all the investment jargon, both ETFs and index-based mutual funds are virtually the same. They both invest in a basket of stocks that are constituents of an index, and then methodically track that index over time.

Apart from this issue around pricing, there are no real substantive differences between the ETF and index mutual fund. However, a couple of smaller differences exist, including the following:

>> **An index tracking mutual fund is structured as a conventional mutual fund or unit trust that can be bought via a fund supermarket or platform whereas an ETF is actually a security or share that can be traded on a stock market.** Most financial advisers tend to prefer using unit trust funds, so if you're an advised client with an independent financial adviser (IFA), the chances are they'll mostly use unit trust funds.

>> **An index tracking mutual fund tends to offer end of day pricing, whereas an ETF can be traded in real time whenever the market is open.** This sounds complicated, but isn't. With an ETF the value of each unit in the fund – the share – is in effect in real time. In an index mutual fund, the price you buy and sell at is worked out (and transacted) at the end of the day.

REMEMBER

Access to index mutual funds is usually done through a fund's supermarket platform, in many cases using an IFA. You can't buy an index mutual fund through an online broker. Just to confuse matters, some robo wealth advisory services invest in both ETFs and index tracking mutual funds.

TIP

In the past many index tracking mutual funds have been cheap with low single digit (basis points) fees – with many sub 0.20 per cent per annum. Over the last few years though ETF charges have tumbled, so honestly there really isn't any big difference in pricing now. But the choice of markets you can invest in through index mutual funds is usually a great deal more limited to major markets and geographies. You won't find any specialist index funds investing in say the US energy sector, whereas in ETF land, you can find plenty.

Adopting a core satellite approach

Tracking major stock market indexes isn't for everyone. As you can see from the list of questions to ask about a tracker fund provided in the nearby sidebar, you need to do some due diligence of your own and you absolutely shouldn't invest in a note or certificate if you don't understand its structure. Crucially, you also need to understand that index tracking funds should only ever form a part of your portfolio of funds and individual stocks and bonds. Even the greatest fans of index tracking in the academic community accept that, in certain markets, a fund manager can provide some value, some of the time. That might be because the market is complex or because it's far away and subject to lots of regulatory interference. In fact, an active fund manager may make some sense for a whole host of reasons, but most academics suggest that index tracking is a great idea for the core of your portfolio (tracking those large markets), whereas managed funds and individual stocks (or bonds) make sense for the satellite parts of your portfolio where you're willing to take more risk.

In this satellite part of your portfolio – a smaller percentage of the overall funds than the core – you should consider a huge range of options but you shouldn't lose sight of our very first point in this chapter: *cost*. Hiring a fund manager to add value in, say, complex real estate funds, is perfectly acceptable, but you still don't want to be paying over the odds for duff management. Even in the satellite, if you do have actively managed funds you need to keep costs to the minimum, which tends to suggest that you focus on the great rival to index tracking, the investment trust.

More Competition Means Lower Fees for ETF Investors

When ETFs were first introduced to the world in the 1990s, they tended to track well-known, very mature markets and indices. Think the big geographically located indices: The S&P 500 for the US, the FTSE 100 for the UK, the Stoxx 50 index for the Eurozone.

Over the last ten years though, the ETF market has become hugely more important with an exponential growth in the number of ETF and markets (and indices) tracked. Thousands of ETFs are now listed on the London market with those numbers growing by the week. This growth has resulted in one very obvious development: You can launch only so many S&P 500 and FTSE 100 trackers. For example, at one stage there were 36 different Eurozone Stoxx 50 ETFs. As competition intensifies, fees charged have dropped, but in the competitive main markets, margins are now razor thin.

TIP

Fees for ETFs have dropped measurably. When we first talked about the iShares FTSE 100 ETF back in 2011, the fee was 0.40 per cent or 40 basis points. Now it's 0.07 per cent or 7 basis points! Across the board fees for main market ETFs have dropped like a stone, and honestly any fee for a well-known index much above 0.30 per cent is now regarded as expensive. More specialist ETFs might charge between 0.30 per cent and 0.50 per cent whereas very specialised thematic ETFs might charge between 0.50 per cent and 1 per cent. We recommend you avoid at all costs any ETF charging above 1 per cent a year.

This massive competition has left the ETF issuers in a bit of a pickle. Why launch another standard index tracker that pays them smaller and smaller amounts of money in fees? That has resulted in ETF issuers – big fund management businesses – diversifying into ever more exotic markets and indices. In simple terms, we've observed a number of waves to explain this a bit:

» The first big diversification was into new sectors such as energy sector stocks or tech sector stocks. The idea here was to move from big, well-known, location specific (the FTSE is based in London) to popular industrial sectors that spanned regions and even the global markets.

» The next wave of ETFs went ever more local, ever more specific. For example, in the first wave, a number of global property sector funds launched investing in commercial property. In this next phase, you had European- or American-specific funds launched or perhaps more specialist infrastructure–based funds.

As more and more big institutional investors jumped into the ETF space, they brought with them their more sophisticated, quantitative-driven ideas. For decades big money managers on both sides of the pond have been investing in say value-driven funds where investors use fundamental analysis to work out if a business's shares are cheap – or not. Warren Buffett started off like this. Other investors look for more dividend focused businesses or shares which don't move around in price much (low volatility strategies). These quantitative driven ETFs even sported their own niche terms such as Smart Beta or Fundamentals based ETFs.

>> More recently, *thematic ETFs* have emerged. These, usually global, funds try and capture big macroeconomic or technological themes – the kind of things we talk about in Chapter 22. These could range from aging society ETFs to digitisation ETFs to space ETFs. They look and feel like sector ETFs, but in reality, they span a number of old-fashioned sectors. Take robotics ETFs. These can include industrial businesses, as well as tech businesses and also software businesses.

TIP

Thematic EFTs have become hugely popular and have produced some amazing returns. But you really to understand what's going on under the bonnet. These are frequently tech-focused baskets of stocks with lots of volatile, fast-growing, expensive growth stocks. There's nothing wrong with that, but if confidence ebbs, expect a lot of share price volatility. Smart beta ETFs by contrast were once very popular but have become less so in recent years, in part because many investors don't really understand them and also because returns haven't for the most part been stellar.

>> The latest craze is for ESG ETFs. ESG stands for environmental, social and governance-based strategies designed to focus on businesses with a more sustainable business model. Refer to the section 'Looking at Another Acronym: The Remorseless Rise of ESG', later in this chapter for more details. These ESG ETFs can look a bit like the quantitative-driven ETFs from an earlier phase, in that they use numbers driven strategies to screen through the broad universe of stocks to find the right kind of sustainable businesses.

Examining the Importance of Leveraged Trackers

Leveraged trackers, also known as *short and leveraged products*, aren't ETFs but rather exchange traded products (ETPs). They can leverage up – or down – the daily returns from an index. The usual leverage or gearing is around three times those daily returns from the index. Refer to Chapter 17 for more information about leveraged trackers.

How does this work in practice? Here's an example: Assume you want to invest in an S&P 500 tracker with three times leverage, short and long. The key thing to understand here is that you get three times the *daily* returns form that index. Table 21-3 explains what those returns over a period of just three days might look like.

TABLE 21-3 **Predicting Returns over Three Days**

Index or Product	Leverage	Day 1 Start Price	Day 1 Change	Price at End of Day 1	Day 2	Price at End of Day 2	Day 3
S&P 500	None	£100	5%	£105	3%	£108	−7.5%
Three times long	Three times daily	£100	15%	£115	9%	£125	22.5%
Three times short	Three times daily	£100	15%	£85	−9%	£77	−22.5%

These three days have been hugely volatile, and after three days the index is back where it started. But both the leveraged trackers have lost you money because of the big daily price moves.

REMEMBER

The key point to understand is that when markets become volatile, they tend to stay very volatile for a number of days, if not weeks. An average big bout of heightened volatility can last for around one to two months and in that period, price moving 5 to 10 per cent might not be an unusual. On paper that move of 5 to 10 per cent sounds great, but remember that those big moves can go in *both* directions. So, if you're invested in a short-leveraged tracker – making money on the downside – even if markets are trending downwards, you could be caught by a sudden, unexpected rally on the upside, crushing the share price.

WARNING

By and large, don't use daily leveraged trackers as long-term buy-and-hold products. They aren't designed for that purpose, and over time intense volatility in share prices can eat away at returns. Also, the cost of running these leveraged trackers can build up over time, eating into your returns.

TIP

Leveraged trackers can be a useful alternative to spread betting accounts. Most mainstream online brokers will allow you to trade in these leveraged shares after signing various risk notices. You can also use leveraged shares within an SIPP dealing account. And remember, you can only ever lose your initial investment and nothing more unlike with spread betting accounts where losses can keep mounting.

Despite all our cautions, leveraged trackers can be useful if a market in a short (or even long) period of time trends largely in one direction. In other words, leveraged trackers can be valuable if a share moves steadily up or down in price for many weeks if not months, mostly in the same direction.

If markets stay relatively *trend bound* (stuck within a broad upwards and downwards track), then leveraged trackers can come into their own. Table 21-4 illustrates how this worlds. The table summarises price returns over various periods (in early 2021) for the S&P 500 and FTSE 100 indices against two long 3 times leveraged ETPs from Wisdom Tree, the largest player in the S&L (short and leveraged) space here in the UK.

TABLE 21-4 **How Leveraged Shares Can Amplify Returns over Months**

Returns % for 3 times ETP vs Benchmark	1 month	3 months	6 months	9 months	12 months
3USL	6.56	34	61.2	175	10.2
S&P 500	1.99	12.2	18.6	41.6	16.2
3UKL	14	50.2	28.2	71.9	-39.9
FTSE 100	4.61	15.2	9.03	22.8	-9.53

What's interesting is that right up to the nine-month mark these leveraged trackers have provided roughly what they said they would do in the biscuit tin. They have provided three times the cumulative returns from the benchmark index. And if one dips down into day-by-day returns, the pattern holds steady.

Looking at Another Acronym: The Remorseless Rise of ESG

ETFs focused on only investing in stocks where the underlying business is more sustainable have become hugely popular. More and more investors are switching to the idea of investing in funds where companies are scored based on environmental, social and governance-based criteria (referred to as ESGs). By some estimates many hundreds of billions are now invested in funds with some kind of ESG criteria.

These ESG ETFs sound like acronym wonkiness, but the ideas behind them are actually very simple. Fund managers search through a broad universe of stocks and focus on three bundles of criteria:

>> **Environmental measures:** These could include carbon footprints or environmental sustainability policies.

THE UN'S SUSTAINABLE DEVELOPMENT GOALS

For the last few decades, the United Nations (UN) has been taking the lead in mapping out some broad policy goals to make the world a better place. These were first aimed more at governments, but during the last decade they have become the focus of more corporate interest.

According to the UN, The 2030 Agenda for Sustainable Development, adopted by all United Nations Member States in 2015, provides a shared blueprint for peace and prosperity for people and the planet, now and into the future. At its heart are the 17 Sustainable Development Goals (SDGs), which are an urgent call for action by all countries – developed and developing – in a global partnership. They recognize that ending poverty and other deprivations must go hand-in-hand with strategies that improve health and education, reduce inequality, and spur economic growth – all while tackling climate change and working to preserve our oceans and forests.

You can find out more about these goals at https://sdgs.un.org/goals.

The following figure illustrates the practical challenges involved with these goals, ranging from ending poverty to more focused initiatives such as taking climate action.

Source: Sustainable Development Goals: 17 Goals to Transform Our World, United Nations, Retrieved from: www.un.org/sustainabledevelopment/blog/2015/12/sustainable-development-goals-kick-off-with-start-of-new-year/.

- **Social measures:** These could be gender or race diversity or worker engagement numbers.

- **Governance criteria:** These measure how a business shapes up in corporate governance terms: Have there been any pay scandals? How responsive to shareholders is the board?

These broad categories are usually based on a broader set of objectives listed in something like the UN's own sustainable development goals (see the nearby sidebar).

The ESG movement is so broad that this short section really doesn't do it justice. Not just ETFs have embraced these goals. Many active fund managers are also incorporating ESG ideas into their process. But it's worth noting that most of the ESG ETFs tend to focus more on the climate change and environmental agenda.

Keeping Your Eyes Open When Investing in ETFs

ETFs have taken the world by storm. By and large, they've been a force for the good, and you should welcome them, even if you don't use them. They've given investors much more choice, and they've forced all managers to cut their fees – so, more competition, improved diversification and lower costs.

But ETFs aren't perfect, and they're certainly not for everyone. Some useful ETFs are available, whereas some are less useful. Here is a useful checklist of things to watch out for:

- **Think through whether an ETF or index tracking fund makes sense for the underlying investments.** For well-known, broad, liquid markets they can work a treat. But for less liquid, more opaque, difficult-to-trade-in markets such as up-and-coming frontier markets or highly specialist investment classes, they might be of less value.

- **Remember that cost isn't everything, but in ETF land it does matter.** If you're investing in a *bog standard,* well-known, liquid market and paying more than 0.50 per cent per annum, you may not be getting much value from the fund.

>> **Look at the small details.** For instance, pay attention to the *bid offer spread* – the difference between the buying and selling price of the shares. The smaller the bid offer spread, the better. Also work out the tracking error, which is the difference between the returns from the index and the returns from the ETF tracking that index. If there is a big tracking error (much more than the cumulative fees), then you should investigate further.

>> **Be careful of fads and marketing hype.** ETF firms are quick to jump on popular ideas. That's good in that they're responsive, but market sentiment is fickle and sometimes today's hot idea is tomorrow's has-been. ETF firms are quick to issue new funds and also (less) quick to close funds. Beware these big momentum trends and ask yourself whether the underlying investment idea makes sense.

>> **If you can't be bothered with all the choice, go for the robot.** The sheer proliferation of choice in ETF land has become confusing for many investors. Even after you've picked an investment market you like, you still have seemingly endless choices. If this all sounds a bit too much, then think about getting someone else to do the heavy lifting for you, by choosing their right ETFs and markets. Some funds invest across ETFs and some are also online, app-based robo advisers that will do this hard work for you. (Refer to Chapter 7 for more about robo advisers.)

Chapter **22**

Recognising the Relentless Rise of Technology

Technology is moving at a fearsome rate and in this chapter we navigate around the key trends, figuring out what's worth focusing on as an investor. Consider this fact: More than likely just ten years ago mobile phone penetration rates in China were probably well below 40 per cent. According to Statista, they were 43 per cent in 2015. This same source reckons that that number will be well above 60 per cent by 2023. Ponder that for a moment. China has many poor people especially in rural area who can't afford phones. Furthermore, many older Chinese probably don't want a mobile phone (who can blame them – emails, text messages, endless photos and videos). In urban areas most informed guesses are that mobile phone penetration – almost all of which will be smartphone based – is probably closer to 80 per cent or more. And China is a country within touching distance of being a middle-income country.

Even in Africa – which as a continent is definitely nowhere near middle income – had 477 million unique mobile phone subscribers and 272 million mobile Internet users. Go to small villages in central African highlands, and you'll find someone with a phone as well as a few solar panels and a few laptops.

These global statistics underline an essential point. Globalisation is important, but globalisation *and* technological transformation together are truly disruptive. What's happening at a global scale really is disruptive, revolutionary, ground-breaking stuff – pick your adjective. This digital transformation is about turning information into lots of 1s and 0s and then finding ever quicker ways of sharing said data at the click of a button or the touch of a screen. This transformation is having cascading impacts into everything from modern medicine – using data-driven research techniques – through to traditional consumer products. Talk to the likes of VW and Tesla, and they see the car as a one giant set of processors with an engine and wheels. It's even cascading down into food. Science fiction writers used to conjure worlds of flying drone delivery units and robotic farming devices, but now they're real – and everywhere. Even the food you eat is being grown in vats with the taste and texture manipulated using advanced bio informatic techniques and testing.

Just because everything is being digitised doesn't mean that every business with a share price will benefit equally. Technology favours the scale, global players, with the quickest technology and the biggest data sets. Yet, even these giant scale players can sometimes be upended by ark horse players who come out of nowhere with shiny new ideas. And even when you find your favourite player in whatever niche you focus on, always be vigilant about the price you're paying for buying into this glittering future.

This chapter explores these big trends and flags the key trends to watch – and the bear traps to avoid!

Looking Closer at How Digitisation Has Changed Everything

First came the humble personal computer. Then the Internet. Hook a PC up to the World Wide Web, and you have a connected swarm machine that harnesses the collective power of many machines. The next step is miniaturisation (turning a computer into a small handheld device that can be tucked away in your pocket). These three recent developments – measured in just a few decades – have helped power astonishing growth in global Internet penetration.

However, this digitisation process has much further to go. One obvious growth area is that most things can now be digitised. It started with music, and then hit film. TV followed quickly. In the world of business, many work-based processes are now being turned into digital processes, allowing faster processing times and increased output. One practical example helps explain this digitisation process: public transport. This used to be a highly physical, analogue industry. Paper tickets, mechanically powered devices. People businesses.

Public transport is just the tip of the digitisation iceberg. Even resolutely old-fashioned industries such as construction are starting to go digital. Across the industrial spectrum, new processes are being devised to run online. And a parallel shift is underway with devices – connected fridges, toasters, train carriages, planes, cars – are digital and connected. The 5G mobile networks of tomorrow – or today in some big cities – will allow a new Internet of Things (IoT) to emerge. Engineers even imagine a future where every bridge has its own IP address, its own access to point to a monitoring network, its own real-time monitoring. The message is plain to see: Myriad processes and things are being networked, connected and measured. And in this connected, digitised world, investors have huge opportunities not only in hardware solutions – networked cars, for instance – but also in software solutions.

Focusing on the Remorseless Rise of e-Commerce

Shopping used to be a social enterprise conducted on high streets and in crowds. That still happens but more and more spending is heading online, to e-commerce websites, and the High Street is faltering. This section maps out the opportunities of this big trend.

The coronavirus pandemic has had many side effects, but one stands out in business terms: It turbocharged an existing trend away from the bricks and mortar high streets to online e-commerce. Perhaps the simplest way of explaining this shift is to look at the stunning success of Amazon. According to Statista

>> In 2010 Amazon's revenues were $34 billion. By 2020 that had hit $386 bn

>> Amazon was responsible for 45 per cent of US ecommerce spending in 2019 and has an inventory of about 12 million items across all its categories and services.

>> There are more than 100 million Amazon Prime members around the world (more Prime members than non), and they typically spend more than $1,000 a year.

But the rise of e-commerce isn't just about Amazon. According to Statista approximately 55 per cent of the UK population shops online and people's favourite items to buy online are clothes and sports goods. According to the 2020 interview conducted by the Office for National Statistics, 32 per cent of UK online shoppers purchased deliveries from restaurants, fast-food chains or catering services.

E-commerce is also sweeping the globe. Market research firm eMarketer reckons that global ecommerce is expected to exceed $3.9 trillion in 2020 whereas in the US online sales increased by 32 per cent to $794 billion versus previous growth forecasts of 18 per cent growth. Similar surveys show that online grocery sales in 2020 grew by 43 per cent. Unsurprisingly the traditional High Street is a disaster zone. In the US, 30 retailers filed for bankruptcy in 2020, compared to 17 major retail bankruptcies in 2019, before the pandemic.

Cynics argue that after the pandemic ends, the High Streets might bounce back. That may be true to a degree, but in reality, more and more product categories are now going online. Take one small example – second-hand cars. These were traditionally sold via myriad dealers just off the High Street, but one of the fastest growing businesses today is Internet car supermarkets. This example based on selling a humble car speak to the fact that e-commerce is now spreading out from its start selling say books and electronics to selling anything and everything. And that's all before you begin to think through e-commerce's impact on the developing world.

Considering China's Influence

Everyone knows that China is big, very big (in population at least), but this section explores why its fast growing economy is crucially important for the rest of the world as well.

This chapter's introduction mentions the amazing technological transformation underway in China, led by smartphone penetration. But this revolution is only one part of a much bigger story – the concurrent modernisation, urbanisation *and* consumerisation of modern Chinese society. A few years ago, the US investment bank Goldman Sachs produced a handy short guide to the Chinese consumer that contained some astounding numbers. China had at that point a working population of at least 770 million (compared to 146 million in the US) of which 11 per cent were regarded as middle class. The fast-growing urban middle class comprised 146 million with an annual income per capita of $11,733 whereas below them sat an urban working class of 236 million with an annual average income of just under

46,000. These statistics are almost certainly woefully out of date by the time you read them in this book, and in fact we'd be tempted to add at least 25 per cent to pretty much all those numbers now!

What's most interesting about the report is the list of seven key consumer desires, topped in terms of spending by eating better, having a better home and looking more beautiful. We're sure that Marx and Mao are turning in their graves. The Goldman Sachs analysts also suggested that the potential fastest growing category was having more fun nicely summed up by charts showing exponential growth (pre Covid) in travel.

REMEMBER

Investors need to take all these findings with a big dollop of salt, but you don't need to be a genius to work out what Chinese consumers like to spend their money on – brands, especially technology brands, nice cars, travel, takeaway food delivered by a growing army of home delivery platforms, and IKEA. And we might also add another category – wealth and money management.

Although relations between the US and China deteriorate, you may notice one area of business cooperation that seems to be booming: Western banks, insurers, wealth businesses and fund managers are scrambling to get into the lucrative Chinese markets either on their own or through partnerships. They've collectively realised that as more and more Chinese acquire substantial wealth, they'll need someone to manage that wealth.

The only slight hitch is that existing Chinese businesses such as Ping An Insurance, a tech-powered financial services giant, are already building their market share by using clever technology to provide more and more products to tens of millions of clients. This insurance business is just one of a handful of domestic giants battling it out for control of the world's most lucrative fintech market.

WARNING

The potential in China is huge, but the risks are equally huge. The obvious one is that relations between China and the West break down so much that the Chinese communists in charge start hitting western shareholders. That hasn't happened yet, but you'd have to be hopeless optimist to think that at some point the Chinese government might decide to turn on foreign investors. Chinese consumers have already boycotted a long list of western businesses in core consumer markets, but the Chinese government is also perfectly capable of causing trouble for its own market leading firms. For instance, Alibaba had to pull the IPO of its hugely successful fintech unit Ant Financial at the last minute because of a backlash by local regulators.

Even if you find a Chinese business that somehow manages to keep western investors *and* the Chinese government on side, you still run into some other practical problems. Corporate governance is usually fairly dismal in most big companies.

If the Chinese communist party doesn't call the shots in the board room – perhaps via enormous Chinese state-owned banks – you'll usually find some complex share structure that allows the business founder to ignore everyone else.

Delving Deeper into the World of AI, Big Data and Robotics

Although artificial intelligence (AI) and robotics may once have been only the imagination of science fiction writers, the average automated voice service – trained on machine learning – is a long way from sci-fi dreams. In fact, investors need to consider the real opportunities within these related markets.

TIP

Watch carefully how developers and manufacturers bring new products to market in places like Japan, where an aging population and reluctance to import immigrant workers makes for the perfect test bed for new ideas around automation and robotics.

Consider one example: machine learning and voice calls. Microsoft recently purchased a business called Nunance that specialises in services such as automated transcription of documents. It's based around ever more complex machine learning that's now invading specialist markets such as healthcare – Nuance plays a big role in automating doctor's notes.

Equally in robotics, humanoid androids aren't wandering around the average High Street, but plenty of industrial robotics businesses are making solid profits. For example, Roboglobal is a specialist research firm focused on the robotics (and AI) space that also provides indices that are in turn tracked by a series of exchange traded funds (ETFs). Their market-leading intelligence reports reckon that the industrial automation market is estimated to reach $438 billion in value by 2027, whereas the Smart Robot Market might reach $16 billion plus by 2025. Other specialist markets they track (in their indices) include the computer Vision Market, which they think will hit $19 billion plus (by 2025) as well as the Healthcare AI Market, which could be worth $6 billion by 2021.

Dozens of firms are making solid profits in fast expanding robotics and AI markets, and the number of firms is likely to exponentially increase as the automated machines they produce gather ever more insights from the huge amounts of Big Data flowing into their processors. Over time, those machine learning codes that sit inside machine brains and systems will crunch that data and make ever more decisions that result in new products.

Understanding Investment Opportunities in the Cloud and Online Gaming

As everything goes digital, someone has to store that data somewhere. This section explores the business opportunities that are already emerging.

The *cloud* is a slightly broad term to describe a very real transformation. Here we try to explain what the cloud is. Consider email. Most people have stored thousands of emails on a server somewhere, which they access via an Internet gateway. That email 'library' sits in the cloud, on a server, probably thousands of miles away from where you live. Imagine the same principle being applied to not only movies on demand (think Netflix and Amazon Prime Video) or music but also software that runs a business. Or manages a health service. Or runs educational learning software.

The net result is largely the same. Data sits on computers, servers, somewhere on the planet connected by fibre optic cables to the Internet. These vast farms full of servers need huge cool warehouses that gobble up power to keep cool. More than likely giant tech corporations like Amazon and Microsoft operate them.

According to research firm IDC Worldwide whole cloud revenues will reach $554 billion by 2021. Consider Amazon, which started selling books online and then moved to selling other items. Over time, it started offering access to its e-commerce platform to third-party marketplaces. Soon Amazon realised it was also providing two other things: services to manage a store and computer servers to run the marketplace. And so, its Amazon Web Services (AWS) cloud business was born. Over the last decade AWS has grown into a cloud-based leviathan. AWS revenues amounted to $45 billion in 2020, and growth rates in sales and profits have been running at double digit growth rates for much of the last 15 years of its existence.

However, the cloud is more than just Amazon and its closest competitor Microsoft (Azure). Other leading cloud players and a myriad of businesses support a complex ecology of business processes situated on the web. Arguably the big shift is the move towards software as a service and infrastructure as a service as enterprises become more digital in their approach. An increasing demand for cloud-hosted applications such as video-conferencing has been accelerated by the Covid pandemic. Within this broad trend you can identify a number of distinct subthemes such as Infrastructure as a Service (IaaS), Platform as a Service (PaaS) and Software as a Service (SaaS).

Arguably the fastest growing market within this broad spectrum of services is online gaming. In the good old days, fans sat at home on their game consoles playing games (via DVD or downloads). However now more and more games are played online, multiplayer, in real time, via the cloud and what are called *edge media servers*. According to one data source, competitive video gaming audiences are expected to reach 495 million people globally, driven in part by rising population of digital natives. Within that cloud gaming market e-sports – competitive tournament-based gaming online – have also emerged with revenue growth increasing on average 28 per cent yearly since 2015.

Going Green – How Renewables Are Creating New Investing Prospects

The need to transition to a more sustainable economy, and transition away from fossil fuels, is already sparking a huge investment land grab. This section highlights the niches worth focusing on.

If you ever have a bit of spare time and want to examine up close the energy transition – from hydrocarbons to renewables – pay a visit to OurWorldInData, and in particular their section on renewable energy. On this site you can see a wide array of maps and data showing the rocketing share of power generated first by wind power – where the UK is very much in the lead, offshore at least – and then solar power. The story is obvious. The cost of manufacturing solar panels – and wind turbines – has collapsed (at least in terms of cost per unit of power generated), and in many parts of the world these renewable forms of grid-connected power are now cheaper than natural gas and coal. As a result, coal-fired power stations are closing at a rapid rate with the UK, boasting only a handful of working stations, and possibly none at all by the time you read this book. Even in India coal-fired power stations are closing down whereas in the US natural gas power stations are also starting to close. A new national grid is emerging, with more and more of the power generated by renewables. Who knows, the UK may even manage to replace its aging nuclear power fleet of generators with new units?

REMEMBER

This seismic change in how electricity is being generated has already had some major investment implications. Money has flooded into income-oriented renewable energy funds in the UK. But this is only the first ripples of a much longer wave of transformation that will span the next few decades. Renewable power needs to be generating at least 70 per cent of the country's power if the UK is to meet global decarbonisation deadlines, and some countries such as the US have a lot of catching up to do. But as renewables become ever more important, there are other problems. Both wind and solar power are intermittent – in other words, they don't always produce electricity when people need it. That means that on some occasions there's not enough power and on others too much. Cue the rise of energy storage technologies, and especially grid-connected battery plants that soak up spare power when it's cheap and plentiful and feed it back into the grid when power is desperately needed.

Batteries, whether connected to the gird and plonked in your electric car, will also need to carry on evolving and getting cheaper and more powerful. For electric cars that means having batteries that have more capacity to cover longer distances as well as charging faster. Technology will help, but ever more rare earths and metals such as lithium and cobalt will need to be dug from the ground. Another metal that will be absolutely crucial in this energy transformation is copper, plenty of which go into electric cars and wind power turbines.

TIP

Stepping back from these big transformations, you should keep your eye on three investment strategies:

>> Be defensive and focus on buying into income-generating assets from infrastructure assets like power generation and energy storage.

>> Invest in transformational commodities such as rare earths and copper if you're more adventurous and willing to bet mining equities.

>> If you're technology-focused, look at disruptive new ideas such as new materials for batteries, green (environmentally friendly) hydrogen and next-generation geothermal and mini-nuclear technologies.

Looking at Digital Currencies and the Blockchain

Confused by the crypto revolution? Can't figure whether Bitcoin or Ether is for you? Think of this section as a basic primer for the uninitiated.

It's remarkable to think that a little more than ten years ago, no one had even heard of crypto currencies and Bitcoin. It was only on 3 January 2009 that the first bitcoin network running on a blockchain first emerged, courtesy of the mysterious creator Satoshi Nakamoto, whoever he or she may be. For many years this digital currency ploughed its own farrow until a programmer called Vitalik Buterin switched on the Ethereum platform as arrival. Most older investors tend to be very cynical about the whole digital/crypto currency mania/craze, lambasting its recent origins, its decentralised basis of organisation and its frequent outrages and hacks.

But go online and check out the price of say Bitcoin over the last few years to see a very different story. Check out `https://crypto.com/price/bitcoin`. These upward sloping charts remind us that the price of Bitcoin has been on a bumpy ride with plenty of precipitous price falls, but the message is clear – more and more investors ascribe real value to Bitcoin.

As Bitcoin has become ever more mainstream, with investment banks jumping on the bandwagon, we have also seen a proliferation of rival currencies and platforms to Ethereum (and its currency ether) and Bitcoin. The big name is of course Bitcoin, which clearly dominates the market with a total value of a little less than $1 trillion. It's twice as big, in value terms, as its nearest rival Ethereum, which in turn is more than four times as big as the number three currency Binance Coin. After that there's a long list of other currencies, some of which are more well know – like DogeCoin for arguably less than positive reasons – and Tether – a stable coin pegged to the value of the dollar – through to currencies that are arguably really rather niche as Polkadot.

But the digital currency revolution is not only about just currencies. Sitting behind these digital creations is a complex ecology of innovations, most of which sit on something called a blockchain. According to its cheer leaders, this electronic distributed ledger is the centrepiece of a new form of decentralised finance. Rather than rely on central bankers, lawyers and accountants to verify every transaction, blockchain introduces an automated form of security and administration, powered by millions of computers around the globe checking and double checking ledger entries. Blockchain theoretically has almost limitless possibilities to upend existing administrative systems although practical implementations are somewhat rarer than the hype.

One practical implementation is the NFT, or non-fungible token. This builds on the block chain to in effect provide what is in effect a digital library which houses records or in this case tokens which in turn prove ownership of any asset. The most high-profile example of an NFT is in digital art involving creators such as Beeple who sold one piece of art for $69m via an NFT (which converted into 42 million ether). We don't as of now know who bought the collage but there's a fair chance that a crypto currency billionaire (of which there are plenty) probably used some of their digital wealth to fund the purchase.

Again, the cynic can easily build a case against all this innovation and its certainly true that anything priced in crypto currencies is likely to be a tad volatile in pricing but if it's all just a passing fad (valued in the hundreds of billions?), why is it that central banks are looking to launch their own digital currencies?

Going Global — Fintech Is Here

Money isn't what it used to be! As you discover in this section, cash is vanishing, and a whole new online financial system is emerging. To understand how that future might take shape, think about China.

China is speeding ahead when it comes to mass market adoption of online financial services. Cash is an increasingly rare sight in many major Chinese cities. But China isn't alone in adopting new online financial services, otherwise known as *fintech*. The UK is also a pioneer when it comes to fintech. Our small little island was one of the first to embrace a myriad of innovations to do with money. UK embraced peer-to-peer online lending early on. UK-based start-ups were also pioneering in building online only, app-based digital banks (such as Revolut, Starling and Monzo). The UK has also led the way with online filing of business and personal taxes, and UK businesses were also pioneers behind alternative online payments processes such as WorldPay. Boring old London is also the home of myriad investment-oriented digital finance businesses ranging from at least a half a dozen leading robo wealth advisers through to two of the world's leading digital crowdfunding platforms.

In truth, many of these businesses are still small scale and no match for the giant, traditional High Street banks. But those banks have also been embracing technological change, closing more and more branches and encouraging their customers to bank online. That's helped cut their bloated costs and improve profits. It has also channelled lucrative revenues to specialist technology firms that can help enable this change.

Preparing for the Coming Biotech and Genomics Revolution

Decoding human DNA seemed like a big deal at the time, but it's now clear this was just the start of a genomics revolution, as you discover in this section. The whole healthcare sector is now being turned into one giant digital research project with huge investment implications. There's even a term called *bioinformatics* used to describe how DNA data and therapeutic initiatives are giving us all an unprecedented understanding of how the human genome can be repaired or even rejuvenated.

In turn, this data-led revolution is founded on the new discipline of *genomics*, which is the study of the structure, the function and inheritance of the genome of an organism. This fast-emerging discipline relies on recombinant DNA and DNA sequencing methods plus all that data-led bioinformatics to sequence, assemble and analyse the structure and function of genomes. And there is plenty of data to analyse as every human contains a genome sequence of 3.2 billion letters!

On one level, these advances can seem rather abstract, but as tech fund management firm ArkInvest points out, there have already been huge advances. They observe that the cost to sequence a genome, once a nine-figure nation-state-worthy project, has dropped into the hundreds of dollars. They also note that for the first time, living therapies are likely to cure some diseases with just one dose.

One powerful new way of understanding this bioinformatic data is using a technology called Clustered Regularly Interspaced Short Palindromic Repeats (CRISPR), which refers to DNA sequences naturally found in the genomes of bacteria and other microorganisms. The CRISPR immune system defends itself from viral attack by destroying the genome of the invading virus. CRISPR technology now focuses on the portions of the DNA strand that has remnants of invaders or was defective by cutting and replacing the DNA stand itself.

Looking more broadly at the genomic space, you can see a number of new applications emerging. The most well-known is *genome sequencing*, which involves studying the DNA of an organism with the aim of uncovering gene mutations and abnormalities. There's also gene therapy that involves DNA editing or *gene therapy*, removing the defective piece and then replacing it with a healthy strand. Lastly in the mass market you can also see a profusion of genetic data services that involve testing for genetic data – via DNA tests – and then aggregating that data. According to the MIT Technology review by 2019, more than 26 million people had taken an at-home ancestry test.

The genomics sector itself is roughly worth around $19 billion in terms of revenue according to Motley Fool.

But if you invest in this space, you also need to be realistic about how you'll make money on very speculative ideas and stocks. One way is through big drug companies buying smaller, faster moving research-oriented biotech firms. Many smart investors have focused on putting money to work in businesses that are then taken over by much bigger drug leviathans.

Growing and Raising Food in the Food Revolution: Food 2.0

The food you eat is about to change, sparking a revolution in the whole food chain that will quite literally change the face of the Earth (consider all those fields full of food!). A new age of food is dawning, as we discuss in this section.

If the developing world carries on enriching more and more middle-class consumers, then a problem could emerge. If the developed world is anything to go by, middle class consumers like eating more meat, especially red meat. In China, it's pork, and in other countries it's beef. People also crave more sea food. So, imagine what will happen if after a decade hundreds of millions more consumers eat significantly more red meat and fish? Cattle and pig farming is energy intensive, gobbles up huge quantities of plant-based feedstock, produces huge methane emissions and in the case of fishing, destroys pristine oceanic habitats. One doesn't have to be a raging vegan to be slightly concerned about the impact of this growing consumer demand.

However, the food industry is also changing at breakneck speed, which we focus on a number of specific niches. Farming is being digitised at a rapid rate. Robots are emerging on farms, drones are flying over them, and the Internet and its information flows are being embedded in working practices. A typical day for a farmer in the not-too-distant future might consist of checking the weather feeds and commodity market price feeds first thing, followed by reports back from drones overnight. They might then head off to the fields on their tractor that has been upgraded with new technology and is guided by GPS. In the fields they might encounter robots weeding, and then they might stop by the closed loop greenhouses and indoor farms where they're growing high value produce such as salad greens.

These types of changes may impact some farmers more than others, especially if the farmers rear livestock. Plant-based meat alternatives are already becoming more popular, and every year seems to bring lower prices for these protein alternatives. Meatless burgers are now on sale in most geographies, and although you may question that the taste isn't quite there yet compared to traditional red meat, it's moving ever closer. But cultured meat, grown in bioreactors, might make that final leap. In Singapore you can already buy (expensive) lab-grown, cultured chicken nuggets that taste like the real chicken nuggets but are essentially cultured.

All these growing number of meat alternatives need to find their way into your home. The obvious distribution channel is through the local supermarket that might in turn choose to deliver via a home delivery service. You might also subscribe to postal-based food kits and plans that also offer sustainable alternatives. On High Street you'll also increasingly encounter fast-food outlets that sell meat alternatives – all the major, well-known fast-food outlets are experimenting with these products. And in the not very distant future, your meat alternatives might be delivered by drones or land-based mini-robots. And of course, these last mile technologies to the home don't have to deliver just meat alternatives – they can deliver traditional foodstuffs as well. There is a huge growth market in last mile technologies, which aim to cut out the local supermarket all together.

Whatever technology triumphs, you can be sure that the food you eat won't be quite the same in decades to come.

5

The Part of Tens

Know how to identify potential warning signs that a share price is about to decline.

Recognise ten signs that a share price is about to increase.

Find out how you can protect yourself against fraud.

Discover challenges and opportunities for stock investors.

Chapter **23**

Ten Warning Signs of a Share's Decline

Have you ever watched a film and noticed that one of the characters coughs excessively throughout? To us, that's a dead giveaway that the character is a goner. Or maybe you've seen a film in which a bit-part character annoys a crime boss, so right away you know that it's time for him to 'sleep with the fishes'. Shares aren't that different. If you're alert, you can recognise some definite signs that your investment may be ready to kick the bucket.

Let the tips in this chapter serve as a symptoms checklist on your share investments. This chapter will help you catch your share as it starts to 'cough', so that you can get out before it 'sleeps with the fishes'. (We just can't help you with mixed metaphors.)

Earnings Slowdown

Profit is the lifeblood of a company, so lack of profit is a sign of a company's poor financial health. Watch the earnings. Are they increasing or not? If they aren't, find out why. If the general economy is experiencing a recession, stagnant earnings are still better than hefty losses – everything is relative. Earnings slowdowns for a company may very well be a temporary phenomenon. If a company's earnings are holding up better than its competitors' and/or the market in general, you don't need to be alarmed.

Nonetheless, a company's earnings are its most important measure of success. Keep an eye on the company's P/E ratio. It could change negatively (go up) because of one of two basic scenarios:

>> The share price goes up as earnings barely budge.

>> The share price doesn't move, yet earnings drop.

Both of these scenarios result in a rising P/E ratio that ultimately has a negative effect on the share price.

REMEMBER

A P/E ratio that's lower than industry competitors' P/E ratios makes a company's shares favourable investments.

Don't buy the argument, 'Although the company has losses, its sales are exploding'. This argument is a variation of, 'The company may be losing money, but it'll make it up on volume'. For example, say that R.U.B. Bish PLC (RUBB) had sales of £1 billion in 2021 and that sales expect to be £1.5 billion in 2022, projecting an increase at RUB of 50 per cent. But what if RUB's earnings were £200 million in 2021 and the company was actually expecting a loss for 2022? The company wouldn't succeed because sales without earnings isn't enough – the company needs to make a profit. Remember that if you put your money in the shares of a company that has losses, you're not investing, you're speculating.

WARNING

Profit warnings are a particularly serious example of an earnings slowdown. Big companies spend inordinate amounts of time 'guiding' the profit estimates devised by analysts in the broking and banking firms. This low-level, steady drum beat of off the record activity gives 'reassurance' to the market that the company bosses are in control and the company is progressing steadily. Every once in a while, though, everything goes pear-shaped and that guidance turns out to be utter tosh, prompting the lesser-spotted profits warning. This situation is bad news on a number of levels. The first is that analysts feel as though they've been led up the garden path and lied to. Cue selling of the shares. The next bad thing to happen is that outside investors reckon that management are losing the plot. Cue more selling. Long-term investors tend to be focused on a rather more humdrum concern; namely, that profit warnings resemble London buses and tend to come in threes. It's very rare for a company to issue a single profit warning and most tend to come in threes and fours. The market is aware of this scenario and punishes the shares accordingly. Bargain hunters think that this punishment is sometimes overdone, but most analysts reckon that companies that issue a profit warning are deadly value traps and should be avoided at all costs.

Sales Slowdown

Sales figures may not give you the whole picture of a company's health, but you can't generate profit without them. Before you invest in a company, make sure that sales are strong and rising. If sales start to decline, that downward motion ultimately affects earnings (refer to the previous section). Although the earnings of a company may go safely up and down, sales should consistently rise. If they cease to rise, a variety of reasons may be to blame. First, the slowdown may be temporary because the economy in general is having tough times. However, the situation may be more serious. Perhaps the company is having marketing problems, or a competitor is eating away at its market share. Maybe a new technology is replacing its products and services. In any case, falling sales raise a red flag you shouldn't ignore.

Exuberant Analyst Reports That Defy Logic

Sometimes, analysts give glowing praise to companies that any logical person with some modest financial acumen would avoid like the plague. Why is this? In some cases, the reasons are murky (or you could argue that plain stupidity is to blame). In any case, remember that analysts are employed by companies that earn hefty investment banking fees from the very companies that these analysts tout. You can see why some analysts might feel pressurised into modifying their opinions.

You should be wary of analysts' views, especially the analysts who make positive recommendations even when the company in question has worrisome features, such as no income and tremendous debt. It may seem a paradox: sell a share when all the pros say buy it. How can that be? Remember, the merits of any share should speak for themselves. When a company is losing money, all the great recommendations in the world can't reverse its fortunes. Also, keep in mind that if everybody is grabbing a particular share – the current analysts' favourite – who's left to buy it? When it turns out to be a dud, you aren't able to sell it because all the other suckers already own it (thanks to analysts' recommendations!). And, if they already own it, they're probably already aware of the company's flaws. What happens then? You got it: more and more people end up selling this particular share. And when more people are selling than buying a share, its price declines.

Insider Selling

Heavy insider selling is to a company's shares what garlic, sunrises and crosses are to vampires: an almost certain sign of doom! If you notice that increasing numbers of insiders (such as the chairperson, the finance director and the chief executive of the company) are selling their holdings, you can consider it a red flag. In recent years, massive insider selling has become a tell-tale sign of a company's imminent fall from grace. After all, who better to know the company's prospects for success (or lack of) than the company's high-level management? What management does (selling shares, for example) speaks louder than what management says. (Do you hear that loud and persistent coughing again?) For more information on insider trading, see Chapter 19.

Dividend Cuts

For investors who own income shares, dividends are the primary consideration. But, income shares or not, dividend cuts are a negative sign. Of course, if a company is having modest financial difficulty, perhaps a dividend cut is a good thing for the overall health of the company. However, usually analysts see a dividend cut as a sign that a company is having trouble with its earnings or cash flow. In either case, a dividend cut is a warning sign that trouble may be brewing for the firm as it becomes . . . uh . . . less firm.

If the company you own shares in announces a dividend cut, find out why. The cut may simply be a temporary measure to help the company out of some minor financial difficulty, or it may be a sign of deeper trouble. Check the company's fundamentals and then decide. (Refer to Chapter 11 to find out how to read and interpret company financial documents.)

Increased Negative Coverage

You may easily see unfavourable reports of a company's shares as a sign to unload them. Or you may be a contrarian and see bad press as an opportunity to scoop up some shares in a company victimised by negative reporting. In any case, take the negative reports as a signal to investigate further. Maybe the negative coverage really does provide you with an opportunity for a bargain. Or, alternatively, selling these shares so that you can make room in your portfolio for a more promising choice of shares may be the best outcome.

Industry Problems

Sometimes, being a strong company doesn't matter if that company's industry is having problems; if the industry is in trouble, the company's decline probably isn't that far behind. Tighten up those trailing stops. (See Chapter 17 to find out how.) Also, try to be aware of industries that are intimately related to your industry. Very often, problems in one industry can affect or spread to a related industry. If car sales are plummeting (for example), then that's likely to have a negative effect on prospects for car parts or car servicing companies.

Political Problems

Political considerations are always a factor in investing. Be it taxes, regulations or other government actions, politics can easily break a company and send its shares plummeting. If your company's shares are sensitive to political developments, be aware of potential political pitfalls for your choice of company (or industry). Reading the *Financial Times* and regularly viewing major financial websites can help you stay informed. (We give you lists of sources in Appendix A.)

In recent years, energy stocks (oil and gas businesses) have had a tough time because of prevailing political attitudes around climate change. Also, certain shares in particular (Facebook currently springs to mind) have seen their share prices drop drastically because they were targets of government actions for reasons ranging from antitrust concerns to public safety issues.

Too High or Unsustainable Debt

Excessive debt is the kiss of death for a struggling company. Record numbers of companies are going bankrupt through debt, including companies that experts thought were invincible.

The most obvious recent example is the story of Enron. Many analysts and investment advisory publications actually touted Enron as a strong buy – even though the amount of problematic data could have made Godzilla gag. Not many investors get a kick out of reading old issues of financial magazines that listed the defunct company the year before its demise as one of ten shares 'for the long haul'. Blimey. Writers like that probably have hobbies such as hang-gliding during hurricane season. Chapter 11 and Appendix B can help you read and understand a company's financial data so that you can make an informed decision about buying or selling its shares.

Funny Accounting: No Laughing Here!

Throughout this book, we discuss the topic of accounting as an important way to see how well (or how poorly) a company is doing. Understanding a company's balance sheet and income statement, and making a simple comparison of these documents over a period of several years, can give you great insights into the company's prospects. You don't have to be an accountant to grasp key concepts.

So, what signs should you look out for? Try these:

>> **Off-balance sheet nonsense:** Look through the detailed notes at the end of the accounts and see what financial entities the company has constructed to hide . . . sorry . . . displace financial liabilities in vehicles usually registered in the West Indies. Companies are required to report these entities and, although they're not usually effusive about the nitty-gritty detail, you can get some idea of the full horrors that are hidden away.

>> **Pension fund deficits:** These are also reported in the notes section at the back of the reports and accounts. Most big companies have accumulated large deficits in their pension schemes and they'll state that fact in black and white. What they're more reluctant to tell you is the changing dynamic of those 'liabilities' – for that is what a pension fund deficit is. These deficits need to be funded by shareholders and eventually the bill will need to be paid! Look to see how that deficit has changed over time and how big it is relative to the accumulated equity in the company.

>> **Company provenance:** Lots of foreign companies, and especially those based in the emerging markets, have listed on the UK and US stock markets and used all manner of clever devices to have a shiny Anglo-Saxon ticker attached to their name. While nothing's intrinsically wrong with this situation, you do need to understand these companies' underlying financial structures, especially Chinese companies. Do two sets of accounts exist, one for you and one for the local tax inspector? Is a big accounting firm working on those numbers or some hokey-pokey small firm in deepest Florida that no one's ever heard of?

>> **The cash trail:** Lots of respectable companies play all sorts of tricks when it comes to reporting their profits. Many companies have been producing exceptional items on their accounts every year for the last 20 years. One never quite knows what's exceptional, normal or just odd. Our best tip is to follow the cash. Look at what's coming in and what's going out. If too much is going out on a regular basis, that can only mean an increase in debt and eventual trouble. Companies are like everyone else – they have to live within their means!

To understand these points more fully (along with other equally incisive and lucid accounting and financial points), and to know how to use the information to avoid similar mistakes in the future, see Chapters 10 and 11 and Appendix B.

For more info on understanding the detail of company documents, check out *Interpreting Company Reports For Dummies*, by Ken Langdon, Alan Bonham and Lita Epstein (John Wiley & Sons, Inc.).

Chapter **24**

Ten Signals of a Share Price Increase

I f you find a share that has all ten signals listed in this chapter, start getting to know the company and maybe even think about including it on your watch-list of shares so that you're ready and able to pounce if the price is right. The odds are that you won't need all ten to indicate that it's a share worth a closer look. Probably five or more signals are enough to merit further consideration. In any case, the more signals, the better your chances of choosing a successful share.

REMEMBER

Regardless of market conditions and investor sentiment (how investors 'feel' about shares and the economy), remember the three rules of investment success: profits, profits, profits, also known as earnings, earnings, earnings. This advice is as important as property's location, location, location. It's that important . . . uh . . . important, important.

Rise in Earnings

If a company earned £1 per share for the past three years and its earnings are now £1.20 per share (a 20 per cent increase), consider this increase a positive harbinger. As the saying goes, 'Earnings drive the market', so you need to pay attention to the company's profitability. The more a company makes, the greater the chance that its share price will increase.

Some people wonder whether to invest in a company that was losing money and then finally turns a profit. Perhaps you're considering shares in a company involved in new, untested technology. Our advice is that you need to be careful in this situation. In such a case, predicting whether a second year of profits will show up is difficult, but, of course, that's what investors are hoping for.

For the serious investor, a track record of positive earnings is important. Several years of earnings (especially growing earnings) are crucial in the decision-making process. As earnings rise, make sure that the growth is at a rate of 10 per cent or higher.

Say that you're looking at Buckets-o-Money PLC (BOM). BOM had earnings of £1 per share in 2009, £1.10 in 2010 and £1.21 in 2011. First, you can see that the company is a profitable enterprise. Second (and more importantly), you can see that the earnings grew 10 per cent each year. The fact that earnings are growing consistently year after year is important because it indicates that the company is being managed well. Effective company management has a very positive effect on the share price because the market notices the company's progress.

Growing earnings are important for another reason – inflation. If a company earns £1 per share in each year, that's of course better than earning less or losing money. But inflation erodes the purchasing power of money. If earnings stay constant, the company's ability to grow decreases because the value of its money will decline as a result of inflation.

Increase in Assets Because Debts Are Stable or Decreasing

Increasing assets while decreasing debts (or at least stabilising them) is key to growing the book value of a company. *Book value* refers to the company's value as it appears on a balance sheet – equal to total assets minus liabilities. Book value usually differs significantly from market value (or market capitalisation) because market value is based on supply of and demand for the company's shares in the marketplace. For example, a company may have a book value of £10 million (assets of £15 million less liabilities of £5 million) but a market value of £19 million (if, for example, it has 1 million shares that are currently trading at £19 per share). Usually, market value is higher (sometimes much higher) than book value.

Rising book value has a positive impact on market value, which, in turn, tends to drive the share price up as well. Therefore, watch book value. Rising book value can be accomplished in one of two ways:

>> Debt stays level as assets rise.

>> Assets stay level as debts decline.

TIP

When looking at a company's assets and debts, the best scenario you can find is assets rising and debts declining.

At the most basic level, total assets should exceed total debt. Preferably, the company should have a ratio of at least 2-to-1 in terms of assets to debt. A ratio of 3-to-1 is better, and so on.

The best way to figure out a company's asset to debt ratio is to look at the company's most recent balance sheet and compare it to its balance sheet from prior periods (such as the year before or the same quarter last year). By comparing the figures over three or more years, you can see a trend developing. If the asset to debt ratio has been stable or improving over these three balance sheets, the company is showing growing financial strength, which will help the company's share price increase in value.

Positive Publicity for the Industry

When the media report that a company is doing well financially or that its products and services are being well received by the market, that news lets you know that this company's shares may be going places. This positive publicity ties in nicely with the point we make in the section 'Consumer Desire for the Brand', later in this chapter about consumer acceptance of the company's products and services.

Positive press and consumer acceptance are important because they mean that the company is doing what's necessary to please its customers. The positive media coverage also may attract new customers to the company. Gaining customers means more sales and more earnings, which translate into a higher price for the shares. You can find corporate publicity on individual company websites and on the RNS (Regulatory News Service) run by the London Stock Exchange, www.londonstockexchange.com.

Heavy Insider or Corporate Buying

Company insiders (such as the chief executive and the finance director) know more about the health of a company than anyone else. If insiders are buying shares by the boatload, then these purchases are certainly a positive sign for investors. Chapter 19 covers insider trading, but we highlight the main points here. Insiders can do one of two things:

>> **Buy shares for themselves:** If individuals such as the chief executive or the finance director are buying shares for their personal portfolios, you can assume that they think the shares are a good investment.

>> **Buy shares as a corporate decision:** When the company buys its own shares, it's usually considered a positive move. The company may see its own shares as a good investment. Additionally, corporate share buybacks reduce the number of shares available in the market, potentially pushing the share price higher.

All things being equal, both of these approaches should have a positive impact on the share price. The odds are that you won't see a stampede of insiders buying the shares in one day or week, but you will see a buying pattern over a period of months. This is generally true simply because each insider has different circumstances, and insider buying is usually done on an individual basis. An accumulation of purchases tells you that members of the management team believe so strongly that the company will do well that they're willing to put their own money at risk.

Increased Attention from Analysts

Many good analyst reviews, and the public's opinion of a single influential analyst, can make a share's price move dramatically.

WARNING

Analyse a share according to its own merits first. Then watch the share's price as more and more analysts start to direct the public's attention to it. In a sense, they're promoting your shares, an action that tends to boost their price. Don't let the analysts' views sway you, though, because analysts may tout a share for unsavoury reasons. Perhaps the company is a client of the brokerage firm, or maybe the brokerage firm owns a lot of the company's shares and wants to unload them. Analysts have to declare interests such as these if they have them.

Rumours of Takeover Bids

A company that's rumoured to be a takeover candidate (a company that may potentially be bought out by another company) may have an attractive aspect, such as a promising new patent or exclusive rights to certain properties, that could make it worthy for investors as well.

Rumours of a buyout are always welcome, but the bottom line is still that such talk should merely alert you to the possibility of valuable shares. Regardless of whether the buyout rumour proves true, you shouldn't even consider the shares if they aren't worth owning on their own merits. If it's a good company, the rumour tends to increase its visibility and the chance of a takeover is actually more likely. Rumour or not, the attention does tend to increase the share price.

Consumer Desire for the Brand

A company is only as good as the profit it generates. The profit it generates is only as good as the revenues that the company generates. The revenues are based on whether customers accept (and shell out money for) the company's products or services. Therefore, if what the company offers is popular with consumers, it bodes well for profits and consequently higher share prices.

When you're ready to invest in shares, look for high consumer satisfaction. Review consumer publications and websites and read the surveys and consumer feedback information. Good publicity and word-of-mouth consumer satisfaction are things that investors should be aware of. Share-picking expert Peter Lynch (formerly of Fidelity Magellan fund fame) sees this popularity with consumers as very valuable share-picking information. He likes to see what consumers buy because that's where the company's success starts.

Strong or Improving Bond Rating

In Chapter 9, we point out that a poor or deteriorating bond rating is a warning sign for the company. The creditworthiness of a company is a critical factor in determining the company's strength. Most people presume that the bond rating is primarily beneficial for bond investors, and they're correct. However, because the bond rating is assigned according to the company's ability to pay back the bond plus interest, it stands to reason that a strong bond rating (usually a rating of AAA or AA) indicates that the company is financially strong.

The work of independent bond rating firms, such as Standard & Poor's and Moody's, is invaluable for investors in shares.

Powerful Demographics

If you found out that a company generates lots of profit from the teenage market and you find out that the teenage market is going to expand by 10 per cent per year for the foreseeable future, what would you do? Exactly – you'd buy shares in that company. If a company has strong fundamentals and appealing products or services and its market is expanding, that company has a winning combination.

TIP

Stay alert to growing trends in society. How are demographics changing? Which sectors of the population are growing? Shrinking? What shifts are expected in society in terms of age or ethnicity? Check out the data freely available at the Office for National Statistics. You can simply call up with a query or check out the results of the latest census – taken in 2011 – at www.ons.gov.uk.

The census statistics, for instance, show that people are living longer. Companies that target their products and services at elderly consumers are increasing their earnings. Saga, founded by the son of a shoe factory worker from London's East End, has grown from a firm selling short breaks to the over-fifties to a 'grey giant' selling insurance and travel services. The company was bought by venture capitalists in October 2004 for £1.7 billion. In 2007 their investment was shown to be a sound one when motoring organisation the AA bought Saga in a deal which valued it at just under £3 billion. They then floated on the London stock market in 2014 at 185p a share valuing them at more than £1 billion. At one point the shares had hit nearly £35 a share but in recent years – especially after the COVID pandemic – that share price crashed down and as of April 2021 was only at 370p a share.

A market that's growing in size isn't an indicator all by itself (in fact, no indicator gives you the green light all by itself), but it should encourage you to do some research. The fact that a strong company sees improving demographic shifts in its marketplace is a big plus.

Low P/E Relative to Industry or Market

The price-to-earnings (P/E) ratio is a critical number for investors. Value investors in particular scrutinise it. Because the share price's future ability to rise is ultimately tied to the company's earnings (profits), you want to know that you're not paying too much for it. A low P/E ratio (low relative to some standard, such as the industry's average or the average P/E for the S&P 500) is generally considered safe, and the shares are a potential bargain.

If the industry's P/E ratio is 20 and you're looking at a share that has a P/E of 15, all things being equal, that's great. The company has room for growth, and you're getting good value.

Chapter **25**

Ten Ways to Protect Yourself from Fraud

M aking money is tough enough without worrying about who's out to get your cash. The usual suspects, such as Her Majesty's Revenue and Customs (HMRC) and other government agencies, are trying to take your money legally. Fortunately, most of that money goes to apparently beneficial pursuits. However, others are out to take your money by illegal methods. Fraud and theft schemes have always existed. If you that hedge-fund cheat Bernie Madoff was one of a kind – think again! Scammers are most prevalent during two economic conditions: when times are really, really good and when times are really, really bad. During the Great Depression and manic bull markets alike, fraudsters were and are part of the human condition. Bottom line: be alert and use the tips in this chapter to avoid being scammed.

Be Wary of Unsolicited Calls and Emails

Phone calls or emails out of the blue to solicit money from you are always a bit questionable, but if they offer investments, you need to be particularly careful. But you knew that, right? You've read countless consumer reports warning you about investing via call centres and bogus emails. If the investment that's being pitched is so good, why is someone calling to sell you on it? Hasn't the financial press reported it? It probably has, but only as a warning to turn down any such offers. Find out more at websites such as www.scambusters.org and www.actionfraud.police.uk.

Get to Know the FCA

Long before you invest your first pound, whether in shares or any other financial investment, get to know the Financial Conduct Authority (FCA). It's there primarily to protect investors from fraud and other unlawful activity designed to fleece them. The UK government created the FCA – then called the FSA – during the late 1990s to bring together several organisations that regulated different types of financial transactions and the people who carried them out. The aim of the FCA was and is to crack down on abuses that harmed consumers and the reputation of financial services companies.

TIP

The FCA has an excellent website at www.fca.org.uk. The site offers plenty of great articles and resources for both novice and experienced investors to help you watch out for fraud and better understand the financial markets and how they work. You can call the FCA to ask if any broker or company you're dealing with is regulated and if any action has been taken against them. The FCA carries out a number of activities designed to help you invest with confidence. If it has penalised a company for regulatory failures it makes the sanction or fine public. And it maintains a database on file about fines levied against brokers and companies that have committed fraud or other abuses against the investing public.

Your tax pays for this important agency. Find out about its free publications, services and resources before you invest. If you've already been victimised by unscrupulous operators, call the FCA for assistance and advice.

Don't Invest If You Don't Understand

Investments frequently come in complicated forms that promise a great return but can be hard to understand. The premise of the investment – how it works and how it will create a great return on your money – may be hard to figure out. Scammers count on people being overwhelmed by the details to the point that they ignore the mechanics of the deal. Don't fall for such approaches. You should understand exactly what you're investing in, how it makes money and what the risks are. If you still can't understand the investment (even if it's legitimate), then you're probably better off not plunging in with your hard-earned money.

If the investment still sounds intriguing, then at the very least get a second opinion by reviewing the details with advisors you trust.

Question the Promise of Extraordinary Returns

In good times and bad, people want to make as much money as possible with their investments. Hey, who doesn't? If your money is in a bank account earning a paltry 1 per cent, what's wrong with putting some of it into an investment earning 17 per cent compounded hourly? The extraordinary returns promised either end up being illusory or the result of great risk.

Misrepresenting or inflating promises of a great return on your money is common; sometimes even good brokers can unwittingly make such promises. Higher returns mean more exposure to risk.

If the investment is genuine and is quoted as having a high rate of return (either in income or capital gains potential), then you can expect commensurate risk. The risk may not be immediately apparent, but it's there. As the broken record that we are in this chapter, we recommend that you seek independent third parties for an informed second opinion. Appendix A has an extensive list of places and people to turn to.

REMEMBER

A notable investment pro once remarked, 'Sometimes, a return *on* your money is not as important as a return *of* your money'. In other words, until you pick up more investing knowledge, keeping your original investment safe is better than risking it for questionable, pie-in-the-sky promises.

Verify the Investment

If anyone asks you to invest, first verify that the investment exists. Sounds weird, huh? Not really. Yes, many people have lost money in a bad or dubious investment, but you'd be surprised at how many people have been willing to fork over hard-earned money for phantom investments.

Most share investment scams are perpetrated by so-called boiler rooms. This is a set up that appears to be legit but which exists solely to separate hapless – and probably greedy – punters from their money. These dodgy investment 'opportunities' are generally pushed by email.

When someone offers you an investment and you're not certain what type of investment it is or where it's traded, ask questions of the person presenting the investment and of third parties who can offer verification. Here are some questions to ask:

>> What exchange or market is this investment traded or sold on?

>> What government agency oversees this investment, and how can I contact that agency?

>> Have articles on this investment been published by major media sources, such as *the Financial Times* and *Investors Chronicle* magazine?

>> Can I find documents filed by this company on RNS (the Regulatory News Service) or one of the other approved services?

>> What literature do you have that I can present to my accountant and lawyer, if I need to?

Check Out the Broker

Sometimes the investment is legitimate, but the broker or dealer isn't. Scammers don't let the absence of a licence stop them. When an unfamiliar financial product marketer contacts you, do some homework first. Contact one of the following to check the status of a broker or dealer:

>> **The FCA:** Are these marketers properly registered? The FCA can inform you about whether these marketers have been penalised or banned from further activity.

>> **Professional associations:** Do you want to know whether a marketer is a member in good standing? Associations help the public deal with unethical parties in the industry.

>> **The London Stock Exchange (LSE):** Visit its great website at www.london stockexchange.com. This site informs the public about the stockbrokers who are members of the exchange.

Beware of the Pump-and-Dump

The pump-and-dump is a classic scam that usually shows up in bull markets. The scam works best with small-cap or (even better) penny shares – in other words, small companies that have relatively few shares or small capitalisation. Scams are at their most effective when they can play on the two most overworked emotions in the financial markets: greed and fear. In the pump-and-dump, greed is the operative emotion. In this example, the investor to be plucked is called Jim Nicebutdim (no relation to the popular comic character Tim Nicebutdim).

The insiders at the dubious company first try to promote the shares as a 'hot investment'. The company activates the 'pump' when insiders and/or a stockbroker, in cahoots with the insiders, call up investors such as Mr Nicebutdim to tout this fantastic chance. They promise an opportunity to get into a profitable share that will skyrocket in value. As a result of the high-pressure sales tactics, investors start buying the shares. This demand pushes up the price easily because so few shares are available on this thinly-traded company. Perhaps Mr Nicebutdim didn't bite the first time the broker called, but the broker calls again.

'Hello again, Mr Nicebutdim! This is Barry Kuda, account representative from the brokerage firm of Fleecem & Scarper. Do you remember that share investment I brought to your attention last week? That's right . . . Titanic Bio-Tech, Inc. Have you seen the way its price has zoomed since then? When I last spoke to you, it was at £3 a share. Now it's already at £47! Our respected research department tells me it should be at £93 by lunchtime and will probably triple again before the weekend. You don't want to miss this opportunity of a lifetime! Now, how many shares would you like?'

Indeed, the price certainly went up dramatically as Mr Kuda said it would. Mr Nicebutdim puts the order in immediately while pound signs dance in his head. The 'pump' is working very well. After the fraudulent operators see that the share has gone as high as possible, they immediately sell their shares at grossly inflated prices. The 'dump' is complete, and they disappear into the woodwork. Mr Nicebutdim and the other investors watch as their 'hot' investment turns stone cold and the shares plummet to pennies in the pound. Investors can be so blinded by their greed that the pump-and-dump scam has been successfully executed even in cases when no shares existed at all!

WARNING

How can we offer a warning about something legal in a chapter about fraud? Actually, isn't this entire chapter a warning? Yes, but sometimes you need a warning for things that aren't immediately apparent. As odd as this may sound, we want to warn you about something that technically isn't fraud. What is it? Well, a legal version of the pump-and-dump scheme does exist. It's not unusual for brokers and analysts to 'pump' up a share in the media. For example, a celebrated market strategist or high-profile CEO may talk up the wonderful potential of XYZ shares on a financial show. Then later you find out (through RNS filings, for instance) that, while these people were recommending that people buy the shares, they'd actually been furtively selling their holdings in them. You were hearing 'buy, buy' but they were really saying 'bye-bye'.

Watch Out for Short-and-Abort

Short-and-abort works on the same premise as pump-and-dump. The difference is that, instead of playing on greed, the con works on fear. To understand this scam, you should keep in mind that one can profit even when a share falls in price by 'going short'. Chapter 17 goes into detail about making money from going short on shares, but here we want to briefly describe the process.

Going short is a strategy that an investor can use in a margin account with a broker. An investor may consider going short on a share if she expects the share's price to fall. Say that you think the shares of Plummet PLC (at £50 per share) will sink fast. When you tell the broker that you want to go short on 100 shares of Plummet PLC, the broker borrows 100 shares from the market, sells those shares and credits £5,000 to your account (100 shares at £50 per share). Because this transaction is based on 'borrowed shares', sooner or later you have to return the shares. Say that the share price falls to £30; you could then instruct your broker to 'close out the position'. This order means that the broker debits your account to the tune of £3,000 (to buy 100 shares at £30) and returns the shares to the source. In this case, you make a £2,000 profit (the original £5,000 less the £3,000).

In the case of short-and-abort, the scammers want to make money from a share's plummeting price. They may contact shareholders directly or plant phoney stories or press releases in the media to cause concern and panic over a company's prospects. Naturally, shareholders in that particular company get anxious about their investment and decide to sell. The sudden, mass selling causes the share's price to fall. The scammer then closes out the short position, takes the money and runs.

Remember That Talk Is Cheap (Until You Talk to an Expert)

A fertile area for misleading investors is in the world of independent, third-party information sources. As one recent bull market reached its zenith, some people were running expensive share-investing seminars and selling newsletters that promised get-rich-quick results. One promoter in the US sold basic information (some of which was inaccurate) in a £5,000 seminar programme. After many complaints, the authorities investigated and found out that the presenters certainly made a lot of money from their seminars but actually lost money as a result of their investment strategies! (It figures.)

Another information marketer published an expensive newsletter that promised lucrative share picks. It was discovered that he wasn't recommending shares found through diligent and honest research but was actually touting shares in companies that paid him to do so.

Seminars and newsletters are excellent sources of information and expertise on a given topic, but you should stay away from marketers that use hard-sell approaches for outrageously priced seminars and other information products.

Recovering (If You Do Get Scammed)

If, despite your best efforts to invest wisely, you have that sinking feeling that you've been conned, it's time to gain assistance from the authorities. The FCA is a good place to start, but you can turn to other agencies, too.

If a scheme was promoted by phone, especially on a premium rate line, you can contact the phone-paid Services Authority (psauthority.org.uk), the regulatory body for the premium rate telecommunications industry. It has the power to fine companies abusing premium phone lines or supplying misleading content.

Local trading standards offices will always be interested to hear of scams being carried out in their areas. See Appendix A for more resources.

Chapter **26**

Ten Challenges and Opportunities for Stock Market Investors

O ver the years, we've found that the easiest way to make (or avoid losing) money with shares is to simply be aware of the economic environment in which they operate. Shares can be the best (or worst) investment given the economic/political climate. Many economic challenges face the stock market and they include what's happening with government policy, societal trends and national/international geopolitical conditions. You need to be aware of the big picture by staying in touch with the news and regularly checking in with great websites such as Breaking Views (www.breakingviews.com), the *Financial Times* (ww.ft.com) and Bloomberg (www.bloomberg.co.uk).

In this chapter, we discuss the most important issues or megatrends that can affect you and your loved ones as well as your share investments.

Debt, Debt and More Debt

After the global financial crisis, the developed world became painfully aware that excessive debt levels might pose long-term challenges. What followed was a decade of some belt tightening – with the UK government cracking down on the fiscal debt. Some, though not all, corporates also made progress while many individuals also tightened their belts. And then along came the coronavirus pandemic. And guess what happened? Debt levels shot back up again.

According to the government's own statisticians, general government gross debt hit £1,876.8 billion at the end of the financial year ending (FYE) 2020, equivalent to 84.6 per cent of gross domestic product (GDP) and 24.6 percentage points above the level of 60.0 per cent, which in earlier years had been set as an 'excessive deficit' level. On a side note, general government gross debt first exceeded 60.0 per cent at the end of FYE 2010, when it was 69.0 per cent of GDP.

Corporate debt levels are also on the rise as a consequence of the pandemic. According to Statista, corporate debt levels as a percentage share of GDP rose in every major G8 country between the second quarter of 2019 and 2020. In France it had hit 167 per cent, China 162 per cent, the US 83 percent and 77.7 per cent in the UK.

Very few commentators disagreed with the idea that after the coronavirus pandemic, a large part of the UK economy has been kept afloat by a massive tsunami of debt, both at the governmental and the corporate level. Debt in just about every category is at record levels. The global financial crisis finally put a halt to some of this debt expansion – the banks were busily trying to reduce their balance sheets and many big corporations were awash with cash. But after the pandemic, it seems that the painful period of adjustment has only just begun. The problem is that the vast levels of remaining debt must be either paid off or wiped out through bankruptcy. Either one will have its negative consequences for the economy. Either one can do great harm to shares in general and/or your portfolio in particular.

TIP

Make sure that you're dealing with your debt level now. Reduce it as much as possible and make sure that you're analysing your shares in the same light. Companies that carry too much debt will be at great risk. If the company sinks, your shares will follow. If the company goes into bankruptcy, your shares' value will be vaporised.

A New Monetary Norm

Care to guess when in history interest rates last went negative or close to zero? It's a trick question. They have never gone negative or to zero in the entire history of the UK. And that's from Bank of England data stretching back over hundreds of years.

In Denmark, negative interest rates are now common, and many homeowners can borrow at negative rates although they still have to pay fees for arranging the mortgage. But the innovative monetary policy isn't restricted to just interest rates.

Central bank balance sheets have also exploded in size as more money is printed and then used to buy debt. In 2008 the aggregate Bank of England balance sheet amounted to a little under £100 billion. By the middle of the last decade that debt had hit around £500 billion and at the last count – June 2020 – it was within spitting distance of £800 billion.

The debt isn't a huge danger as long as the economy can grow faster than the debt can grow in the next decade. But that debt has inflated the price of nearly all mainstream bonds, making them distinctly unattractive as an investment. It has also probably contributed towards exuberance in stock markets.

WARNING

However, there's also a dark side. What happens when central banks want to reel that monetary intervention back in — for instance by slimming balance sheets and increasing interest rates. They might start selling bonds – which implies lower prices – which might also encourage nervous investors to sell their shares. Keep a close eye on those central bank balance sheets and keep a beady eye on market temperaments. The global markets might suffer from many more 'taper tantrums' as these banks change course.

Central Banks Mess Up

Cynics may come to a different conclusion about this central bank largesse. Many of the traditional tools for fighting future recessions have now been used and arguably abused. Lower interest rates? How can they do that when rates are already zero. Buy more government bonds? What happens if the central banks are already the main buyers? It's possible that in future recessions central banks might not be able to fight a liquidity freeze. Or they might try even more radical measures such as printing more money and then sending it electronically to consumers as a form of e-money. China is already experimenting with e-money from the central bank – as is the Bahamas – and most expect more similar experiments. This might all be jolly useful, but the risks are also becoming more obvious.

The one that worries most investors is inflation, which we discuss in the next section, but there are plenty of other undesirable challenges. What happens if ordinary private banks find themselves crowded out of deposit-taking by central banks? How will government's work through vast piles of bad debt post Covid? Will currency markets be quite so sanguine about this innovation? Could they start to mark down currencies they regard as playing fast and loose? In these circumstances you can begin to understand why so many investors want alternatives to traditional central bank–issued money (called *money fiat*). Might this propel more interest in gold and crypto currencies, such as private sector digital money.

The Return of Inflation

The last time inflation was a major problem was the late 1980s and . . . you guessed it . . . the market was having a rough time. Interest rates soared to close to 10 per cent and everyone experienced economic headaches. And no one needs reminding that inflation post-pandemic has made a return, with different measures suggesting that prices are rising at anything between 2 and 3 per cent per annum, well in excess of any tepid wage rises.

TIP

The *consumer price index* (CPI) is one of several indexes used by the Office for National Statistics to measure the daily cost of living. Pay close attention to this data when it's released each month because, as well as the headline figure, inflation in different industry sectors is also examined. The *retail price index*, also worth watching, is quoted in two forms: including mortgage costs (RPI) and excluding them (RPIX). The difference that including mortgage costs can make may surprise you – another sign of the power of debt!

For share investors, inflation shows that having your money grow is more important than ever. Understanding the pernicious effects of inflation should be factored into your share choices. Some shares are more likely to suffer (mortgage companies with fixed-debt portfolios), while others (precious metals mining companies) are more likely to prosper.

Pension Crisis

You've seen all the headlines: 'Pensions black hole', 'Pension crisis means we must work til we drop', 'People are living for longer', 'People are not saving enough for retirement' . . . Many governments and large companies will experience shortfalls in their financial ability to meet retirement plan obligations. Millions of people will, at the very least, not get as much as they expect when they retire. Thousands of workers already have been left without any pensions when their companies went bust. And although the Financial Protection Fund is now in place to help pay minimum pensions when this happens in future, many pensioners will still suffer serious hardship.

But the trouble with pensions doesn't stop with the vast accumulated deficits clocked up by corporate and state pension schemes. You also need to worry about something called *longevity*. On paper, the fact that people are living much longer after retirement at 65 (the state pension age for men and women will now increase to 67 between 2026 and 2028) is great news. The average life expectancy of a retired 65-year-old-male is now 18.8 years, and that number is constantly increasing. Some analysts reckon this timespan will hit 25 years within a decade or so, and maybe even rise to 30 years. Cause for celebration? Wait one minute – who's going to pay for all those extra years? People will surely have to accumulate even more money for their twilight years.

REMEMBER

Shares are wealth-building tools well suited to long-term needs such as your retirement concerns. Start now because the future has a way of sneaking up on you faster than you think.

Emerging Markets

Over the last 40 years many developing countries have turned into exciting emerging markets. These developments have been great in many ways, but you also need a heavy dose of caution. Much of that globalisation has helped fuel populist anger, especially around immigration and offshoring of jobs. And many economists are concerned as the push to free up trade withers on the fine that growth rates in many emerging markets might start to slow down.

That may happen just as traditional routes to modernisation – through extensive industrialisation – start to look unattainable for many regions (especially Africa where the pace of industrialisation is already painfully slow). Some regions by contrast, especially in Southeast Asia, look like they might be jumping existing stages of development and embracing a technological society where everything from mobile phones to constant CCTV is pervasive.

REMEMBER

To make matters complicated, over the last decade the returns from investing in emerging markets have proved distinctly under whelming. Frankly, you may as well have stuck your money in the US and made more. The idea that investing in emerging markets equities is a sure-fire way of capturing future growth is now a tad problematic to say the least. But don't give up hope. Many of these markets do have huge potential, especially around consumer markets. You'll just have to work harder to find the opportunities.

China's Rise

In 2014 the Chinese technology giant Alibaba listed on the US stock market, with each share priced at $68. In total, the business raised $21 billion and at the time its IPO was the biggest in US history. Its listing was a signal that investors had finally woken up to the huge potential that China offers, especially in technology and consumers markets. Sure, many investors had worried about corporate governance and the influence of the Chinese Communist Party (CCP), but investing in Asia has always presented governance challenges – just ask any Japanese investor.

Over the next few years, the share price drifted a bit lower, pushing below $67 in 2016, but by autumn 2020 the share price was more than $305 as China seemed to shrug off the pandemic. Within six months that share price was down a third as investors started to panic about the CCP's influence and its increasingly interventionist policies. Alibaba's financial unit called Ant had its IPO pulled at the last moment by Chinese regulators.

Alibaba's fortunes on the US stock market serve as a parable for the wider opportunities and risks presented by China. At some stage in the next few decades, China may have a larger domestic economy – on purchasing power parity terms – than the US. Its growth rate is allegedly running at an average clip of more than 6 per cent per annum, and its consumer markets are experiencing rapid disruption as technology adoption speeds up. But investors are also waking up to the risks. Some have reacted by choosing to focus on Western businesses that sell into Chinese markets. However, when consumer boycotts hit the likes of H&M and Burberry, that strategy can sometimes seem just as risky. Others focus on Taiwan to the east as an island of opportunity. Certainly, its semiconductor giant Taiwan Semi-Conductor Company, TSMC, is a world leader. But what happens if the CCP decides to invade Taiwan and forcibly reunite the country? China is the ultimate challenge for investors. Do the risks outweigh the obvious upside opportunities?

The Green Energy Transition

In the early 2010s, many investors were worrying about something called *peak oil*. This term described scenarios in which the world had run out of oil. Today the term now describes a peak in oil demand followed by a long, remorseless decline in demand for the black stuff. As this narrative has changed, so have attitudes to all that oil in the ground.

In the past, oil companies were eager to bid up estimates of the value of their huge oil reserves. Now they talk of stranded oil reserves and oil majors, starting to write down the value of their reserves and cut back on capital expenditure. OPEC states remain committed to providing cheap oil if necessary as they battle the energy upstarts fracking for oil (and gas) in Texas and the Midwest.

Lurking in the background is a globally epic transformation. If the developed world is to hit its carbon reduction targets and keep global temperatures from increasing by more than 2 degrees Celsius, then drastic changes are needed. Oil, and to a lesser extent natural gas, will have to be phased out aggressively – as has already happened with coal where coal-fired power stations are closing at a rapid rate in the developed world. The UK has now had many days and weeks where virtually no power is generated by coal or oil, and even generated power from natural gas contribution is being pushed down as offshore wind exponentially increases its output.

Working out how to play these constantly changing dynamics challenges even the professional stock pickers. It's not immediately obvious that oil prices will collapse, and oil prices may in fact increase. Natural gas will continue to be intensively used for another decade or so, even as battery-powered cars increase their market share. The developing world may continue to use huge amounts of oil and gas, even as countries such as the UK try and push towards ambitious carbon reduction targets.

Our own tentative conclusion is that many things could be true at the same time. By this we mean clean energy businesses could experience a huge boom as well as a real opportunity in bombed-out oil and gas stocks. Another way to look at it: Oil prices could carry on increasing even as wind and solar output costs keep declining. At some point though the transition will happen, and a new energy economy will start to emerge.

Dangers from Out of the Blue

Investing in shares is a brave, new world fraught with dangers for the clueless, but filled with wealth-building opportunities for the 'clued in'. No one knows what disasters will affect the economy and society in general. Events such as 9/11, Hurricane Katrina and the Covid-19 pandemic certainly show the world holds unseen perils for everyone's prosperity. The point is that terrorism and other factors will have an impact. Fortunately, you can make changes . . . even slight changes . . . that can protect or grow your wealth.

TIP

Stay informed and understand that successful share investing doesn't happen in a vacuum.

The One Certainty

This section focuses on the one big issue that can be described with absolute certainty. That 'certainty' is that the investment industry is one giant machine largely dedicated to the task of making you poorer by charging unwarranted and excessive fees. The financial services sector loves to make everything seem complicated and dangerous, to justify the employment of lots of clever people and their frequently excessive salaries and bonuses. Don't believe a word of it.

Most investment should be about simple ideas, cheaply executed with the minimum of fuss. Of course, expert advice is essential for personal planning or tax advice, but high fees charged by fund managers and stockbrokers are simply inexcusable and should be resisted at all costs. High costs are guaranteed to destroy your wealth over the long term. Keep your costs down and scrutinise all the charges made to your investment and savings accounts.

6 Appendixes

Find resources that aid you in making informed investment decisions. Whether the topic is share investing terminology, economics, or avoiding capital gains taxes, we include a treasure trove of resources for you.

Examine what financial ratios mean. These important numbers help you better determine whether or not to invest in a particular company's shares.

Appendix A

Resources for Investors in Shares

Getting and staying informed is an ongoing priority for investors in shares. The lists in this appendix represent some the best information resources available.

Financial Planning Sources

To find a financial planner to help you with your general financial needs, contact the following organisations. Be sure to ask for a financial planner who specialises in investing.

Chartered Institute for Securities and Investment: www.cisi.org

Independent Financial Adviser Promotion (IFAP): Email: contact@unbiased.co.uk, website: www.unbiased.co.uk

The Language of Investing

The world of investing can sometimes seem really very confusing, what with all the complex jargon and acronyms, but these sources help guide you through the maze of investing terminology.

The New Penguin Dictionary of Business: By Evan Davis, Paul Trott, Graham Bannock, and Mark D. Uncles. Published by Penguin Reference Books. A nicely laid out A-to-Z publication for investors mystified by financial terms. It explains the important investing and business terms you come across every day.

Investopedia: (www.investopedia.com): An excellent site with plenty of information on investing for beginners and intermediate investors.

Textual Investment Resources

Share investment success isn't an event; it's a process. The periodicals and magazines listed (along with their websites) have offered many years of guidance and information for investors, and they're still top-notch. The books and pamphlets provide much wisdom that is either timeless or timely (covering problems and concerns every investor should be aware of now).

Periodicals and magazines

These publications offer a wide range of news, analysis, and investment, whether online or in print. We give you the web addresses here to get you started:

Barron's: www.barrons.com/

Citywire: www.citywire.co.uk

The Financial Times: www.ft.com

Forbes: www.forbes.com

Investment Week: www.investmentweek.co.uk

Investor's Chronicle: www.investorschronicle.co.uk

MoneyWeek: www.moneyweek.com

Books and pamphlets

These books and pamphlets go into greater detail about investing:

The Financial Times Guide to Using the Financial Pages by Romesh Vaitlingam (6th Edition), published by FT Prentice Hall

Guide to Analysing Companies by Bob Vause, published by Economist Books

How to Pick Stocks Like Warren Buffett: Profiting from the Bargain Hunting Strategies of the World's Greatest Value Investor by Timothy Vick, published by McGraw-Hill Professional Publishing

The Intelligent Investor: A Book of Practical Counsel by Benjamin Graham (preface by Warren Buffett), published by HarperCollins

The Little Book of Common Sense Investing by John C. Bogle, published by John Wiley & Sons, Ltd.

The Little Book of Behavioral Investing by James Montier, published by John Wiley & Sons, Ltd.

The Financial Times Guide to Investing: The Definitive Companion to Investment and the Financial Markets **(The FT Guides)** by Glen Arnold, published by FT Prentice Hall

Investor's Guide to Analysing Companies & Valuing Shares by Michael Cahill, published by FT Prentice Hall

The Investors Guide to Understanding Accounts by Robert Leach, published by Harriman House Publishing

How to Own the World: A Plain English Guide to Thinking Globally and Investing Wisely by Andrew Craig, published by John Murray

The Little Book That Still Beats the Market: Your Safe Haven in Good Times or Bad by Joel Greenblatt, published by John Wiley and Sons, Ltd.

Magic Numbers for Stock Investors by Peter Temple, published by John Wiley & Sons, Ltd.

Anatomy of the Bear: Lessons from Wall Street's four great bottoms by Russell Napier, publisher Harriman House

Extraordinary Popular Delusions and the Madness of Crowds (Harriman Definitive Edition): The classic guide to crowd psychology, financial folly and surprising superstition by Charles Mackay, Daed Authors Society

Harriman's Financial Dictionary by Simon Briscoe and Jane Fuller, publisher Harriman House

Special books of interest to share investors

These titles provide more in-depth information for Chapters 13 and 23:

Ethical Money: How to Invest in Sustainable Enterprises and Avoid the Polluters and Exploiters by John Hancock, published by Kogan Page

The Ultimate ETF Guidebook: A Comprehensive Guide to the World of Exchange-Traded Funds – Including the Latest Innovations and Ideas for ETF Portfolios by David Stevenson and David Tuckwell, publisher Harriman House

The Investment Trusts Handbook 2021: Investing essentials, expert insights and powerful trends and data by Jonathan Davis, publisher Harriman House

Beyond the Zulu Principle: Extraordinary Profits from Growth Shares by Jim Slater, publisher Harriman House

Investing Websites

How can any serious investor ignore the Internet? You can't and you shouldn't. The following are among the best information sources available.

General investing websites

Start with these websites:

Bloomberg: www.bloomberg.com

Breaking Views: www.breakingviews.com

Citywire: www.citywire.co.uk

Motley Fool: www.fool.co.uk

Stock investing websites

These sites focus more on stock investing:

Economist: www.economist.com

ETF Stream: www.etfstream.com

Investing.com: uk.investing.com

Investing for Good: www.investingforgood.co.uk

JustETF: www.justetf.com

MarketWatch: www.marketwatch.com

Stockopedia: www.stockopedia.com

Trustnet: www.trustnet.com

World Gold Council: www.gold.org

Yahoo! Finance www.finance.yahoo.com

Investor Associations and Organisations

Someone needs to fight the investors corner – these organisations might be just the ticket:

Financial Ombudsman Service: Exchange Tower, 1 Harbour Exchange Square, London, E14 9SR. Telephone: 0300 123 9123, email complaint.info@financial-ombudsman.org.uk, website: www.financial-ombudsman.org.uk

Financial Services Compensation Scheme: PO Box 300, Mitcheldean, GL17 1DY. Telephone: 0800 678 1100, website: www.fscs.org.uk

The United Kingdom Shareholders Association (www.uksa.org.uk): Outspoken independent organisation representing private shareholders

Stock Exchanges

The main stock exchanges in the UK and the US boast surprisingly useful websites, full of information

Aquis Market: www.aquis.eu

London Stock Exchange (and Alternative Investment Market): www.london stockexchange.com

Nasdaq: www.nasdaq.com

New York Stock Exchange: www.nyse.com

Finding Brokers

Here we give you more information about finding the broker right for you.

Choosing brokers

Some context about which broker to use is essential – these websites might give you some useful clues about which brokers to pick.

Broker Chooser: https://brokerchooser.com/compare-brokerage

Compeer: www.compeer.com

Monevator: https://monevator.com/compare-uk-cheapest-online-brokers/

Brokers

You'll need a broker to buy and sell shares. These are the main national brokers, all available online.

AJ Bell's YouInvest: www.youinvest.co.uk

Barclays Stockbrokers Smart Investor: www.barclays.co.uk/smart-investor/

DeGiro: www.degiro.co.uk/

eToro: www.etoro.com

Freetrade: www.freetrade.io

Halifax: www.halifax.co.uk/investing/start-investing/share-dealing-services/share-dealing-account.html

Hargreaves Lansdown: www.h-l.co.uk

IG Markets: www.ig.com/uk/share-trading-ig-stockbrokers

Interactive Investor: www.ii.co.uk

James Brearley & Sons: www.jbrearley.co.uk/individual-investors/dealing-services/

Trading 212: www.trading212.com

Investment Sources

The following are fee-based subscription services. Many of them also offer excellent free email newsletters tracking the stock market and related news.

Motley Fool: www.fool.co.uk

Sharepad: www.sharepad.co.uk

Stockopedia: www.stockopedia.com

The Value Line Investment Survey: www.valueline.com

Sources for Analysis

The following sources give you the chance to look a little deeper at some critical aspects regarding stock analysis. Whether it's earnings estimates and insider selling or a more insightful look at a particular industry, these sources are among our favourites.

Earnings and earnings estimates

Need to find out the latest updates on corporate earnings? Search here:

Zacks Summary of Brokerage Research: www.zacks.com

Briefing.com: http://briefing.com

Industry analysis

Need to understand how an industry or sector works? These sites could be useful:

Hoover's: www.hoovers.com

Mergermarket: www.mergermarket.com

Standard & Poor's: www.standardandpoors.com

Factors that affect market value

Understanding basic economics is so vital to making your investment decisions that we had to include this section. These great sources have helped us understand 'the big picture' and what ultimately affects the stock market.

Economics and politics

Investors can't ignore how government policy impacts markets, and these websites should give you some background official information that could come in handy.

The Bank of England (www.bankofengland.co.uk): *Note:* Learn how the Monetary Policy Committee decides on interest rates. This can give you a great insight into the predictions of the UK's foremost economists.

They Work for You: www.theyworkforyou.com

Office of National Statistics (www.ons.gov.uk): Here you can find all the numbers that count – from the government's official bean counters.

Securities and Exchange Commission (SEC) (www.sec.gov): The SEC has tremendous resources for investors who have shares in companies listed in the US. In addition to information on investing, the SEC also monitors the US financial markets for fraud and other abusive activities. For stock market investors, it also has EDGAR (Electronic Data Gathering, Analysis, and Retrieval system), which is a comprehensive, searchable database of public documents that are filed by public companies.

Changing laws

Go to these sites to find out about new and proposed laws. The on-site search engines will help you find the laws that are likely to affect your investments.

House of Lords and House of Commons: http://www.parliament.uk/

UK Government: www.gov.uk

Technical analysis

Technical analysis can be extremely useful for active investors looking for trends, and these websites should give you some starters for ten:

Barchart: www.barchart.com

Stock Charts: www.stockcharts.com

UK Society of Technical Analysts: www.technicalanalysts.com/

Directors' share dealing and other tips

It's always worth checking on which shares directors are buying and selling, and these sites should give you some ideas.

Financial Times Directors Deals: www.ft.com/personal-finance/directors-deals

Sharecast: www.sharecast.com

Tax Benefits and Obligations

Here are some handy sites that tell you what you have to pay and give you some advice on how to go about it:

HM Revenue & Customs: www.gov.uk/government/organisations/hm-revenue-customs

TaxationWeb: www.taxationweb.co.uk

Tax Café: www.taxcafe.co.uk

Fraud

Here is a selection of sites to help you ensure that no one gets their hands on your money who shouldn't:

Action Fraud: actionfraid.police.uk; Action Fraud is the UK's national reporting centre for fraud and cybercrime.

Cardwatch: www.cardwatch.org.uk

CIFAS: www.cifas.org.uk; the UK's Fraud Prevention Service

Financial Conduct Authority: www.fca.gov.uk

The Fraud Advisory Panel: www.fraudadvisorypanel.org

Serious Fraud Office: www.sfo.gov.uk; responsible for prosecuting cases of illegal insider dealing and other serious frauds

Appendix **B**

Financial Ratios and Accounting Terms

A s dull or cumbersome as the topic sounds, financial ratios are indeed the 'meat' of analysing shares. Sadly, most investors don't exercise their due diligence when it comes to doing some relatively easy things to make sure that the company they're investing in is a good place for their hard-earned investment pounds. This appendix lists the most common ratios that investors should be aware of and use. A solid company doesn't have to pass all these ratio tests with flying colours, but at a minimum, it should comfortably pass the ones regarding profitability and solvency:

>> **Profitability:** Is the company making money? Is it making more or less than it did in the previous period? Are sales growing? Are profits growing?

You can answer these questions by looking at the following ratios:

- Return on Equity

- Common Size Ratio (P&L)

- Return on Capital Employed

>> **Solvency:** Is the company keeping debts and other liabilities under control? Are the company's assets growing? Is the company's net equity (or net worth or shareholders' funds) growing?

You can answer these questions by looking at the following ratios:

- Debt-to-Equity
- Working Capital
- Quick Ratio

While you examine ratios, keep these points in mind:

>> Not every company and/or industry is the same. A ratio that seems problematic in one industry may be just fine in another. Investigate.

>> A single ratio isn't enough on which to base your investment decision. Look at several ratios covering the major aspects of a company's finances.

>> Look at two or more years of a company's numbers to judge whether the most recent ratio is better, worse, or unchanged from the previous year's ratio. Ratios can give you early warning signs regarding the company's prospects.

Liquidity Ratios

Liquidity means the ability to quickly turn assets into cash. Liquid assets are simply assets that are easier to convert to cash. Property, for example, is certainly an asset, but it's not liquid because converting it to cash could take weeks, months, or even years. Current assets such as cheque accounts, savings accounts, marketable securities, accounts receivable and stock are much easier to sell or convert to cash in a very short period of time.

Paying bills or immediate debt takes liquidity. Liquidity ratios help you understand a company's ability to pay its current liabilities. The most common liquidity ratios are the current ratio and the quick ratio; the numbers to calculate them are located on the balance sheet.

Current ratio

The *current ratio* is the most commonly used liquidity ratio. It answers the question 'Does the company have enough financial cushion to meet its current bills?' It's calculated as follows:

Current Ratio = Total Current Assets ÷ Total Current Liabilities

If Holee Guacamolee PLC. (HG) has £60,000 in current assets and £20,000 in current liabilities, the current ratio is 3 because the company has £3 of current assets for each pound of current liabilities.

REMEMBER

As a general rule, a current ratio of 2 or more is desirable. A current ratio of less than 1 is a red flag that the company may have a cash crunch that could cause financial problems. Although many companies strive to get the current ratio to equal 1, we like to see a higher ratio (in the range of 1–3) to keep a cash cushion should the economy slow down.

Quick ratio

The *quick ratio* is frequently referred to as the *acid test ratio*. It's a little more stringent than the current ratio in that you calculate it without taking into account stock. We use the current ratio example discussed in the preceding section. What if half of the assets are stock (£30,000 in this case)? Now what? First, here's the formula for the quick ratio:

Quick Ratio = (Current Assets Less Stock) ÷ Current Liabilities

In the example, the quick ratio for HG is 1.5 (£30,000 divided by £20,000). In other words, the company has £1.50 of 'quick' liquid assets for each pound of current liabilities. This amount is okay. *Quick liquid assets* include any money in the bank, marketable securities, and accounts receivable. If quick liquid assets at the very least equal or exceed total current liabilities, that amount is considered adequate.

TIP

The acid test that this ratio reflects is embodied in the question 'Can the company pay its bills when times are tough?' In other words, if the company can't sell its goods (stock), can it still meet its short-term liabilities? Of course, you must watch the accounts receivable as well. If the economy is entering rough times, you want to make sure that the company's customers are paying invoices on a timely basis.

Operating Ratios

Operating ratios essentially measure the company's efficiency. 'How is the company managing its resources?' is a question commonly answered with operating ratios. If, for example, a company sells products, does it have too much stock? If it does, that could impair the company's operations. The following sections present common operating ratios.

Return on equity (ROE)

Equity is the amount left from total assets after you account for total liabilities. (This can also be considered a profitability ratio.) The *shareholders' funds* (also known as *net equity*, or *net worth*) is the bottom line in the company's balance sheet, both geographically as well as figuratively. It's calculated as

Return on Equity (ROE) = Operating Profit ÷ Shareholders' Funds

The operating profit (from the company's income statement) is simply the total income less total expenses. Operating profit that isn't spent or used up increases the company's net equity. Looking at operating profit is a great way to see whether the company's management is doing a good job growing the business. You can check this out by looking at the shareholder's funds from both the most recent balance sheet and the one from a year earlier. Ask yourself whether the current net worth is higher or lower than the year before. If it's higher, by what percentage is it higher? Use the ROE in conjunction with the ROA ratio (see the following section) to get a fuller picture of a company's activity.

Return on capital employed (ROCE)

The ROCE may seem similar to the ROE, but it's actually a widely used measurement of management performance expressed as a percentage. The formula for working out ROCE is

Return on Capital Employed (per cent) = (Pre-tax Profit × 100) ÷ Capital Employed

The ROCE reflects the relationship between a company's profit and the assets used to generate it. If the company HG makes a profit of £10,000 and has used assets of £100,000, the ROCE is 10 per cent. This percentage should be as high as possible.

Say that the company has an ROE of 25 per cent but an ROCE of only 5 per cent. Is that good? It sounds okay, but a problem exists. If the ROCE is much lower than the ROE, it indicates that the higher ROE may have been generated by something other than total assets – debt! The use of debt can be a leverage to maximise the ROE, but if the ROCE doesn't show a similar percentage of efficiency, then the company may have incurred too much debt. In that case, investors should be aware that it could cause problems (see the section 'Solvency Ratios', later in this appendix).

Solvency Ratios

Solvency just means that the company isn't overwhelmed by its liabilities. Insolvency means 'Oops! Too late'. You get the point. Solvency ratios have never been more important than they are now. Solvency ratios look at the relationship between what the company owns and what it owes. Here are two of the primary solvency ratios.

Debt to equity ratio

The *debt to equity ratio* is an indicator of the company's solvency. It answers the question 'How dependent is the company on debt?' In other words, it tells you how much the company owes and how much it owns. You calculate it as follows:

Debt to Equity Ratio = Total Debt ÷ Shareholders' Funds

But you can also calculate it with this formula:

Debt to Equity Ratio = Total Debt ÷ (Shareholders' Funds + Total Debt)

Using the first calculation method, if the company HG has £100,000 in debt and £50,000 in net worth, the debt to equity ratio is 2. The company has two pounds of debt to every pound of net worth. In this case, what the company owes is twice the amount of what it owns. Whenever a company's debt to net equity ratio exceeds 1 (as in the example), that isn't good. In fact, the higher the number, the more negative the situation. If the number is too high and the company isn't generating enough income to cover the debt, the company runs the risk of bankruptcy. But be sure of how this ratio is being calculated before you make any decisions based on it.

Working capital

Technically, working capital isn't a ratio, but it does belong to the list of things that serious investors look at. *Working capital* means what the company has in current assets and its relationship to current liabilities. It's a simple equation:

Working Capital = Total Current Assets – Total Current Liabilities

The point is obvious: Does the company have enough to cover the current bills? Actually, you can formulate a useful ratio. If current assets are £25,000 and current liabilities are £25,000, then that's a 1-to-1 ratio, which is cutting it close. Current assets should be at least 50 per cent higher than current liabilities (say, £1.50 to £1.00) to have enough cushion to pay bills and have some money for other purposes. Preferably, the ratio should be 2 to 1 or higher.

Common Size Ratios

Common size ratios offer simple comparisons. You have common size ratios for both the balance sheet (where you compare total assets) and the profit and loss account (where you compare total sales or turnover):

>> **To get a common size ratio from a balance sheet,** the total assets figure is assigned the percentage of 100 per cent. Every other item on the balance sheet is represented as a percentage of total assets. For example, if Holee Guacamolee PLC. (HG) has total assets of £10,000 and debt of £3,000, you know that total assets equal 100 per cent, while debt equals 30 per cent (debt divided by total assets or £3,000 ÷ £10,000, which equals 30 per cent).

>> **To get a common size ratio from an income statement (or profit and loss account),** you compare total sales or turnover. For example, if a company has £50,000 in total sales and a net profit of £8,000, then you know that the profit equals 16 per cent of total sales.

Keep in mind the following points with common size ratios:

>> **Net profit:** What percentage of sales is it? What was it last year? How about the year before? What percentage of increases (or decreases) is the company experiencing?

>> **Expenses:** Are total expenses in line with the previous year? Are any expenses going out of line?

>> **Shareholders' funds:** Is this item higher or lower than the year before?

>> **Debt:** Is this item higher or lower than the year before?

REMEMBER

Common size ratios are used to compare the company's financial data not only with previous balance sheets and income statements but also with other companies in the same industry. You want to make sure that the company is not only doing better historically but also as a competitor in the industry.

Valuation Ratios

Understanding the value of a share is very important for investors. The quickest and most efficient way to judge the value of a company is to look at valuation ratios. The type of value that you deal with throughout the book is the *market value* (essentially the price of the company's shares). You hope to buy it at one price and sell it later at a higher price — that's the name of the game. But what's the best way to determine whether what you're paying for now is a bargain or is fair market value? How do you know whether your share investment is undervalued or overvalued? The valuation ratios in this appendix can help you answer these questions. In fact, they're the same ratios that value investors have used with great success for many years.

Price-to-earnings ratio (P/E)

The *price-to-earnings ratio* can also double as a profitability ratio because it's a common barometer of value that many investors and analysts look at. We cover this topic in Chapter 10, but because it's such a critical ratio, we also include it here. The formula is

P/E Ratio = Price (Per Share) ÷ Earnings (Per Share)

For example, if a company's share price is £10 and the earnings per share are £1, the P/E is 10 (10 divided by 1).

The P/E ratio answers the question 'Am I paying too much for the company's earnings?' Value investors find this number to be extremely important. Here are some points to remember:

>> Generally, the lower the P/E ratio, the better (from a financial strength point of view). Frequently, a low P/E ratio indicates that the shares are undervalued (or the company is failing).

>> A company with a P/E ratio significantly higher than its industry average is a red flag that its share price is too high (or that it is growing faster than its competitors).

>> Don't invest in a company with no P/E ratio (it has a share price, but the company experienced losses). Such a share may be good for a speculator's portfolio but not for your retirement account.

>> Any shares with a P/E higher than 40 should be considered a speculation and not an investment. Frequently, a high P/E ratio indicates that the shares are overvalued.

REMEMBER

When you buy a company, you're really buying its power to make money. In essence, you're buying its earnings. Paying for a share that's priced at between 5 and 15 times earnings is a conservative strategy that has served investors well for nearly a century. Make sure that the company is priced fairly and use the P/E ratio in conjunction with other measures of value (such as the other ratios in this appendix).

Price to sales ratio (PSR)

The *price to sales ratio (PSR or P/R)* is another method for valuing the company. It helps to answer the question 'Am I paying too much for the company's shares based on the company's sales?' This is a useful valuation ratio that we recommend using as a companion tool with the company's P/E ratio. You calculate it as follows:

PSR = Share Price (Per Share) ÷ Total Sales (Per Share)

This ratio can be quoted on a per-share basis or on an aggregate basis. For example, if a company's market value (or market capitalisation) is £1 billion and annual sales are also £1 billion, the PSR is 1. If the market value in this example is £2 billion, then the PSR is 2. For investors trying to make sure that they're not paying too much for the shares, the general rule is that the lower the PSR, the better. Shares with a PSR of 2 or less are considered undervalued.

WARNING

Be very hesitant about buying a share with a PSR greater than 5. If you buy a share with a PSR of 38, that means you're paying £38 for each pound of sales – not exactly a bargain.

Price to book ratio (PBR)

The *price to book ratio* (PBR) is yet another valuation method. This ratio compares the market value to the company's accounting (or book) value. Recall that the book value refers to the company's net equity or shareholders' funds (assets minus liabilities). The company's market value is usually dictated by external factors such as supply and demand in the stock market. The book value is indicative of the company's internal operations. Value investors see the PBR as another perspective to valuing the company to determine whether you're paying too much for the shares. The formula is

Price to Book Ratio (PBR) = Share Price ÷ Shareholders' Funds Per Share

An alternate method is to calculate the ratio on a capitalisation basis, which yields the same ratio. If the company's share price is £20 and the book value (per share) is £15, then the PBR is 1.33. In other words, the company's market value is 33 per cent higher than its book value. Investors seeking an undervalued share like to see the market value as close as possible to (or even better, below) the book value.

REMEMBER

Keep in mind that the PBR may vary depending on the industry and other factors. Also, judging a company solely on book value may be misleading because many companies have assets that aren't adequately reflected in the book value. Software companies are a good example. Intellectual properties, such as copyrights and trademarks, are very valuable yet aren't fully covered in book value. Just bear in mind that, generally, the lower the market value is in relation to the book value, the better for you (especially if the company has strong earnings and the outlook for the industry is positive).

Other Useful Accounting Terms

The more you read up on shares and investment the more likely you are to come across new accounting terms that are likely to bamboozle rather than bedazzle you.

EBITDA

The first mouthful you might encounter is EBITDA, which is pronounced as a word (EE-Bit-Dah). It stands for *Earnings Before Interest, Tax, Depreciation,* and *Amortisation.* Although it sounds very important it is pretty meaningless – except to highlight what could be an investment to avoid. Analysts in the US used EBITDA to value the telecommunications group WorldCom. This wasn't considered such a good move when an $11 billion accounting fraud was revealed in June 2002 and the company filed for bankruptcy protection a month later. However some seasoned share pickers still take note of EBITDA when making selections.

Gearing

Gearing isn't about fashion, but you should pay attention to the gearing on your Marks and Spencers shares. It's a ratio that expresses the company's level of borrowing. It's calculated by dividing the percentage of interest-bearing loans and preference share capital by ordinary shareholders' funds. Take care if the gearing is more than 50 per cent.

Index

B

baby boomers, 203
bachelor/single investor, 214
balance, within investment, 16
balance sheet
  analysing, 22–23, 130
  within the annual report, 150–151
  common size ratio from, 356
  of company, 70
  composing, 16
  considerations regarding, 312
  defined, 16, 109
  example of, 110
  overview of, 134–136
bank, interest rates of, 43
Bank of England, 43, 208, 333, 348
bank statement, 261
Bankers Investment Trust, 183
banking industry, 168
Barchart, 349
Barclays Stockbrokers, 85, 262
Barclays Stockbrokers Smart Investor, 346
bargain hunting, 205
barriers to entry, 107
Barron's, 342
bear market
  bargain hunting following, 205
  beginnings of, 209–211
  caution within, 176–178
  debt and, 208
  defined, 16
  economic downtrend and, 201
  example of, 7
  government intervention and, 208–209
  history regarding, 206–207
  international/national conflict and, 209
  optimism and, 207
  overview of, 206–211
  PCA within, 243
  secular, 207
  technology industry within, 156

tips regarding, 108
  tracking, 207
  uncertain markets as, 212
bed-and-breakfasting (B&B), 261
bellwether industry, 166
Berkshire Hathaway, 94
beta measurement, 225–226
Beyond the Zulu Principle (Slater), 344
bid-offer spread, 92, 289
big data, 296
Binance Coin, 300
binary problem, 118
bioinformatics, 301
biotechnology industry, 114, 174–175, 301–302
Bitcoin, 300
BlackRock, 175, 278
blank cheque company, 112
Blockchain, 195, 299–300
Bloomberg, 62, 74, 250, 331, 344
blue chips, 10, 59
bog standard, 288
boiler room, scams within, 325–326
bond
  within asset allocation, 53
  central banks and, 173
  defined, 124
  interest rates of, 43
  rating, 124–125, 319–320
  selling of, 333
bonus issue, 254
book value, 132, 316–317
borrowing, for shares, 229–232
bottom line, 42, 137
boycotts, consumer, 336
Breaking Views, 331, 344
Brewin Dolphin, 89
Briefing.com, 348
broker
  advisory, 87, 88
  charges of, 270–272
  choosing, 94–95
  churning by, 89

G

gamblers, investors *versus,* 13, 29
gaming, online, 297–298
gearing, 359
genome sequencing, 302
genomics, 174, 301–302
Getty, J. Paul, 202
GlaxoSmithKline, 107
Glencore, 226
Global Financial Crisis (GFC), 7, 48, 49–50
globalisation, 171, 292
glossary, 68
Go-Ahead, 163
goal, financial, 28–29, 32, 33–35, 53
goals, share strategies with, 32–33
going long, 232
going public, 112, 113
going short, 232–235, 328
gold industry, 166, 173–174
Goldman Sachs, 294
good-till-cancelled (GTC) order, 224–225, 228–229
Google, 7, 8, 94
Google Finance, 154
Gosimpletax, 261
government
  debt of, 177, 332
  direct funding by, 164
  economic effects from, 71–72
  energy influence of, 189
  funding from, 188
  intervention increases by, 208–209
  research regarding, 75–76
  spending of, 173
  targeting by, 80, 163–164
governmental risk, 47
greed, 48–49, 327
green energy, transition within, 337
Green Paper, 75
grey pound, 174
Grobaby PLC, 109
gross domestic product (GDP), 75

growth, rates of, 214
growth component, 206
growth investing, 35–36, 104–105
growth shares, 104, 105–111
Guide to Analysing Companies (Vause), 343

H

half-yearly dividend, 83
Halifax, 7, 347
Hargreaves Lansdown, 85, 347
Harriman's Financial Dictionary (Briscoe and Fuller), 344
Healthcare AI Market, 296
healthcare sector, 160, 174–175, 188, 189
hedge fund, 196
Henderson, Janus, 183
H&M, 336
HM Revenue & Customs (HMRC), 261, 350
hold recommendation, 97
home equity, for consumer debt, 23
Hoover's, 348
House of Lords and House of Commons, 349
housing sector, 188, 190, 191
How to Own the World (Craig), 343
How to Pick Stocks Like Warren Buffett (Vick), 343

I

IG Markets, 91, 347
illiquid investments, 17
imaginary investing, 51
incentive shares, 263
income, 24–25, 70, 192–193, 266
income and expense statement, 24
income component, 206
income investing, 36–37
income investor, 81
income shares
  analysing, 119–125
  disadvantages of, 117–119
  diversification of, 123–124
  overview of, 116

About the Authors

David Stevenson is the Adventurous Investor columnist for the *Financial Times* and also writes a regular column for *MoneyWeek* magazine and Citywire. He has also a written a number of books on the subject of investing, including the main European book on investing in ETFs. David is the founding editor of FutureFoodFinance. com and executive editor of Altfi.com and ETFStream.com. He also finds some time to be a magistrate and to run his own investment portfolios.

Paul Mladjenovic is a certified financial planner practitioner, writer, and public speaker who has a website at www.mladjenovic.com. His business, PM Financial Services, has helped people with financial and business concerns since 1981. In 1985 he achieved his CFP designation. Since 1983, Paul has taught thousands of budding investors through popular national seminars such as 'The $50 Wealth-builder' and 'Stock Investing Like a Pro'. Paul has been quoted or referenced by many media outlets such as Bloomberg, MarketWatch, CNBC, and many financial and business publications and websites. As an author, he has written the books *The Unofficial Guide to Picking Stocks, Stock Investing For Dummies, Affiliate Marketing For Dummies, Investing in Gold & Silver For Dummies,* and *Micro-Entrepreneurship For Dummies* (John Wiley & Sons, Inc.), and *Zero-Cost Marketing* (Todd Publications). In recent years, Paul accurately forecasted many economic events, such as the rise of gold and the decline of the US dollar.

Dedication

David: For Vanessa, Rebecca and Zac and not forgetting Jake and Harvey!

Paul: For my beloved Fran, Adam, Joshua, and a loving, supportive family, I thank God for you. I also dedicate this book to the millions of investors who deserve more knowledge and information to achieve lasting prosperity.

Authors' Acknowledgements

David: Thank you to Vanessa and the Stevenson pack – Rebecca, Zac and the hounds Jake and Harvey . . . not forgetting Mum of course who to this day doesn't understand a word about investment and 'all that stuff'. Sensible lady.

Thanks also to John Stepek for his kind comments and observations. Also many thanks to my varied line editors and my colleagues at www.altfi.com and www.etfstream.com for their helpful comments.

Paul: First and foremost, I offer my appreciation and gratitude to the wonderful people at Wiley. It has been a pleasure to work with such a top-notch organisation that works so hard to create products that offer readers tremendous value and information. I wish all of you continued success! There are some notables there whom I want to single out.

My gratitude goes out to the acquisitions editor Tracy Boggier for making this *For Dummies* book happen. *For Dummies* books don't magically appear at the bookstore; they happen due to the foresight and efforts of people like Tracy. Wiley is fortunate to have her (and the others also mentioned)!

Fran, Lipa Zyenska, you helped make those late nights at the computer more tolerable, and you helped me focus on the important things. Te amo and I thank God that you are by my side. With you and the rest of my loving family, I know that the future will be bright.

Lastly, I want to acknowledge you, the reader. Over the years, you have made the *For Dummies* books what they are today. Your devotion to these wonderful books created a foundation that played a big part in the creation of this book and many more yet to come. Thank you!

Publisher's Acknowledgments

Senior Acquisitions Editor: Tracy Boggier

Project Manager and Editor: Chad R. Sievers

Technical Editor: John Stepek

Proofreader: Debbye Butler

Production Editor: Mohammed Zafar Ali

Cover Image: © IR Stone/Shutterstock

Take dummies with you everywhere you go!

Whether you are excited about e-books, want more from the web, must have your mobile apps, or are swept up in social media, dummies makes everything easier.

Find us online!

dummies.com

Leverage the power

Dummies is the global leader in the reference category and one of the most trusted and highly regarded brands in the world. No longer just focused on books, customers now have access to the dummies content they need in the format they want. Together we'll craft a solution that engages your customers, stands out from the competition, and helps you meet your goals.

Advertising & Sponsorships

Connect with an engaged audience on a powerful multimedia site, and position your message alongside expert how-to content. Dummies.com is a one-stop shop for free, online information and know-how curated by a team of experts.

- Targeted ads
- Video
- Email Marketing

- Microsites
- Sweepstakes sponsorship

20 MILLION
PAGE VIEWS
EVERY SINGLE MONTH

15 MILLION
UNIQUE
VISITORS PER MONTH

43%
OF ALL VISITORS
ACCESS THE SITE
VIA THEIR MOBILE DEVICES

700,000 NEWSLETTER
SUBSCRIPTION
TO THE INBOXES OF
300,000 UNIQUE INDIVIDUALS
EVERY WEEK

# of dummies

Custom Publishing

Reach a global audience in any language by creating a solution that will differentiate you from competitors, amplify your message, and encourage customers to make a buying decision.

- Apps
- Books
- eBooks
- Video
- Audio
- Webinars

Brand Licensing & Content

Leverage the strength of the world's most popular reference brand to reach new audiences and channels of distribution.

For more information, visit dummies.com/biz

PERSONAL ENRICHMENT

9781119187790
USA $26.00
CAN $31.99
UK £19.99

9781119179030
USA $21.99
CAN $25.99
UK £16.99

9781119293354
USA $24.99
CAN $29.99
UK £17.99

9781119293347
USA $22.99
CAN $27.99
UK £16.99

9781119310068
USA $22.99
CAN $27.99
UK £16.99

9781119235606
USA $24.99
CAN $29.99
UK £17.99

9781119251163
USA $24.99
CAN $29.99
UK £17.99

9781119235491
USA $26.99
CAN $31.99
UK £19.99

9781119279952
USA $24.99
CAN $29.99
UK £17.99

9781119283133
USA $24.99
CAN $29.99
UK £17.99

9781119287117
USA $24.99
CAN $29.99
UK £16.99

9781119130246
USA $22.99
CAN $27.99
UK £16.99

PROFESSIONAL DEVELOPMENT

9781119311041
USA $24.99
CAN $29.99
UK £17.99

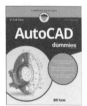
9781119255796
USA $39.99
CAN $47.99
UK £27.99

9781119293439
USA $26.99
CAN $31.99
UK £19.99

9781119281467
USA $26.99
CAN $31.99
UK £19.99

9781119280651
USA $29.99
CAN $35.99
UK £21.99

9781119251132
USA $24.99
CAN $29.99
UK £17.99

9781119310563
USA $34.00
CAN $41.99
UK £24.99

9781119181705
USA $29.99
CAN $35.99
UK £21.99

9781119263593
USA $26.99
CAN $31.99
UK £19.99

9781119257769
USA $29.99
CAN $35.99
UK £21.99

9781119293477
USA $26.99
CAN $31.99
UK £19.99

9781119265313
USA $24.99
CAN $29.99
UK £17.99

9781119239314
USA $29.99
CAN $35.99
UK £21.99

9781119293323
USA $29.99
CAN $35.99
UK £21.99

dummies.com

dummies
A Wiley Brand

Learning Made Easy

ACADEMIC

9781119293576
USA $19.99
CAN $23.99
UK £15.99

9781119293637
USA $19.99
CAN $23.99
UK £15.99

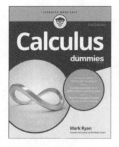

9781119293491
USA $19.99
CAN $23.99
UK £15.99

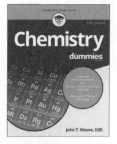

9781119293460
USA $19.99
CAN $23.99
UK £15.99

9781119293590
USA $19.99
CAN $23.99
UK £15.99

9781119215844
USA $26.99
CAN $31.99
UK £19.99

9781119293378
USA $22.99
CAN $27.99
UK £16.99

9781119293521
USA $19.99
CAN $23.99
UK £15.99

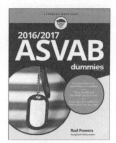

9781119239178
USA $18.99
CAN $22.99
UK £14.99

9781119263883
USA $26.99
CAN $31.99
UK £19.99

Available Everywhere Books Are Sold

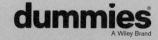

Small books for big imaginations

9781119177173
USA $9.99
CAN $9.99
UK £8.99

9781119177272
USA $9.99
CAN $9.99
UK £8.99

9781119177241
USA $9.99
CAN $9.99
UK £8.99

9781119177210
USA $9.99
CAN $9.99
UK £8.99

9781119262657
USA $9.99
CAN $9.99
UK £6.99

9781119291336
USA $9.99
CAN $9.99
UK £6.99

9781119233527
USA $9.99
CAN $9.99
UK £6.99

9781119291220
USA $9.99
CAN $9.99
UK £6.99

9781119177302
USA $9.99
CAN $9.99
UK £8.99

Unleash Their Creativity

dummies.com

dummies
A Wiley Brand